Envisioning the National Health Care Quality Report

Committee on the National Quality Report on Health Care Delivery

Margarita P. Hurtado, Elaine K. Swift, and Janet M. Corrigan,
Editors

Board on Health Care Services

INSTITUTE OF MEDICINE

NATIONAL ACADEMY PRESS
Washington, D.C.

NATIONAL ACADEMY PRESS • 2101 Constitution Avenue, N.W. • Washington, DC 20418

NOTICE: The project that is the subject of this report was approved by the Governing Board of the National Research Council, whose members are drawn from the councils of the National Academy of Sciences, the National Academy of Engineering, and the Institute of Medicine. The members of the committee responsible for the report were chosen for their special competences and with regard for appropriate balance.

Support for this project was provided by the Agency for Healthcare Research and Quality, U.S. Department of Health and Human Services (Contract No.282-99-0045, Task Order No. 2). Additional support was provided by the Commonwealth Fund, a New York City-based private, independent foundation. The views presented in this report are those of the Institute of Medicine Committee on the National Quality Report on Health Care Delivery and are not necessarily those of the funding agencies.

International Standard Book Number 0-309-07343-X

Additional copies of this report are available for sale from the National Academy Press, 2101 Constitution Avenue, N.W., Box 285, Washington, D.C. 20055. Call (800) 624-6242 or (202) 334-3313 (in the Washington metropolitan area), or visit the NAP's home page at **www.nap.edu.**

For more information about the Institute of Medicine, visit the IOM home page at **www. iom.edu.**

*"Knowing is not enough; we must apply.
Willing is not enough; we must do."*

—Goethe

INSTITUTE OF MEDICINE

Shaping the Future for Health

THE NATIONAL ACADEMIES

National Academy of Sciences
National Academy of Engineering
Institute of Medicine
National Research Council

The **National Academy of Sciences** is a private, nonprofit, self-perpetuating society of distinguished scholars engaged in scientific and engineering research, dedicated to the furtherance of science and technology and to their use for the general welfare. Upon the authority of the charter granted to it by the Congress in 1863, the Academy has a mandate that requires it to advise the federal government on scientific and technical matters. Dr. Bruce M. Alberts is president of the National Academy of Sciences.

The **National Academy of Engineering** was established in 1964, under the charter of the National Academy of Sciences, as a parallel organization of outstanding engineers. It is autonomous in its administration and in the selection of its members, sharing with the National Academy of Sciences the responsibility for advising the federal government. The National Academy of Engineering also sponsors engineering programs aimed at meeting national needs, encourages education and research, and recognizes the superior achievements of engineers. Dr. William A. Wulf is president of the National Academy of Engineering.

The **Institute of Medicine** was established in 1970 by the National Academy of Sciences to secure the services of eminent members of appropriate professions in the examination of policy matters pertaining to the health of the public. The Institute acts under the responsibility given to the National Academy of Sciences by its congressional charter to be an adviser to the federal government and, upon its own initiative, to identify issues of medical care, research, and education. Dr. Kenneth I. Shine is president of the Institute of Medicine.

The **National Research Council** was organized by the National Academy of Sciences in 1916 to associate the broad community of science and technology with the Academy's purposes of furthering knowledge and advising the federal government. Functioning in accordance with general policies determined by the Academy, the Council has become the principal operating agency of both the National Academy of Sciences and the National Academy of Engineering in providing services to the government, the public, and the scientific and engineering communities. The Council is administered jointly by both Academies and the Institute of Medicine. Dr. Bruce M. Alberts and Dr. William A. Wulf are chairman and vice chairman, respectively, of the National Research Council.

v

REVIEWERS

The report was reviewed by individuals chosen for their diverse perspectives and technical expertise in accordance with procedures approved by the National Research Council's Report Review Committee. The purpose of this independent review is to provide candid and critical comments to assist the authors and the Institute of Medicine in making the published report as sound as possible and to ensure that the report meets institutional standards for objectivity, evidence, and responsiveness to the study charge. The review comments and draft manuscript remain confidential to protect the integrity of the deliberative process. The committee wishes to thank the following individuals for their review of this report:

Lu Ann Aday, University of Texas, Houston Health Science Center
Ann Arvin, Stanford University School of Medicine
Donald M. Berwick, Institute for Healthcare Improvement
Morris F. Collen, Kaiser Permanente Medical Center
Colleen Conway-Welch, Vanderbilt University, School of Nursing
Robert A. Greenes, Brigham and Women's Hospital
E.A. Hammel, University of California, Berkeley, Department of Demography
Pamela H. Mitchell, University of Washington, School of Nursing
Patricia Riley, National Academy for State Health Policy
Patricia Salber, General Motors Corporation, Health Care Initiatives
Shoshanna Sofaer, Baruch College, School of Public Affairs

Although the reviewers listed above have provided many constructive comments and suggestions, they were not asked to endorse the conclusions or recommendations nor did they see the final draft of the report before its release. The review of this report was overseen by **Richard Bonnie**, John S. Battle Professor of Law and Director of the Institute of Law, Psychiatry, and Public Policy at the University of Virginia, who was responsible for making certain that an independent examination of this report was carried out in accordance with institutional procedures and that all review comments were carefully considered. Responsibility for the final content of this report rests entirely with the authoring committee and institution.

Preface

After several decades of close attention to the cost of health care and to the uneven access to this care across the United States, we are now beginning to seriously examine health care quality. A wide range of individual studies suggests that the quality of the health care we receive is often less than optimal, if not downright poor. Yet we lack information that would allow us to systematically examine how we are doing, to determine which aspects of our health care are better or worse, and to assess whether the quality of our care is improving over time. To help fill these knowledge gaps, the Institute of Medicine (IOM) was asked by the Agency for Healthcare Research and Quality (AHRQ) to undertake a planning effort for a "national quality report on health care delivery." In the 1999 legislation that reauthorized and renamed the agency, Congress mandated that such a report be developed and published annually starting in 2003.

Specifically, the IOM and the committee appointed to conduct this study were asked to take a long-term view and to suggest how best to measure the overall quality of health care in the nation. We were to develop a format that would allow both policy makers and the general public to make year-to-year comparisons of how the health care system is doing, allowing them to determine just how much the quality of care varies or diverges from desired levels when these are specified. Furthermore, our effort is supposed to encompass the spectrum of health care settings, not just the inpatient hospital environment. Eventually, it is also supposed to allow for state- or regional-level measures, as well as measures that compare the quality of care received by various racial, ethnic, or other groups in the population.

The committee brought together expertise in health care quality measurement, health care financing and delivery, health information systems, communications, health economics, biostatistics, medicine, and public policy, as well as the perspectives of state-level health policy makers and health care purchasers. We met four times and sponsored a workshop on the state of the art in health care quality measurement and reporting that gave us the opportunity to hear from a variety of groups and experts. Through their presentations, we learned about quality measurement in other sectors, international experiences with national health care quality reports, the availability of measures to assess diverse aspects of health care quality, and other technical and policy issues related to quality measurement. The results of these efforts are the following general and specific recommendations to AHRQ on the National Health Care Quality Report. Recognizing that the Quality Report will be a dynamic document, evolving over time and that evaluation of the report and its impact should guide subsequent efforts, we sought to give broad guidance on how to undertake the vital task of assessing the quality of health care most effectively. In addition to offering a framework for thinking about health care quality, we give specific examples of the types of measures the Quality Report should include. We also provide suggestions on the criteria for making decisions about which specific measures to include or exclude and where to obtain that information. Lastly, we provide advice on how to reach the intended audiences with this valuable information.

We believe that if properly prepared and communicated, the National Health Care Quality Report can become a mainstay of our nation's effort to improve health care quality. For just as today everyone from the stockbroker on Wall Street to the person in the street follows the economic indicators, someday soon the Congress, executive branch agencies, providers, consumers, and the public at large will be tracking trends in health care quality via the National Health Care Quality Report. We eagerly look forward to that new era.

William L. Roper
Chair

Arnold M. Epstein
Vice-Chair

Acknowledgments

During the course of the study, the committee and study staff were assisted by many individuals and groups who generously shared their valuable expertise. The Agency for Healthcare Research and Quality (AHRQ) made this study possible through both financial support and the technical assistance it provided. Many people at AHRQ facilitated our efforts including Nancy Foster, Project Officer and Coordinator of Quality Activities; Gregg Meyer, Director, Center for Quality Measurement and Improvement; Tom Reilly, Director, National Quality Report; Eileen Hogan, Program Analyst; Steve Cohen, Director, Division of Statistical Research and Methods; Steven Clauser, Director, Quality Measurement and Assessment Group; and, Doris Lefkowitz, Director, Division of Survey Operations, Center for Cost and Financing. Additional information and insights came from Irma Arispe, Associate Director for Science, National Center for Health Statistics; Edward Sondik, Director, National Center for Health Statistics; other members of the federal intragency working group on the National Quality Report; and the others at the Department of Health and Human Services, the Health Care Financing Administration, and other agencies and organizations who responded to our inquiries.

The committee also wants to acknowledge the participants at the workshop on "Envisioning a National Quality Report on Health Care" held on May 22 and 23, 2000, in Washington, D.C. Their important contributions greatly facilitated the committee's thinking on the subject and helped to guide the committee's work. They included Irma Arispe, National Center for Health Statistics; David Bates, Brigham and Women's Hospital; Christina Bethell, Foundation for Accountability; Cybelle Bjorklund, Senate Committee on Health, Education, Labor, and Pensions; Robert Brook, The RAND Corporation; Peggy Carr, National Center for Education Statistics; John M. Colmers, Maryland Health Care Commission; Suzanne Delbanco, Leapfrog Group; Claes Fornell, University of Michigan School of Business Administration; Nancy Foster, Agency for Healthcare Research and Quality; Marsha Gold, Mathematica Policy Research; Jessie Gruman, Center for the Advancement of Health; Sherrie Kaplan, Tufts University School of Medicine; Jason Lee, House Committee on Commerce; Mark McClellan, Stanford University; Elizabeth McGlynn, The RAND Corporation; Gregg Meyer, Agency for Healthcare Research and Quality; Michael Millenson, William M. Mercer, Inc; R. Healther Palmer, Harvard School of Public Health; Lee Partridge, American Human Services Association; Robert Rubin, Lewin Group; Barbara Starfield, The Johns Hopkins University; Ora Strickland, Neil Hodgson Woodruff School of Nursing, Emory University; Jack E. Triplett, Brookings Institution; John Ware, Jr., QualityMetric, Inc.; John E. Wennberg, Dartmouth Medical School; David Williams, University of Michigan; and Donald Young, Health Insurance Association of America.

The committee would also like to recognize the authors of the four commissioned papers: Christina Bethell on measures of patient centeredness; Marsha Gold on potential data sources for the National Health Care Quality Report; Mark McClellan on measures of efficiency; and Elizabeth A. McGlynn, Robert H. Brook, and Paul Shekelle on measuring effectiveness and appropriateness of care. Their input was extremely valuable to the committee's deliberations.

The committee benefited as well from the expert testimony of individuals and representatives from a variety of organizations experienced in quality measurement. Special thanks are extended to Donald M. Berwick, Institute for Healthcare Improvement; Christina Bethell, Foundation for Accountability; Robert J. Blendon, Harvard School of Public Health and the John F. Kennedy School of Government; Maria Hewitt, National Cancer Policy Board; Kenneth W. Kizer, National Quality Forum; Jeffrey Koshel, Office of the Assistant Secretary for Planning and Evaluation, U.S. Department of Health and Human Services; Peggy O'Kane, National Committee for Quality Assurance; Paul Schyve, Joint Commission on Accreditation of Healthcare Organizations; and Reed Tuckson, formerly of the American Medical Association. Those who responded to the committee's call for measures on quality of care also provided very valuable input on potential measures for the Quality Report (see Appendix C).

The committee and study staff would like to thank colleagues at the Institute of Medicine for their support throughout this project. Janet Corrigan, Director, Board on Health Care Services, provided guidance throughout the study. We are also grateful for the assistance of Linda Kilroy, Office of Contracts and Grants; Jennifer Cangco and Kay Harris, Office of Finance and Administration; Claudia Carl, Mike Edington, and Jennifer Otten, Office of Reports and Communications; and Sally Stanfield and Dawn Eichenlaub, National Academy

Press. We would also like to thank Christine Coussens, Andrea Kalfoglou, and Tracy McKay for their assistance.

Support for this study was provided by the Agency for Healthcare Research and Quality, U.S. Department of Health and Human Services. Additional support was provided by the Commonwealth Fund, a New York City-based private, independent foundation.

Contents

Tables, Figures, and Boxes

TABLES

FIGURES

BOXES

Envisioning the National Health Care Quality Report

Executive Summary

The quality of health care received by the people of the United States falls far short of what it should be (Advisory Commission on Consumer Protection and Quality in the Health Care Industry, 1998; Chassin and Galvin, 1998). A large body of literature documents serious quality problems. There is a gap (some say a "chasm") between the health care services that should be provided based on current professional knowledge and technology and those that many patients actually receive (Institute of Medicine, 2001; Institute of Medicine and National Research Council, 1999; Schuster et al., 2001). For example, the National Cancer Policy Board of the Institute of Medicine (IOM) has concluded that "for many Americans with cancer, there is a wide gulf between what could be construed as the ideal and the reality of their experience with cancer care" (Institute of Medicine and National Research Council, 1999). Another IOM report documented that tens of thousands of Americans are seriously harmed as a result of errors in health care (Institute of Medicine, 2000).

Enormous resources are invested in health care. In 1998, national health care expenditures topped $1.1 trillion or 13.5 percent of the gross domestic product (Levit et al., 2000). Americans spend $4,270 per person per year on health care, an amount in excess of that spent by any other country (Anderson et al., 2000). Is this money well spent? Is it translated into quality care and improved health? Today, it is not possible to answer these questions satisfactorily.

It is clear that all resources are not used effectively or safely. Study after study documents the *overuse* of many services—the provision of services when the potential for harm outweighs possible benefits. At the same time, studies

1

also document the *underuse* of other services—the failure to provide services from which the patient would likely have benefited (Chassin and Galvin, 1998).[1] Patient safety was the subject of a landmark report by the IOM (2000).

It is these and other shortcomings in quality that led the President's Advisory Commission on Consumer Protection and Quality in the Health Care Industry to call for a national commitment to improve quality involving both the private and the public sectors and every level of the health care system (Advisory Commission on Consumer Protection and Quality in the Health Care Industry, 1998). To help guide this process and track progress, the Advisory Commission recommended that there be an annual report to the President and Congress on the nation's progress in improving health care quality. Shortly thereafter, Congress enacted the Healthcare Research and Quality Act of 1999, directing the Agency for Healthcare Research and Quality (AHRQ) to prepare an annual report on national trends in the quality of health care provided to the American people.

AHRQ contracted with the IOM to assist in the design of the new national health care quality report. The IOM Committee on the National Quality Report on Health Care Delivery was established in 1999 and was charged with laying out a *vision* of the National Health Care Quality Report (also referred to as the Quality Report), including both its content and its presentation. Specifically, the committee was asked to

- identify the most important questions to answer in evaluating whether the health care delivery system is providing high-quality health care and whether quality is improving over time;
- identify the major aspects of quality that should be reflected in the Quality Report;
- provide examples of specific measures that might be included in the Quality Report; and
- provide advice on the format and production of the report.

PURPOSE OF THE NATIONAL HEALTH CARE QUALITY REPORT

The National Health Care Quality Report should serve as a yardstick or barometer by which to gauge progress in improving the performance of the health care delivery system in consistently providing high-quality care. Similar tools have been applied and found useful in other areas and industries. For example, the Bureau of Labor Statistics produces economic indicators, such as the

---

[1] For a review of more than 70 articles documenting shortcomings in quality of care see Schuster et al., 2001.

Consumer Price Index (CPI), to track the state of the economy. This information is used to establish economic policies that promote sound economic growth (Bureau of Labor Statistics, 2000). In another sector, the National Assessment of Educational Progress (NAEP) report tracks educational performance. This information is used to guide educational reform, including changes in curriculum and instruction (National Center for Education Statistics, 2000; National Research Council, 1998, 2000, 2001).

The Quality Report should complement other reports produced on the health of the people of the United States by the Department of Health and Human Services (DHHS). *Health United States* examines health status annually (National Center for Health Statistics, 2000). *Healthy People 2010* sets forth 467 public health objectives for the coming decade (U.S. Department of Health and Human Services, 2000a). While these efforts focus on tracking and improving the public's health, the Quality Report should focus on the performance of the health care delivery system with regard to personal health care, rather than public health functions. It should examine the quality of care provided to the general population and major subgroups by the system as a whole and not care delivered in specific health care settings or by specific providers. In this respect, it differs from the comparative "report cards" issued by other organizations, such as the National Committee for Quality Assurance (NCQA), which inform purchaser and consumer choice of health plans (National Committee for Quality Assurance, 2000).

The Quality Report should present a "broad-brush" portrait of quality of care to inform Congress and national policy, while more detailed performance reports at the provider, institutional, and local levels would be used for specific quality improvement efforts. The Quality Report is intended to complement another report mandated by Congress in the same legislation. This second report, which is under development, will address "disparities in health care delivery as it relates to racial and socioeconomic factors in priority populations" (Healthcare Research and Quality Act, 1999:Sec. 902). The importance of articulating these two efforts cannot be overemphasized. While there may be some overlap between the two, the committee recommends that the Quality Report present appropriate information on equity by geographic region and population subgroup, as discussed later. It is the committee's understanding that the disparities report will include in-depth analyses of any differences that may be present in various aspects of health care delivery, including quality. The committee views the Quality Report as one of the components of a multilevel reporting system that will eventually cover local to national levels and span a variety of topics, all of which are needed to examine both health care delivery and the health status of the people of the United States.

The committee believes that the Quality Report should satisfy several objectives:

• *Enhance awareness of quality.* An annual report on the state of quality can serve as an important vehicle of communication to improve awareness and understanding of quality issues by policy leaders, health care professionals, and the lay public.

• *Monitor possible effects of policy decisions and initiatives.* Many efforts are currently underway in both the public and the private sectors to improve quality. Tracking key aspects of the health care system's performance over time will be critical to assessing the impact of these improvement efforts and other policy initiatives, including budgetary changes. For example, if Congress enacts Medicare prescription coverage, the Quality Report could potentially be one of several instruments used to examine whether this change has contributed to improved blood pressure control among seniors.

• *Assess progress in meeting national goals.* If health care leaders choose to develop specific goals for improvement in the health care delivery system (for example, to achieve a 50 percent reduction in adverse drug events over the next five years), the Quality Report can be used to track progress in meeting these goals. The coupling of an annual reporting mechanism with specific goals for improvement is an approach that has worked well in other sectors.

The committee concluded that if these objectives are met, the Quality Report can provide a much-needed source of authoritative information to answer key questions about the quality of care. It should be useful in determining whether the quality of health care is improving, staying the same, or worsening over time. It should help assess whether progress is being made in improving specific aspects of quality, including safety, effectiveness, "patient centeredness," and timeliness. The report should also help ascertain whether the health care system is responsive to consumers' needs and preferences for care. To do so, the Quality Report should include a wide range of measures that reflect consumer perspectives and different needs for care when they are healthy, experience acute illness, need to manage a chronic illness, or are coping with the end of life.

The report design should be flexible enough to allow for exploration of special questions that affect different groups of the population, such as

• variations in the quality of care received by people residing in different geographic areas (for example, states);

• assessment of the quality of care received by people with a specific health problem or condition (for example, diabetes); and

• variations in the quality of care based on personal characteristics unrelated to health (for example, ethnicity, race, gender, age, health insurance coverage).

DEFINING A VISION FOR THE
NATIONAL HEALTH CARE QUALITY REPORT

The committee went through a four-step process to define a vision for the National Health Care Quality Report:

- development of the conceptual framework,
- specification of criteria for selecting measures and identification of sample measures,
- specification of criteria for selecting data sources and identification of potential data sources, and
- development of audience-centered reporting criteria.

First, the committee formulated a conceptual framework for the Quality Report. To do so, the committee considered both the key questions to be answered and the major aspects of quality that should be measured to answer these questions. Conceptual frameworks used by other public- and private-sector groups engaged in quality measurement and improvement were reviewed and built upon whenever possible. Throughout its endeavors, the committee strived to make its work synergistic with that of others and to avoid "reinventing the wheel."

Second, having specified a conceptual framework, the committee turned its attention to the process of selecting examples of the type of measures that should be included in the Quality Report. The committee has developed criteria to guide the final selection of measures that address each of the major components of quality. The committee was also asked to provide examples of measures for the Quality Report. More than 130 measures were submitted by organizations and individuals in response to a call for measures issued to the private sector by the committee in June and July 2000.[2] The committee examined these and other potential measures identified through a review of the literature and selected a limited number to serve as examples of those that might be included in the Quality Report.

Third, potential public and private sector data sources that might be drawn on to produce measures in the Quality Report were identified and evaluated based on specific criteria defined by the committee. The committee concluded that no single existing data source can satisfy all of the requirements of the Quality Report, but much progress can be made by drawing on a mosaic of data sources, including consumer and provider surveys, clinical or medical record data, and administrative data.

Lastly, the committee identified the main audiences for the Quality Report and developed guidelines for the design and production of reports tailored to these audiences. Although its primary audience is intended to be health care

---

[2] AHRQ issued a separate call for measures to federal agencies after the committee had concluded its deliberations.

policy makers and leaders at the national and state levels, the Quality Report should also be of keen interest to the lay public, clinicians, purchasers, researchers, and others. The Quality Report is not envisioned as a single static report, but rather as a collection of annual reports tailored to the needs and interests of particular constituencies.

CONCEPTUAL FRAMEWORK

RECOMMENDATION 1: The conceptual framework for the National Health Care Quality Report should address two dimensions: components of health care quality and consumer perspectives on health care needs. Components of health care quality—the first dimension—include safety, effectiveness, patient centeredness, and timeliness. Consumer perspectives on health care needs—the second dimension—reflect changing consumer needs for care over the life cycle associated with staying healthy, getting better, living with illness or disability, and coping with the end of life. Quality can be examined along both dimensions for health care in general or for specific conditions. The conceptual framework should also provide for the analysis of equity as an issue that cuts across both dimensions and is reflected in differences in the quality of care received by different groups of the population. (See Chapter 2.)

As a starting point, the committee adopted the following IOM definition of health care quality: "the degree to which health services for individuals and populations increase the likelihood of desired health outcomes and are consistent with current professional knowledge" (Institute of Medicine, 1990:21). With its emphasis on "desired health outcomes," this definition incorporates consumer perspectives on quality, while clearly linking quality to making the best use of current medical knowledge and technology. The definition also recognizes that there are population- and individual-level considerations that must be balanced when defining and assessing quality. For example, the health care provided to some patients may be excellent, yet the outcomes for the entire population that should be served by the system may fall short.

To operationalize this definition, the committee developed a two-dimensional framework. The framework is intended to provide a stable foundation for the Quality Report and specifies the aspects that should be measured while the individual measures may change over time in response to new health care practices and improvements in quality measurement. The first dimension of the framework captures the components of health care quality—*safety*, *effectiveness*, *patient centeredness*, and *timeliness*.

• *Safety* refers to "avoiding injuries to patients from care that is intended to help them" (Institute of Medicine, 2001). Improving safety means designing and implementing health care processes to avoid, prevent, and ameliorate adverse outcomes or injuries that stem from the processes of health care itself (National Patient Safety Foundation, 2000). For instance, unsafe care occurs when a pharmacist misreads a hand-written prescription for a patient and dispenses a higher dosage than actually ordered by the physician.

• *Effectiveness* refers to "providing services based on scientific knowledge to all who could benefit, and refraining from providing services to those not likely to benefit (avoiding overuse and underuse)" (Institute of Medicine, 2001). For instance, effective care means that patients who experience a heart attack and do not have specific contraindications should receive beta-blockers.

• *Patient centeredness* refers to health care that establishes a partnership among practitioners, patients, and their families (when appropriate) to ensure that decisions respect patients' wants, needs, and preferences and that patients have the education and support they require to make decisions and participate in their own care. For instance, if a woman with breast cancer undergoes a mastectomy without being fully informed about the various treatment options, given the nature of her cancer, that care was not patient centered.

• *Timeliness* refers to obtaining needed care and minimizing unnecessary delays in getting that care. For instance, a woman who discovers a lump in her breast has received timely care if she is able to see her clinician, have the lump biopsied, and be informed of the results within a short and appropriate period of time.

The second dimension of the framework reflects consumer perspectives on health care needs or reasons for seeking care. It assesses health system performance in meeting changing consumer needs over the life cycle, which—depending on health status—could be to *stay healthy, get better, live with illness or disability,* or *cope with the end of life* (Foundation for Accountability, 1997). These consumer perspectives on health care needs are roughly equivalent to different types of health care as often defined by clinicians—preventive care, acute care, chronic care, and end-of-life care.

In addition to the two dimensions of quality components and consumer health care needs, the framework incorporates *equity* as a crosscutting issue, and the committee recommends that information in the Quality Report be presented by population subgroups when appropriate. The committee understands that the more in-depth, causal analysis, including issues of access and insurance, will be presented in the planned disparities report, mentioned earlier (Healthcare Research and Quality Act, 1999) and in publications related to *Healthy People 2010* (U.S. Department of Health and Human Services, 2000).

For the Quality Report, the committee views *equity* as the provision of health care of equal quality to those who may differ in personal characteristics that are not inherently linked to health, such as gender, ethnicity, geographic location, socioeconomic status, or insurance coverage. Equity means that the quality of care is based on needs and clinical factors. For example, care is provided equitably when an elderly African-American man and an elderly white man with prostate cancer and similar clinical profiles are both presented with complete information on the full range of treatment options and receive surgical and medical care of the same quality. Finally, the framework contemplates the measurement of quality of care for people with specific health conditions, particularly in the context of consumer health care needs. For example, the report can be used to examine whether persons with diabetes are receiving the care they need to manage or "live with their illness" or whether children are "staying healthy" by receiving indicated immunizations at the appropriate ages.

The combination of components of health care quality and consumer perspectives on health care needs defines the types of measures that should be in the National Health Care Quality Report, and can be represented as a matrix (Figure 1). The matrix is a tool to visualize possible combinations of the two dimensions of the framework and better understand how various aspects of the framework relate to each other. Not all combinations will be relevant to evaluate quality, not all cells will be equally important to all audiences, and the availability of measures for each cell will vary. Both health conditions and population characteristics related to equity would be issues that apply within each cell of the matrix.

Consumer Perspectives on Health Care Needs	Components of Health Care Quality			
	Safety	Effectiveness	Patient Centeredness	Timeliness
Staying healthy				
Getting better				
Living with illness or disability				
Coping with the end of life				

FIGURE 1 Classification matrix for measures for the National Health Care Quality Report.

For example, if the Quality Report is to include measures of quality of care for prostate cancer, the *effectiveness–getting better* cell might include a measure of whether patients undergoing prostatectomies were those for whom the likely benefits of the procedure exceeded the risks. The *patient centeredness–getting better* cell could have measures of whether patients were given the opportunity and information needed to make an informed choice between medical and surgical interventions.

The scope of the Quality Report is limited to quality of care. Thus, *efficiency* is not included in the framework. The committee does consider efficiency to be an important goal of the health care system that is related to, but conceptually different from, quality of care. Waste robs the health care system of scarce monetary and other resources that could be used to improve quality (Institute of Medicine, 2001). Specific causes of inefficiency, such as repeat procedures due to error, overuse, fragmentation of care, and unnecessary delays, are included under the appropriate component of quality. In the future, information on costs could be combined with information on the quality of care to provide an indication of whether the country is in effect using these resources to enhance the value received from health care spending.

SELECTING MEASURES FOR THE NATIONAL HEALTH CARE QUALITY REPORT AND DATA SET

RECOMMENDATION 2: The Agency for Healthcare Research and Quality should apply a uniform set of criteria describing desirable attributes to assess potential individual measures and measure sets for the content areas defined by the framework. For individual measures, the committee proposes ten criteria grouped into the three following sets: (1) the overall importance of the aspects of quality being measured, (2) the scientific soundness of the measures, and (3) the feasibility of the measures. For the measure set as a whole, the committee proposes three additional criteria: balance, comprehensiveness, and robustness. (See Chapter 3.)

These are ideal criteria and should not be interpreted as strict requirements for potential measures. In the short term, all criteria referring to feasibility and/or scientific soundness may not always be fulfilled. The evaluation of measures based on the proposed criteria can be used to pinpoint areas for improvement in measure development.

Individual measures selected for the Quality Report should ideally rate highly for all criteria. However, importance and scientific soundness take precedence over feasibility. Feasibility criteria may have to be relaxed initially to allow for new or improved measures, given the fact that many of the aspects of quality that must be addressed have never been measured. The specific questions that can be used to examine whether or not a particular measure should be selected for the Quality Report are listed below.

Importance of What Is Being Measured

- What is the impact on health associated with this problem?
- Are policy makers and consumers concerned about this area?
- Can the health care system meaningfully address this aspect or problem?

Scientific Soundness of the Measure

- Does the measure actually measure what it is intended to measure?
- Does the measure provide stable results across various populations and circumstances?
- Is there scientific evidence available to support the measure?

Feasibility of Using the Measure

- Is the measure in use?
- Can the information needed for the measure be collected in the scale and time frame required?
- How much will it cost to collect the data needed for the measure?
- Can the measure be used to compare different groups of the population (for example, by health conditions, sociodemographic characteristics, or states)?

It is also important that the set of measures as a whole is balanced, comprehensive, and robust. For this purpose, the committee recommends that three questions be asked: (1) Does the measure set reflect both what is being done well and what is being done poorly? (2) Can the measure set be used to portray the state of quality of health care delivery as a whole; that is, does it cover all of the elements in the framework? (3) Is the measure set relatively stable and robust, that is, not extremely sensitive to minor changes in the system not associated with quality?

> **RECOMMENDATION 3: The Agency for Healthcare Research and Quality should have an ongoing independent committee or advisory body to help assess and guide improvements over time in the National Health Care Quality Report.** (See Chapter 3.)

Given the complexity of designing and producing the Quality Report, AHRQ should obtain advice from an independent advisory body. This advisory body should support the agency on the various processes associated with defining and updating the measures for the report, as well as designing and producing the report. It should include experts and representatives from organizations experienced in the development, evaluation, and application of specific quality measures. Members should be drawn from organizations in both the public and the private sectors, and should include national- as well as state-level representatives. The advisory body could be analogous to the National Committee on Vital and Health Statistics (NCVHS) or the National Quality Forum (NQF) (National Quality Forum, 2000; U.S. Department of Health and Human Services, 2000b). It should also serve as a vehicle for collaboration among interested public and private sector parties with the goal of improving quality measurement and reporting at the national level.

> **RECOMMENDATION 4:** The Agency for Healthcare Research and Quality should set the long-term goal of using a comprehensive approach to the assessment and measurement of quality of care as a basis for the National Health Care Quality Data Set. (See Chapter 3.)

A comprehensive system is one in which the majority of care for a given population is assessed using a large number of measures representing the many components of health care quality and consumer perspectives on health care needs in an integrated manner. This approach should result in a more complete and accurate picture of the state of quality in the nation than is now available. To this end, the Agency for Healthcare Research and Quality should evaluate current efforts to develop comprehensive quality measurement systems (for example, in the area of effectiveness) and examine how they may be used and expanded.

One example of a comprehensive approach to measurement is the QA Tools system developed by RAND. The QA Tools system consists of more than 1200 quality measures (or indicators of effectiveness) applicable to 58 clinical areas (including conditions and recommended preventive services) and covering children, adults, and the vulnerable elderly. At present, application of the QA Tools requires abstraction of a sizable sample of medical records. For each medical record in the sample, information is abstracted on the subset of quality measures applicable to the patient given his or her gender, age, condition, and health risk profile. This information is then aggregated across the entire sample of individuals to produce an overall measure of the degree to which the care provided to this population is consistent with the care that should have been provided based on scientific evidence.

The committee sees potential promise in this kind of comprehensive approach to measuring effectiveness but believes that it would be premature to recommend using the QA Tools system in the National Health Care Quality Report at this time. First, the system was developed only recently, is still being revised, and has not yet been subject to an independent evaluation. Second, application at this time would impose a sizable burden in terms of medical record abstraction.

The committee does think that comprehensive approaches to measurement, such as the RAND QA Tools system, merit careful evaluation. The continued development of increasingly standardized, electronic clinical data systems as part of a new health information infrastructure should make comprehensive measurement approaches more feasible and less burdensome in the future. It may also be possible, over time, for such approaches to incorporate measures of safety, patient centeredness, and timeliness, in addition to effectiveness. AHRQ, with the advice of the independent advisory body, should periodically revisit the issue of how best to start implementing a comprehensive approach to measurement for the National Health Care Quality Report.

RECOMMENDATION 5: When possible and appropriate, and to enhance robustness, facilitate detection of trends, and simplify presentation of the measures in the National Health Care Quality Report, the Agency for Healthcare Research and Quality (AHRQ) should consider combining related individual measures into summary measures of specific aspects of quality. AHRQ should also make available to the public information on the individual measures included in any summary measure, as well as the procedures used to construct them. (See Chapter 3.)

The National Health Care Quality Report and Data Set should make use of summary measures to represent each of the framework's measure categories (for example, safety) or subcategories. This will facilitate the presentation of information on a very complex subject. In general, the measures combined should be based on the same population or have the same denominator and unit of measurement. That is, summary measures should combine like with like. The committee does not believe that an overall summary measure of quality would be useful or scientifically sound at this time, given that it would have to combine very disparate aspects of quality.

Summary measures should be specific enough to guide policy. The method and sources behind them should be stated clearly and made available. Presenting these summary measures along with a corresponding reference point or benchmark (for example, past performance, desirable level of performance, or average performance at the national level when presenting information for states) would provide a useful context for interpreting of the actual number being reported.

Summary measures have been used in public reporting in many other fields. Properly presented, they would make information more accessible to the public. In economics, for example, the Consumer Price Index is a summary measure of inflation that reflects the average price of a basket of goods and services purchased by consumers (Bureau of Labor Statistics, 2000). In the Quality Report summary measures could be used to assess specific aspects of safety of care or any of the other quality components. For example, a report could include a summary measure of the safety of surgery based on measures for a variety of surgical procedures.

> **RECOMMENDATION 6: The National Health Care Quality Data Set should reflect a balance of outcome-validated process measures and condition- or procedure-specific outcome measures.** Given the weak links between most structures and outcomes of care and the interests of consumers and providers in processes or practice-related aspects as well as outcome measures, structural measures should be avoided. (See Chapter 3.)

The committee recommends that the National Health Care Quality Report and Data Set rely on a balanced set of process and outcome measures and avoid structural measures. Structural measures of the organizational, technological, and human resources infrastructure of the health care system (Donabedian, 1966) have not been shown to be consistently linked to the quality of care and desired outcomes. A combination of process and outcome measures will satisfy the needs of policy makers, clinicians, and consumers. Any measures for the National Health Care Quality Report and Data Set should not stifle innovation by institutionalizing specific processes or infrastructure that could soon become outdated.

SELECTING SOURCES FOR THE NATIONAL HEALTH CARE QUALITY DATA SET

> **RECOMMENDATION 7: Potential data sources for the National Health Care Quality Data Set should be assessed according to the following criteria: credibility and validity of the data, national scope and potential to provide state-level detail, availability and consistency of the data over time and across sources, timeliness of the data, ability to support population subgroup and condition-specific analyses, and public accessibility of the data. In addition, in order to support the framework, the ensemble of data sources defined for the National Health Care Quality Data Set should be comprehensive.** (See Chapter 4.)

The data sources that are intended to support the long-term goal of a National Health Care Quality Data Set must meet certain high standards to support analysis of the state of health care quality in the United States. Although these criteria are not exhaustive, they do include the essential ideal features that should characterize data sources for the Quality Report in the future. When current data collection efforts do not fulfill these criteria, AHRQ should explore ways to enhance existent data sources and establish new data collection and reporting systems that exhibit these characteristics, in collaboration with the appropriate entities in the public and private sectors.

> **RECOMMENDATION 8: The Agency for Healthcare Research and Quality will have to draw on a mosaic of public and private data sources for the National Health Care Quality Data Set. Existent data sources will have to be complemented by the development of new ones in order to address all of the aspects included in the proposed framework and resulting measure set. Over the coming decade, the evolution of a comprehensive health information infrastructure, including standardized, electronic clinical data systems, will greatly facilitate the definition of an integrated and comprehensive data set for the Quality Report. (See Chapter 4.)**

A preliminary and limited evaluation of several candidate data sources suggests that a combination of the Medical Expenditure Panel Survey (MEPS) and the Consumer Assessment of Health Plans Survey (CAHPS) may have the best potential to supply data for measures of patient centeredness and aspects of timeliness. However, the CAHPS component presently planned for MEPS will have to include additional questions in order to meet the data requirements for these two components of quality and related consumer perspectives on health care needs. To assess effectiveness and safety, as well as relevant health care needs, a combination of public and private data sources should be used, including MEPS, other population surveys, claims and other administrative data, medical record abstraction, and new data sources that will have to be developed.

The committee considers that this effort will require an assessment of the investment needed to create and maintain appropriate data systems to support the annual production of the Quality Report. Whenever possible, the committee recommends that the Agency for Healthcare Research and Quality pursue data strategies that encourage the collection of electronic clinical data as a part of the care process. Although there are many clinical and administrative reasons for the use of standardized electronic information, in the long run, this type of information will also provide the best data on both the system's quality components and consumer health care needs.

Early versions or editions of the Quality Report will have to rely on existent data sources, but they should shed light on some very important aspects of quality. They will also develop consumer and policy-maker expectations for ongoing reports on the quality of health care. Over time, the Quality Report should present a more textured and comprehensive view of quality as the health care sector develops a more sophisticated health information infrastructure.

RECOMMENDATION 9: The data for the National Health Care Quality Report should be nationally representative and, in the long term, reportable at the state level. (See Chapter 4.)

By measuring health care quality at the national and state levels, the National Health Care Quality Report would provide benchmarks to judge how well health care delivery systems are performing at the state level relative to the degree of quality achieved for the nation as a whole. The ability to examine certain quality measures across states would substantially enhance the policy relevance, visibility, and usefulness of the report. In some cases, the sample size may have to be increased in order to produce more precise state-level estimates. States should be given the option of acquiring additional sample size when the data available nationally are not sufficient to conduct state-level analyses for populations of interest. Local-level identifiers such as zip codes can be used to examine specific subpopulations when needed. Since health care is inherently a local phenomenon, further detail on the quality of care for geographic units smaller than states is usually required to address potential problems at the provider and organizational levels. However, this level of detail should generally correspond to regional or specialized reports since the purpose of the National Health Care Quality Report is to examine the quality of care provided by the system as a whole, not by individual providers, localities, or health plans.

DESIGNING THE NATIONAL HEALTH CARE QUALITY REPORT

RECOMMENDATION 10: The National Health Care Quality Report should be produced in several versions tailored to key audiences—policy makers, consumers, purchasers, providers, and researchers. It should feature a limited number of key findings and the minimum number of measures needed to support these findings. (See Chapter 5.)

The Agency for Healthcare Research and Quality should produce a National Health Care Quality Report, or collection of reports, that will attract the attention and interest of national and state policy makers, consumers, purchasers, providers, and researchers. Policy makers should be able to act on the findings presented in the report by formulating legislation or designing programs, for example. The National Health Care Quality Report will be an important tool that AHRQ can use to promote a better understanding of quality, generate support for improvement, and highlight areas that require special attention. The Quality Report should inform the public and provide a context for accountability of the health care system.

To accomplish these goals, AHRQ should make the Quality Report relevant, engaging, easy to read, and easy to understand. The print version should be brief and aimed at key audiences. It should summarize key findings on specific topics. For example, the topics might include quality of care for diabetics, quality of care for children, and quality of preventive care.

There should be different versions of the report, that is, a collection or family of reports, available in print and on a dedicated web site. The web site should also include a user-accessible version of the complete data set to the extent feasible. The family of reports should be tailored to specialized audiences, as well as the general public. The content should be highly selective, relevant to current policy concerns, and fresh from year to year, even while preserving some continuity. Finally, the format employed should be designed so that differences across regions or groups and trends are easily discernible.

CONCLUSION

In this report, the IOM Committee on the National Quality Report on Health Care Delivery provides the Agency for Healthcare Research and Quality with a *vision* of the contents and design of the National Health Care Quality Report. It defines the aspects of quality that should be measured, describes the characteristics of desirable measures and data sources, provides specific examples of measures, and proposes a set of criteria for designing and producing the Quality Report.

The committee recognizes the difficulties involved in achieving the vision presented here, but the changes required are necessary in order to be able to assess and track quality of care adequately. Some measures available do not fit all of the criteria proposed and will have to be improved. For certain elements of the framework completely new measures will have to be developed, but past experience with measures for *Healthy People 2000* has shown that this is feasible (U.S. Department of Health and Human Services, 1991, 2000). For the Quality Report to provide a comprehensive picture of quality, new data sources will be required. Ultimately, a new health information infrastructure, based on uniform data standards and including computerized clinical data systems that are part of the care process, will be necessary. The need to tailor the Quality Report to specific audiences and each year's particular findings makes the task of producing the report more difficult but also optimizes its utility. The obstacles in the path of developing a Quality Report are many, but they are not insurmountable. The recommendations formulated by the committee in this report should help AHRQ make this vision a reality.

REFERENCES

Advisory Commission on Consumer Protection and Quality in the Health Care Industry. 1998. *Quality First: Better Health Care for All Americans.* Washington, D.C.: U.S. Government Printing Office.

Anderson, Gerard F., Jeremy Hurst, Peter Sotir Hussey, and Melissa Jee-Hughes. Health spending and outcomes: Trends in OECD countries, 1960–1998. 2000. *Health Affairs* 19(3):150–157.

Bureau of Labor Statistics. *Consumer Price Indexes* [on-line]. Available at: http://stats.bls.gov/cpihome.htm [Dec. 5, 2000].

Chassin, Mark R., and Robert W. Galvin. 1998. The urgent need to improve health care quality: Institute of Medicine National Roundtable on Health Care Quality. *Journal of the American Medical Association* 280(11):1000–1005.

Donabedian, Avedis. 1966. Evaluating the quality of medical care. *Milbank Memorial Fund Quarterly* 44:166–203.

Foundation for Accountability. 1997. *Reporting Quality Information to Consumers.* Portland, Ore.: FACCT.

Healthcare Research and Quality Act. 1999. *Statutes at Large.* Vol. 113, Sec. 1653.

Institute of Medicine. 1990. *Medicare: A Strategy for Quality Assurance*, Vol. 2. ed. Kathleen Lohr. Washington, D.C.: National Academy Press.

Institute of Medicine. 2000. *To Err Is Human: Building a Safer Health System.* eds. Linda T. Kohn, Janet M. Corrigan, and Molla S. Donaldson. Washington, D.C.: National Academy Press.

Institute of Medicine. 2001. *Crossing the Quality Chasm: A New Health System for the 21st Century.* Washington, D.C.: National Academy Press.

Institute of Medicine and National Research Council. 1999. *Ensuring Quality Cancer Care.* eds. Maria Hewitt and Joseph V. Simone. Washington, D.C.: National Academy Press.

Levit, Katharine, Cathy Cowan, Helen Lazenby, Arthur Sensenig, Patricia McDonnell, Jean Stiller, and Anne Martin. 2000. Health spending in 1998: Signals of change. *Health Affairs* 19(1):124–132.

McGlynn, Elizabeth A., Paul G. Shekelle, and Robert H. Brook. 2000. Commissioned Paper for the Institute of Medicine Committee on the National Quality Report on Health Care Delivery.

National Center for Education Statistics. 2000. *The Nation's Report Card: National Assessment of Educational Progress* [on-line]. Available at: http://nces.ed.gov/ nationsreportcard/site/home.asp [Dec. 8, 2000].

National Center for Health Statistics. 2000. *Health, United States, 2000 with Adolescent Health Chartbook*, Hyattsville, Md.: U.S. Government Printing Office.

National Committee for Quality Assurance. 2000. *The State of Managed Care Quality.* Washington, D.C. Available at: http://www.ncqa.org.

National Patient Safety Foundation. 2000. *Agenda for Research and Development in Patient Safety* [on-line]. Available at: www.npsf.org.

National Quality Forum. 2000. *NQF: About Us* [on-line]. Available at: http://www.qualityforum.org/about/home.htm [Dec. 6, 2000].

National Research Council. 1998. *Grading the Nation's Report Card: Evaluating NAEP and Transforming the Assessment of Education Progress.* eds. James W. Pellegrino, Lee R. Jones, and Karen J. Mitchell. Washington, D.C.: National Academy Press.

National Research Council. 2000. *Grading the Nation's Report Card: Research from the Evaluation of NAEP.* eds. Nambury S. Raju, James W. Pellegrino, Meryl W. Bertenthal, Karen J. Mitchell, and Lee R. Jones. Washington, D.C.: National Academy Press.

National Research Council. 2001. *NAEP Reporting Practices: Investigating District-Level and Market-Basket Reporting.* Eds. Pasquale J. DeVito and Judith A. Koening. Washington, D.C.: National Academy Press.

Schuster, Mark A., Elizabeth A. McGlynn, Cung B. Pham, Myles D. Spar, and Robert H. Brook. 2001. The quality of health care in the United States: A review of articles Since 1987. *Crossing the Quality Chasm: A New Health System for the 21st Century,* Appendix A. Washington, D.C.: National Academy Press.

U.S. Department of Health and Human Services. 1991. *Healthy People 2000: National Health Promotion and Disease Prevention Objectives,* Pub. No. (PHS) 91-50212. Washington, D.C.: Office of the Assistant Secretary for Health.

U.S. Department of Health and Human Services. 2000a. *Healthy People 2010.* Washington, D.C.: U.S. Government Printing Office.

U.S. Department of Health and Human Services. 2000b. *Introduction to the NCVHS* [online]. Available at: http://ncvhs.hhs.gov/intro.htm [Dec. 22, 2000].

1

Introduction

The Agency for Healthcare Research and Quality (AHRQ) will soon produce the first annual report on the quality of health care in the United States. To help formulate the new National Health Care Quality Report (also referred to as the Quality Report), AHRQ commissioned the Institute of Medicine (IOM) to conduct a study that would identify

- the most important questions to answer in evaluating whether the health care delivery system is providing high-quality health care and whether quality is changing over time;
  - the types or domains of information that should be produced; and
  - examples of specific measures that fall into each domain.

The IOM formed the Committee on the National Quality Report on Health Care Delivery to carry out this work. As described in this chapter, the committee studied different approaches to defining and measuring quality. It also reviewed leading national reports on health care quality and major national initiatives on quality measurement. In addition, it examined the ways in which states, other nations, and the World Health Organization (WHO) have formulated quality measurement and reporting frameworks, along with the ways they have presented information on quality to those outside the traditional audience of the health care community. This chapter begins with a brief presentation on the origins of the new National Health Care Quality Report. It also summarizes the origins and work of the IOM Committee on the National Quality Report on Health Care Delivery.

ORIGINS OF THE NATIONAL HEALTH CARE QUALITY REPORT

The President's Advisory Commission on Consumer Protection and Quality in the Health Care Industry issued a number of recommendations in 1998, among them a call for greater public reporting on health care quality (Advisory Commission on Consumer Protection and Quality in the Health Care Industry, 1998). Congress responded with Title IX of the Healthcare Research and Quality Act of 1999, which requires AHRQ to report to the U.S. Senate and House of Representatives "on national trends in the quality of health care provided to the American people" (Healthcare Research and Quality Act, 1999). The publication of the report, or family of reports, to be made annually, is scheduled to start in fiscal year 2003.

THE IOM COMMITTEE ON THE NATIONAL QUALITY REPORT ON HEALTH CARE DELIVERY

In its role of advising AHRQ on the Quality Report, the committee worked to provide a vision of what should be included.[1] As an important part of its work, the committee held four two-day meetings in 2000, during which it considered research on major issues related to its charge and formulated its recommendations. At the first meeting, the committee heard testimony from representatives of a number of organizations working in the area of quality measurement, including Donald Berwick, Institute for Healthcare Improvement; Robert Blendon, Harvard School of Public Health and the John F. Kennedy School of Government; Christina Bethell, Foundation for Accountability (FACCT); John Eisenberg and Gregg Meyer, Agency for Healthcare Research and Quality (AHRQ); Margaret O'Kane, National Committee for Quality Assurance (NCQA); Kenneth Kizer, National Forum for Health Care Quality Measurement and Reporting; Paul Schyve, Joint Commission on Accreditation of Healthcare Organizations (JCAHO); and Reed Tuckson, formerly of the American Medical

---

[1] It should be noted that because of the short amount of time between the slated release of this Institute of Medicine report (March 2001) and the production of the first Quality Report in fiscal year 2003 (which begins October 1, 2002), a Department of Health and Human Services working group was formed and held several meetings at about the same time as the IOM committee. The purpose of the working group is to begin preparations in three major areas—measures, report design and market research, and report writing (Meyer, 2000).

Association (AMA). The committee also heard from IOM staff members involved in other studies relevant to this one including Maria Hewitt and Jeffrey Koshel (now at the U.S. Department of Health and Human Services [DHHS]).

To gather additional information from a variety of perspectives, the committee held a two-day workshop, "Envisioning a National Quality Report on Health Care." Twenty-seven speakers delivered testimony on an array of topics, including the feasibility of measuring safety, effectiveness, "patient centeredness," and efficiency as system aims for quality of care; the availability and appropriateness of public and private data sources to support measures of quality of care; the feasibility of applying experiences in quality measurement and reporting from other sectors; and the need for specific measures to gauge the quality of care for particular populations and to track potential disparities in the quality of care (see Appendix A for the workshop agenda and list of speakers).

As part of the workshop, the committee commissioned four papers on issues of particular importance; it heard testimony and held discussions based on these papers: "Patient-Centeredness Measures for the National Quality Report," by Christina Bethell (FACCT); "Effectiveness and Appropriateness of Care Measures for the National Quality Report," by Elizabeth McGlynn, Paul Shekelle, and Robert Brook (RAND) (see Appendix B for an excerpt from this paper); "Efficiency Measures for the National Quality Report," by Mark McClellan (Stanford University); and "Data Sources and Potential Indicators for a National Quality Report," by Marsha Gold (Mathematica Policy Research).

Following the workshop, the committee issued a limited call to organizations and individuals in the private sector for measures of specific aspects of the quality of health care.[2] Specifically, it requested measures of health care safety, effectiveness, patient centeredness, and timeliness. It also requested measures that addressed consumer perspectives or patient needs for care to stay healthy, get better, live with illness, or cope with changing needs (later renamed "coping with the end of life"). These terms are defined in Chapter 2. In response to its call, the committee received 138 suggested measures from eight organizations and two individuals (see Appendix C). The purpose of the call for measures was to gather information about the type of measures available in the private sector and the aspects they addressed. It was not to produce an exhaustive inventory of quality measures. The results obtained provided the committee with information about potential gaps and reflected the absence of measures to assess certain aspects of the proposed framework. The measures submitted covered many of the aspects of health care quality contained in the call, but the greatest number referred to effectiveness of care and living with illness or getting better. Safety and coping with the end of life had the fewest number of submissions.

---

[2] Public-sector agencies were excluded because AHRQ would be issuing that call directly. It did so after the committee had concluded its work, so the results could not be considered for this report.

DEFINING HEALTH CARE QUALITY

The Committee on the National Quality Report on Health Care Delivery adopted the definition of health care quality first developed by the IOM in 1990: "the degree to which health services for individuals and populations increase the likelihood of desired health outcomes and are consistent with current professional knowledge" (Institute of Medicine, 1990:21). This definition speaks to several key aspects of quality. First, many people, organizations, and institutions provide health care services to patients, and all must be of good quality. Second, quality health care should produce outcomes that patients desire, and patients may vary in their preferences for treatment options (for example, invasive versus noninvasive procedures, limited versus extensive use of lifesaving measures). Third, quality health care does not guarantee desirable outcomes. Factors beyond the control of providers or organizations, such as environmental hazards, can undermine even the best care. It is also true that phenomena such as human resilience may mean that in spite of poor-quality care there may be surprisingly good results. Lastly, it addresses the responsibility that all providers have to inform themselves about the most recent advances in their fields (Chassin and Galvin, 1998).

In its consideration of health care quality, the committee examined the seminal work of Avedis Donabedian (1966, 1980), who defined quality in terms of structure ("the settings in which [health care] takes place and the instrumentalities of which it is the product"), process ("whether what is now known as 'good' medical care has been applied"), and outcomes ("in terms of recovery, restoration of function and of survival") (Donabedian, 1966:167, 169–170).

The committee was also influenced by the work of the Foundation for Accountability, a nonprofit organization that provides support for consumer decision making in health care. Its research has called attention to the need to consider the consumer's perspective on health care quality in communicating messages and measurement results (Foundation for Accountability, 1999). As described in Chapter 2, the committee adopted and slightly revised FACCT's consumer information model as part of the National Health Care Quality Framework. It did this in recognition of the need to measure quality in ways that are meaningful to the consumer.

RECENT INITIATIVES ON HEALTH CARE QUALITY AND QUALITY REPORTING

The work of the committee has drawn from several recent initiatives on health care quality and quality measurement. Increasing attention has been paid to these issues in the past few years. In recent years, several major reports have been released, each addressing serious gaps in the quality of care. In its consensus statement, the IOM's National Roundtable on Health Care Quality declared that "[p]roblems in health care quality are serious and extensive; they occur in all delivery systems and financing mechanisms. Americans bear a great burden of harm because of these problems, a burden that is measured in lost lives, reduced functioning, and wasted resources" (Chassin and Galvin, 1998:1001). One of the aspects highlighted by the roundtable was the need to develop new quality measures, particularly those that would appeal to consumers.

The President's Advisory Commission on Consumer Protection and Quality in the Health Care Industry found major and widespread shortcomings in health care quality. According to its analysis, these problems "endanger the health and lives of all patients, add costs to the health care system, and reduce productivity" (Advisory Commission on Consumer Protection and Quality in the Health Care Industry, 1998). In addition to greater public reporting on quality, the commission recommended standardized reporting by the health care industry on core sets of quality measures; the development of a framework and increased capacity for quality measurement and reporting; industry support for the development of quality measures; and the creation of a private-sector forum to oversee quality measurement requirements, specifications, and reporting (Advisory Commission on Consumer Protection and Quality in the Health Care Industry, 1998).

A review of the scientific literature on the quality of care, conducted by scholars at RAND, further substantiated the statements of both of these groups. Based on an analysis of peer-reviewed publications between 1993 and mid-1997, the review provided strong support for findings of serious deficiencies in health care quality (Schuster et al., 1998; Schuster et al., 2001).

The National Cancer Policy Board of the IOM and the National Research Council (NRC) specifically examined quality of care for cancer patients. They issued a report in 1999 that emphasized the importance of using measures to assess the quality of cancer care and of holding providers accountable for care. The board also recommended that providers be required to report quality measures to qualify for Medicare and Medicaid payment (Institute of Medicine and National Research Council, 1999).

From 1998 to 2001, the IOM Quality of Health Care in America Project studied ways to improve health care quality in the long and short terms. Related activities included

• a literature review and synthesis of findings on health care quality to support continuing research;
• a communications strategy to raise awareness of health care quality on the part of the public and of stakeholders;
• a framework and measurement strategy to estimate the value of investing in health care services; and
• the identification of means by which to encourage continuous quality improvement by purchasers, providers, and other stakeholders.

The first report from the project, *To Err Is Human: Building a Safer Health System*, was released early in 2000. It focuses on ways to improve reporting and prevention (Institute of Medicine, 2000). The second report, *Crossing the Quality Chasm: A Health System for the 21st Century*, was released in the spring of 2001 (Institute of Medicine, 2001). It examines how the health care delivery system can be redesigned to improve the quality of care in all its dimensions.

OTHER NATIONAL AND INTERNATIONAL INITIATIVES ON HEALTH CARE QUALITY MEASUREMENT

The Quality Report is part of a larger national and international movement to measure quality in general, and health care quality in particular, as a necessary step in determining where improvements could and should be made (Epstein, 1996; Hussey and Anderson, 2000). While there have been many developments in this direction in the past few years, health care quality reporting and measurement have been the long-term focus of important state, national, and international initiatives. This section surveys those initiatives to provide background on the larger picture of innovations that have influenced the committee's recommendations on the Quality Report. Many of these initiatives also involve reporting, but the focus of the discussion here is on quality measurement. Quality reporting is discussed in Chapter 5.

National Initiatives

National Committee for Quality Assurance

The National Committee for Quality Assurance (NCQA) is a private, nonprofit organization that accredits managed care plans and reports on the quality of the care they provide. Established in 1990, it assumed responsibility two years later for the Health Plan Employer Data and Information Set (HEDIS) from its original developer, the HMO Group. In 1993, NCQA issued the first update of HEDIS, which would soon become the standard measurement tool for assessing health plan performance. Since then, NCQA has released several versions. To date, it contains 51 measures (including 16 on effectiveness of care) that provide standard ways to assess and compare plan performance (National Committee for Quality Assurance, 2000). HEDIS 2001 also includes a battery of questions from the Consumer Assessment of Health Plans Survey described in this chapter.

Agency for Healthcare Research and Quality

In 1995, the Agency for Healthcare Research and Quality (then the Agency for Health Care Policy and Research [AHCPR]) initiated the development of the CAHPS family of surveys by funding and working with researchers to develop questionnaires, as well as reporting formats, on the experiences that health plan members had in receiving care. The aim of the surveys and the reporting formats was to provide information to consumers that they could use in making decisions on joining health plans. Following the release of CAHPS 1.0 in 1998, AHRQ joined with NCQA and other CAHPS researchers to develop new versions, which include many questions from the original version as well as items from the NCQA's Membership Satisfaction Survey. Since the release of the first version of CAHPS, a variety of groups, including NCQA, the Health Care Financing Administration (HCFA), peer review organizations (PROs), and private sector organizations, have developed their own versions of the survey to fit their objectives (Agency for Healthcare Research and Quality, 2000).

Foundation for Accountability

Founded in 1995, the Foundation for Accountability has sought to bring the consumer perspective to the issue of quality measurement. In particular, it has been engaged in formulating measures that consumers find relevant and easy to understand. To do so, it has worked to identify measures used by other organizations that fit this description, such as HEDIS measures used by NCQA and measures from CAHPS surveys used by NCQA, HCFA, and others. FACCT has developed measure sets for adult asthma, alcohol misuse, breast cancer, diabetes, major depressive disorder, health status, and health risks, and is in the process of formulating measures in other areas, including child and adolescent health, coronary artery disease, end-of-life care, and HIV/AIDS (Foundation for Accountability, 2000a). FACCT uses the measures that it and other organizations have developed as the basis for defining quality reports that consumers can use to compare health plans (Foundation for Accountability, 2000b).

Health Care Financing Administration

As part of its responsibility to administer the Medicare program, HCFA carries out a number of quality improvement and measurement programs. The Health Care Quality Improvement Program (HCQIP) has been a major initiative. The agency sets quality improvement targets in certain clinical areas, and state-based PROs monitor performance and encourage improvements (Health Care Financing Administration, 2000). Recently, HCFA released results from its HCQIP program showing wide variation among states in general. It also showed geographic patterns in state performance: northern and/or less populous states tended to have higher ranking than southern and/or more populous states (Jencks, 2000).

National Quality Forum

The National Forum for Health Care Quality Measurement and Reporting (known as the National Quality Forum) was established in response to the President's Advisory Commission's call for an organization to address pressing issues in health care quality measurement and reporting (Advisory Commission on Consumer Protection and Quality in the Health Care Industry, 1998). It is a public–private partnership among national, state, and local organizations of consumers, purchasers, providers, labor unions, and others (Foster et al., 1999; Miller and Leatherman, 1999). It is now undertaking a project to analyze quality measures for acute care hospitals that have already been applied or are being developed and to assess the need for new ones (National Quality Forum, 2000).

The Leapfrog Group

Founded in 1999, the Leapfrog Group consists of a growing number of Fortune 500 companies and other large health care purchasers that have joined forces to "trigger a giant leap forward in quality, customer service and affordability of health care" (Leapfrog Group, 2000a). Their two-pronged strategy to achieve this goal is educating the public about patient safety and defining a set of purchasing principles designed to promote safety and increase the value of health care. The Leapfrog Group is initially focusing on three hospital safety measures that will be the basis for provider performance comparisons and hospital recognition. The measures identified are (1) the use of computerized physician order entry systems; (2) evidence-based hospital referrals of patients with complex problems to specialized facilities; and (3) staffing of intensive care units with physicians specializing in critical care (Leapfrog Group, 2000b). These measures were selected based on research evidence that indicates their potential to improve safety and save lives (Birkmeyer et al., 2000).

State Initiatives

Almost all states require that health care data be collected, analyzed, and distributed (Gormley and Weimer, 1999). The Vermont Program for Quality in Health Care (VPQHC) illustrates a comprehensive approach—the state contracts with this nonprofit corporation to measure and report quality across several health conditions and dimensions, providing a broad overview of performance (Vermont Program for Quality in Health Care, 2000). Other states such as California, Maryland, Missouri, New Jersey, and New York have adopted more

> **BOX 1.1 Selective Quality Reporting in Pennsylvania**
>
> *Pennsylvania's Guide to Coronary Artery Bypass Graft Surgery* presents risk-adjusted mortality data for individual cardiac surgeons; Medicare and Medicaid; fee-for-service and managed care plans; and public and private hospitals approved by the state to perform the procedure. It also provides risk-adjusted mortality data for length of hospital stay by hospital and by plan. In addition, it presents data on the volume of coronary artery bypass graft surgeries performed in hospitals and by individual surgeons and data on average hospital charges for the procedure. Publication of the report encourages hospitals, surgeons, and health plans to use the information in their efforts to improve quality and encourages consumers to compare quality and price performance in making their choice. Research shows that about one-third of Pennsylvania hospitals approved for the operation have used performance measures to recruit physicians. Some hospitals have also changed practices in marketing and patient care based on the report's results.
>
> SOURCES: Bentley and Nash, 1998; Jollis and Romano, 1998; Pennsylvania Health Care Cost Containment Council, 1998; Schneider and Epstein, 1998.

selective approaches, measuring and reporting on the quality of particular surgical procedures, specific health conditions, or individual health care institutions (Bentley and Nash, 1998; Hannan et al., 1995; Maryland Health Care Commission, 2000; New Jersey Department of Health and Senior Services, 2000; Zach et al., 1997). For example, the Pennsylvania Health Care Cost Containment Council (PHC4) presents quality-of-care measures in separate publications for hospitals and health maintenance organizations (HMOs) overall; different reports on hospital, doctor, and plan performance in heart attack treatment and in coronary artery bypass graft (CABG) surgery; and reports on HMO management of diabetes (Box 1.1) (Bentley and Nash, 1998; Jollis and Romano, 1998; Pennsylvania Health Care Cost Containment Council, 1998; Schneider and Epstein, 1998).

International Initiatives

The World Health Organization, the Organization for Economic Cooperation and Development (OECD), and nations including the United States, England, Canada, and Australia are among those undertaking major initiatives to measure and report on quality and other aspects of health care (Commonwealth Fund, 2000; Hurst and Jee-Hughes, 2001; World Health Organization, 2000). Although these efforts are in different stages of development, all involve the identification of major aspects of quality, followed by measurement formulation, data collection, and reporting. All aim to take a comprehensive approach to quality reporting. While there are strong similarities across countries, there are also strong differences (Department of Health, 2000; Health Canada, 2000; National Health Performance Committee, 2000).

The initiatives by the United Kingdom, Canada, and Australia are in broad agreement on the aspects of health care quality that deserve particular attention and that can be directly—if not solely—influenced by the health care system. These are patient safety, health care effectiveness, patient satisfaction, timely care, efficient care, and equitable care (see Box 1.2 on the United Kingdom's National Health Service) (Department of Health, 2000; Health Canada, 2000; National Health Performance Committee, 2000).

Countries often use a variety of terms for some of these aspects of quality and define them somewhat differently. For example, the Australian initiative defines timeliness in terms of accessibility, continuity, and equity, whereas the Canadian initiative defines it only in terms of accessibility and continuity. As Chapter 2 shows, these definitions can also differ from those formulated by the committee for use in the National Health Care Quality Report. For example, the committee uses the broader concept of patient centeredness rather than patient satisfaction as one of the components of health care quality (Health Canada, 2000; National Health Performance Committee, 2000).

These international initiatives differ in other ways. Perhaps most importantly, different nations emphasize different aspects of quality. The quality initiative in The United Kingdom emphasizes the importance of measuring and reporting on the quality of health service delivery. Canada highlights the importance of public health concerns as well as health system performance (Health Canada, 2000).

Despite these and other differences, the international initiatives commonly recognize the central role that quality measurement plays in efforts to improve quality and the need to develop adequate measures and data sources to make it easier to identify areas in which performance is lagging and reasons for the poor performance. Although they are more implicit, initiatives by The United Kingdom, Canada, and Australia also recognize the significance of consumer information needs, especially those that apply to acute care (Department of Health, 2000a; Health Canada, 2000; National Health Performance Committee, 2000).

**BOX 1.2 The United Kingdom's National Health
Service Quality Performance Reports**

In 2000, the National Health Service (NHS) issued its second annual report on quality performance in hospitals. These annual reports are part of a new national quality initiative launched by the NHS in 1998. The reports are based on a framework that contains six *key areas* that patients most care about: *health improvement; fair access to services; effective delivery of health care; efficiency; patient and carer experience;* and *health outcomes of NHS care.* The report assesses performance at the national and local levels using a growing set of measures in areas such as service utilization, patient satisfaction, care outcomes, and service performance. Future plans call for developing new measures and methods of risk adjustment, which is not currently performed. Also, a National Survey of Patient and User Experience will be conducted to provide a fuller picture of patient satisfaction.

The NHS is developing separate National Service Frameworks for specific conditions and population groups. These frameworks provide the NHS with national standards and service models, create performance measures with timelines for assessing progress, and establish programs to carry them out. The NHS has already produced National Service Frameworks for mental health and coronary heart disease. Frameworks for older people and for diabetes are currently being developed.

SOURCES: Department of Health, 2000a, b; Enthoven, 2000; Mulligan et al., 2000.

QUALITY MEASUREMENT AND REPORTING IN OTHER SECTORS

Although it focused on experiences in the health care sector, the committee also examined quality measurement and reporting initiatives in other areas where such efforts often preceded those in health. In recent years, the popularity of concepts such as Total Quality Management (TQM) have energized efforts to measure quality. TQM and other customer-centered approaches have called attention to the need to measure how well organizations are serving their customers and satisfying their expectations (Dean and Bowen, 1994; Deming, 1982; Drucker, 1993; Merlyn and Parkinson, 1994).

At the May 2000 workshop on envisioning a national quality report on health care delivery, the committee heard testimony regarding the American Customer Satisfaction Index (ACSI) (Fornell, 2000) and the National Assessment of Educational Progress (NAEP) (Carr, 2000). First implemented in 1994, the ACSI is based on customer surveys regarding the goods and services provided by 164 companies and 30 government agencies (Fornell et al., 1996; University of Michigan Business School, 1998). Conducted and published annually, it provides a standard measure of customer satisfaction that can be used to compare service quality across a variety of industries and organizations and guide continuous quality improvement efforts.

At the workshop, the committee also learned about an initiative in another service sector—education—which is more closely related to the National Health Care Quality Report. The National Assessment of Educational Progress has been conducted since 1969 to evaluate academic excellence and gauge the state of education in the country (Box 1.3) (Carr, 2000; National Center for Education Statistics, 2000).

BOX 1.3 The National Assessment of Educational Progress

The NAEP is known as "the Nation's Report Card." The only national evaluation of academic achievement of its kind, it measures how well students perform in reading, mathematics, science, writing, history, geography, and other subjects. Congressionally mandated and conducted since 1969, it reflects the condition and progress of education in the United States over time. One of its main purposes is to provide information for decision making to national- and state-level policy makers as well as school administrators, principals and teachers. It is also widely disseminated by the media and of interest to the general public. Since 1990, a state-level version (conducted in 47 of the 50 states as of the year 2000) has produced accurate estimates so that states can compare their results with those of the nation and other states. The results of the NAEP have also been used to compare the quality of education in the United States to that of other countries. The NAEP is administered by the National Center for Education Statistics in the Department of Education and guided by the policies formulated by the National Assessment Governing Board established by Congress in 1988.

SOURCES: Carr, 2000; National Center for Education Statistics, 2000; National Research Council, 1998, 2000, 2001.

OBJECTIVES OF THE NATIONAL HEALTH CARE QUALITY REPORT

Mandated by Congress, the National Health Care Quality Report should supply a much-needed source of authoritative information on health care quality in the United States. The primary audiences for the Quality Report are national- and state-level policy makers (as is later discussed in Chapter 5). The report should also be of interest to consumers, health care providers, and health care purchasers. More specifically, the Quality Report should play a vital role in badly needed quality improvement efforts by

- supplying a common understanding of quality and how to measure it that reflects the best current approaches and practices;
- identifying aspects of the health care system that improve or impede quality;
- generating data associated with major quality initiatives;
- educating the public, the media, and other audiences about the importance of health care quality and the current level of quality;
- identifying for policy makers the problem areas in health care quality that most need their attention and action, with the understanding that these priorities may change over time and differ by geographic location;
- providing policy makers, purchasers, health care providers, and others with realistic benchmarks for quality of care in the form of national, regional, and population comparisons;
- making it easier to compare the quality of the U.S. health care system with that of other nations;
- stimulating the refinement of existing measures and the development of new ones;
- stimulating data collection efforts at the state and local levels (mirroring the national effort) to facilitate targeted quality improvements;
- incorporating improved measures as they become available and practicable;
- clarifying the many aspects of health care quality and how they affect one another and quality as a whole; and
- encouraging the data collection efforts needed to refine and develop quality measures and, ultimately, stimulate the development of a health information infrastructure to support quality measurement and reporting.

To better understand what the Quality Report should try to achieve, it is also important to understand how it differs from other annual reports on health-related topics. The legislation that mandates the Quality Report also mandates a report on disparities in health care delivery by race and socioeconomic status (Healthcare Research and Quality Act, 1999:Sec. 902). Although its content has not been defined yet, the "disparities report" will probably provide in-depth analyses of possible disparities in the quality of care that may also be indicated in the Quality Report. These two efforts will have to be articulated so that they complement each other. Although the Quality Report may include some of the same measures and draw on some of the same sources of data as other reports, it should be a distinct product tailored to respond to the objectives just outlined.

Health United States, produced annually by the Centers for Disease Control and Prevention (CDC) and the National Center for Health Statistics (NCHS), provides an overview of the health status of the American people (National Center for Health Statistics, 2000). The Quality Report will include related information since the quality of care offered by the health care system can affect health status.

America's Children, produced by the Forum on Child and Family Statistics, and HCFA's annual *Health Care Financing Review Medicare and Medicaid Statistical Supplement*, are examples of documents that focus on specific populations or subpopulations (Federal Interagency Forum on Child and Family Statistics, 2000; Health Care Financing Administration, 1999). In contrast, the Quality Report is concerned with the population of the United States as a whole, although it will also present data for specific subpopulations (for example, by race or ethnicity) as a means of examining equity. In addition, by including information on both the insured and the uninsured, the Quality Report would be more inclusive than current quality reports, which typically include only health plan enrollees.

The Quality Report should also be distinguished from *Healthy People 2010*, produced by the U.S. Department of Health and Human Services (2000). In *Healthy People 2010*, DHHS sets national goals for improvement in targeted areas of public health, specifically 467 objectives in 28 focus areas (Box 1.4). One of the focus areas is "access to quality health services." Others include aspects related to the management of chronic illness that may overlap with measures included in the Quality Report. However, the subject matter of *Healthy People 2010* is public health, whereas the Quality Report's is mainly personal health care services. The majority of the *Healthy People 2010* objectives refer to social, behavioral, environmental, and other factors that affect health status but generally lie outside the influence of the health care delivery system.

The Quality Report should be dynamically linked to the goal-setting processes of the appropriate public- and private-sector actors in the health care arena. It should continually reflect and be used to shape goals for quality improvement by presenting information that is useful to policy makers and others to define clear objectives, assess progress, and define appropriate actions. The Quality Report should differ from other efforts to report on health care quality. A wide range of public- and private-sector organizations have undertaken initiatives to report on health care quality. These include accrediting organizations such as NCQA and JCAHO; national government agencies such as HCFA and AHRQ; state and local government agencies such as the Pennsylvania Health Care Cost Containment Council; and individual health plans, medical groups, and institutions such as hospitals. In addition, national magazines, such as *U.S. News and World Report,* and state and local publications feature information on the health care quality of plans, providers, and organizations. A large number of "third-party" organizations also provide information on health care quality, often through free or fee-based web sites. These organizations include Health Care Choices, HealthGrades, HealthScope, and WebMD, to name a few (Bates and Gawande, 2000).

BOX 1.4 *Healthy People 2010* Focus Areas

1. Access to Quality Health Services
2. Arthritis, Osteoporosis, and Chronic Back Conditions
3. Cancer
4. Chronic Kidney Disease
5. Diabetes
6. Disability and Secondary Conditions
7. Educational and Community-Based Programs
8. Environmental Health
9. Family Planning
10. Food Safety
11. Health Communication
12. Heart Disease and Stroke
13. HIV
14. Immunization and Infectious Diseases
15. Injury and Violence Prevention
16. Maternal, Infant, and Child Health
17. Medical Product Safety
18. Mental Health and Mental Disorders
19. Nutrition and Overweight
20. Occupational Safety and Health
21. Oral Health
22. Physical Activity and Fitness
23. Public Health Infrastructure
24. Respiratory Diseases
25. Sexually Transmitted Diseases
26. Substance Abuse
27. Tobacco Use
28. Vision and Hearing

SOURCE: U.S. Department of Health and Human Services, 2000.

Many of these reporting initiatives are designed primarily to help consumers choose quality health care plans, providers, and organizations by providing ratings, rankings, and other information. Although the Quality Report should also aim to reach consumers, it should do so to engage and inform them about quality trends, developments, and issues at the more general levels of national and state health care systems. This information may provide useful background and comparisons when it comes to making health care choices. However, assisting consumer choice should not be the primary purpose of the report. The main purpose of the Quality Report should be to inform policy makers and consumers, as well as purchasers and providers, about the state and progress of health care quality in the United States. It should examine the quality of care provided by the system as a whole and not care delivered in specific health care settings by specific providers.

ORGANIZATION OF THE IOM REPORT

The remainder of this report builds on the overview of quality presented in this chapter. Chapter 2 introduces the framework for the National Health Care Quality Report. This kind of framework is a tool used to "explain, either graphically or in narrative form, the main things to be studied—the key factors, constructs or variables—and the presumed relationships among them" (Miles and Huberman, 1994:1). The National Health Care Quality Framework presents the categories of measures needed to comprehensively assess the quality of health care in the United States. It forms the basis for the National Health Care Quality Data Set, which contains the measures and data sources used for the Quality Report.

Figure 1.1 illustrates the ways in which the committee defined a framework to guide its vision of the Quality Report and, by extension, the ways in which AHRQ could use that framework to guide production of the actual report. On the left-hand side of the figure are listed the different processes involved in creating the report. On the right-hand side are listed the products generated by these processes. First, the process of determining the framework produces categories of measures. These categories suggest the measures that should be selected for the report, or the measure set. Chapter 3 presents a discussion of specific selection criteria used to examine the pool of potential measures and to define the set of measures that will be applied.

The measure set that is defined, in turn, guides the process of selecting data sources for the data set, which will support the measure set. Chapter 4 contains a discussion of the National Health Care Quality Data Set, including data from existing surveys and new data collection efforts. The discussion includes criteria that can be used in selecting sources for the data set.

The measure set and the data set support the comprehensive approach to measuring quality defined by the framework. A comprehensive approach to measurement is necessary to ensure that major aspects of health care quality are captured. However, the actual report should take a selective approach to communicating about quality, focusing on the most important findings resulting from this comprehensive measurement approach in order to ensure that they receive adequate attention. Chapter 5 contains guidelines on how to choose the findings and measures of quality to be communicated in an annual report or family of reports. Lastly, it includes guidelines on how to promote the Quality Report and how to improve it from year to year.

Process   Product

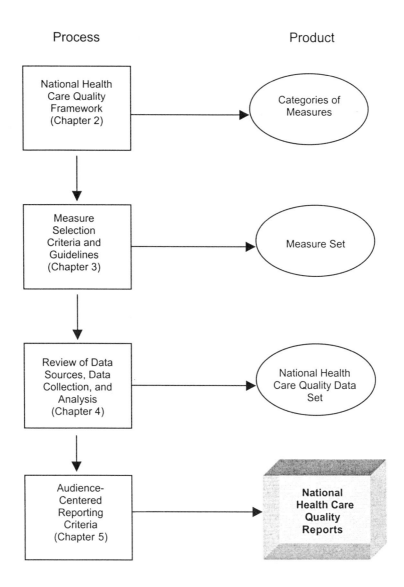

FIGURE 1.1 From the National Health Care Quality Framework to the National Health Care Quality Report.

REFERENCES

Advisory Commission on Consumer Protection and Quality in the Health Care Industry. 1998. *Quality First: Better Health Care for All Americans*. Washington, D.C.: U.S. Government Printing Office.

Agency for Healthcare Research and Quality. 2000. *Consumer Assessment of Health Plans Fact Sheet* [on-line]. Available at: http://www.ahrq.gov/qual/cahpfact.htm [Nov. 28, 2000].

Bates, David W., and Atul A. Gawande. 2000. The impact of the Internet on quality measurement. *Health Affairs* 19(6):104–114.

Bentley, J. Marvin, and David B. Nash. 1998. How Pennsylvania hospitals have responded to publicly released reports on coronary artery bypass graft surgery. *Joint Commission Journal on Quality Improvement* 24(1): 40–49.

Birkmeyer, John D., Christian Birkmeyer, David E. Wennberg, and Michael Young. 2000. *Leapfrog Safety Standards: The Potential Benefits of Universal Adoption*. Available at: http://www.leapfroggroup.org/safety1.htm.

Carr, Peggy G. 2000. Presentation to the Institute of Medicine Committee on the National Quality Report on Health Care Delivery. National Center for Education Statistics, U.S. Department of Education.

Chassin, Mark R., and Robert W. Galvin. 1998. The urgent need to improve health care quality: Institute of Medicine National Roundtable on Health Care Quality. *Journal of the American Medical Association* 280(11):1000–1005.

Commonwealth Fund, Harvard School of Public Health, and Harris Interactive. 2000. *2000 International Health Policy Survey of Physicians*, New York.

Dean, James W., and David E. Bowen. 1994. Management theory and total quality: Improving research and practice through theory development. *Academy of Management Review* 19(3):392–418.

Deming, W. Edwards. 1982. *Quality, Productivity, and Competitive Position*. Cambridge, Mass.: Massachusetts Institute of Technology, Center for Advanced Engineering Study.

Department of Health. 2000a. *NHS Performance Indicators*. Leeds, England: National Health Service (NHS) Executive. Available at: http://www.doh.gov.uk/nhsperfor manceindicators.

Department of Health. 2000b. *National Service Frameworks* [on-line]. Available at: http://www.doh.gov.uk/nsf/about.htm [Feb. 6, 2001].

Donabedian, Avedis. 1966. Evaluating the quality of medical care. *Milbank Memorial Fund Quarterly* 44:166–203.

Donabedian, Avedis. 1980. *Explorations in Quality Assessment and Monitoring*, Vol. 1. Ann Arbor, Mich.: Health Administration Press.

Drucker, Peter F. 1993. *The Practice of Management*. New York: HarperBusiness.

Enthoven, Alain C. 2000. In pursuit of an improving National Health Service. *Health Affairs* 19(3):102–119.

Epstein, Arnold M. 1996. The role of quality measurement in a competitive marketplace. Pp. 201–204 in *Strategic Choices for a Changing Health Care System*. eds. Stuart Altman and Uwe E. Reinhardt. Chicago, Ill.: Health Administration Press.

Federal Interagency Forum on Child and Family Statistics. 2000. *America's Children: Key National Indicators of Well-Being, 2000*. Washington, D.C.: U.S. Government Printing Office.

Fornell, Claes. 2000. Measuring Consumer Satisfaction with Quality Across Industries—The American Customer Satisfaction Index. Presentation at the Institute of Medicine Workshop "Envisioning a National Quality Report on Health Care," May 22.

Fornell, Claes, Michael D. Johnson, Eugene W. Anderson, Jaesung Cha, and Barbara Everitt Bryant. 1996. The American Customer Satisfaction Index: nature, purpose, and findings. *Journal of Marketing* 60:7–18.

Foster, Nancy S., Anthony D. So, and John M. Eisenberg. 1999. *Improving the Nation's Health Care Quality: The President's Quality Commission Report, the Quality Forum and the Quality Interagency Task Force*, U.S. Department of Health and Human Services. Unpublished.

Foundation for Accountability. 1999. *Sharing the Quality Message With Consumers*. Portland, Ore.

Foundation for Accountability. 2000a. *Measuring Quality* [on-line]. Available at: http://www.facct.org/measures.html [Dec. 4, 2000].

Foundation for Accountability. 2000b. *About FACCT* [on-line]. Available at: http://www.facct.org/about.html [Dec. 4, 2000].

Gormley, William T., and David L. Weimer. 1999. *Organizational Report Cards*. Cambridge, Mass.: Harvard University Press.

Hannan, Edward L., Albert L. Siu, Dinesh Kumar, Harold Kilburn, and Mark R. Chassin. 1995. The decline in coronary artery bypass graft surgery mortality in New York State. *Journal of the American Medical Association* 273(3):209–213.

Health Canada. 2000. *Quest for Quality in Canadian Health Care: Continuous Quality Improvement* [on-line]. Available at: http://www.hc-sc.gc.ca/hppb/healthcare/pubs/quest/index.html.

Health Care Financing Administration. 1999. *Health Care Financing Review: Medicare and Medicaid Statistical Supplement, 1999*, Baltimore, Md.: U.S. Department of Health and Human Services.

Health Care Financing Administration. 2000. *Health Care Quality Improvement Program (HCQuIP)* [on-line]. Available at: http://www.hcfa.gov/quality/5b1.htm [Nov. 28, 2000].

Healthcare Research and Quality Act. 1999. *Statutes at Large*. Vol. 113, Sec. 1653.

Hurst, Jeremy, and Melissa Jee-Hughes. 2001. *Performance Measurement and Performance Management in OECD Health Systems*. Paris, France: Organization for Economic Cooperation and Development.

Institute of Medicine. 1990. *Medicare: A Strategy for Quality Assurance*, Vol. 2. ed. Kathleen Lohr. Washington, D.C.: National Academy Press.

Institute of Medicine. 1999. *Measuring the Quality of Health Care*. ed. Molla S. Donaldson. Washington, D.C.: National Academy Press.

Institute of Medicine. 2000. *To Err Is Human: Building a Safer Health System*. eds. Linda T. Kohn, Janet M. Corrigan, and Molla S. Donaldson. Washington, D.C.: National Academy Press.

Institute of Medicine. 2001. *Crossing the Quality Chasm: A New Health System for the 21st Century*. Washington, D.C.: National Academy Press.

Institute of Medicine and National Research Council. 1999. *Ensuring Quality Cancer Care*. eds. Maria Hewitt and Joseph V. Simone. Washington, D.C.: National Academy Press.

Jencks, Stephen F. 2000. Clinical performance measurement—A hard sell. *Journal of the American Medical Association* 283(15):2015–2016.

Jollis, James G., and Patrick S. Romano. 1998. Pennsylvania's focus on heart attack—grading the scorecard. *New England Journal of Medicine* 338(14):983–987.

Leapfrog Group. 2000a. *Fact Sheet* [on-line]. Available at: http://www.leapfroggroup.org/FactSheets/LF_FactSheet.pdf [Feb. 7, 2001].

Leapfrog Group. 2000b. *Patient Safety* [on-line]. Available at: http://leapfroggroup.org/safety1.htm [Feb. 7, 2000].

Maryland Health Care Commission. 2000. *Comparing the Quality of Maryland HMOs*, Baltimore, Md. Available at: http://www.mhcc.state.md.us.

Merlyn, Vaughan, and John Parkinson. 1994. *Development Effectiveness: Strategies for IS Organizational Transition*. New York: John Wiley & Sons.

Meyer, Gregg, 2000. Personal communication, Jan. 18. Agency for Healthcare Research and Quality.

Miles, Matthew B., and A. Michael Huberman. 1994. *Qualitative Data Analysis*. Thousand Oaks, Calif.: Sage.

Miller, Tracy, and Sheila Leatherman. 1999. The National Quality Forum: A 'me-too' or a breakthrough in quality measurement and reporting. *Health Affairs* 18(6):233–237.

Mulligan, Jo, John Appleby, and Anthony Harrison. 2000. Measuring the performance of health systems. *British Medical Journal* 321:191–192.

National Center for Education Statistics. 2000. *The Nation's Report Card: National Assessment of Educational Progress* [on-line]. Available at: http://nces.ed.gov/nationsreportcard/site/home.asp [Dec. 8, 2000].

National Center for Health Statistics. 2000. *Health, United States, 2000 with Adolescent Health Chartbook*. Hyattsville, Md.: U.S. Government Printing Office.

National Committee for Quality Assurance (NCQA). 2000. *HEDIS 2001*, Vol. 1. Washington, D.C.

National Health Performance Committee. 2000. *Fourth National Report on Health Sector Performance Indicators—A Report to the Australian Health Ministers' Conference*, Sydney, Australia: New South Wales Health Department.

National Quality Forum. 2000. *NQF: About Us* [on-line]. Available at: http://www.qualityforum.org/about/home.htm [Dec. 6, 2000].

National Research Council. 1998. *Grading the Nation's Report Card: Evaluating NAEP and Transforming the Assessment of Education Progress*. eds. James W. Pellegrino, Lee R. Jones, and Karen J. Mitchell. Washington, D.C.: National Academy Press.

National Research Council. 2000. *Grading the Nation's Report Card: Research from the Evaluation of NAEP*. eds. Nambury S. Raju, James W. Pellegrino, Meryl W. Bertenthal, Karen J. Mitchell, and Lee R. Jones. Washington, D.C.: National Academy Press.

National Research Council. 2001. *NAEP Reporting Practices: Investigating District-Level and Market-Basket Reporting*. eds. Pasquale J. DeVito and Judith A. Koening. Washington, D.C.: National Academy Press.

New Jersey Department of Health and Senior Services. 2000. *2000 New Jersey HMO Performance Report: Compare Your Choices*, Trenton. Available at: http:// www. state.nj.us/health.

Pennsylvania Health Care Cost Containment Council. 1998. *Pennsylvania's Guide to Coronary Artery Bypass Graft Surgery 1994–1995*. Harrisburg. Available at: http:// www.phc4.org.

Schneider, Eric, and Arnold M. Epstein. 1998. Use of public performance reports: A survey of patients undergoing cardiac surgery. *Journal of the American Medical Association* 279(20):1638–1642.

Schuster, Mark A., Elizabeth A. McGlynn, and Robert H. Brook. 1998. How good is the quality of care in the United States? *Milbank Quarterly* 76(4):517–563.

Schuster, Mark A., Elizabeth A. McGlynn, Cung B. Pham, Myles D. Spar, and Robert H. Brook. 2001. The quality of health care in the United States: A review of articles since 1987. *Crossing the Quality Chasm: A New Health System for the 21st Century,* Appendix A. Washington, D.C.: National Academy Press.

U.S. Department of Health and Human Services. 2000. *Healthy People 2010*. Washington, D.C.: U.S. Government Printing Office.

University of Michigan Business School. 1998. *American Customer Satisfaction Index* [on-line]. Available at: http://www.bus.umich.edu/research/nqrc/acsi.html [Jan. 29, 2001].

Vermont Program for Quality in Health Care. 2000. *The Vermont Health Care Quality Report,* [on-line]. Available at: http://www.vpqhc.org.

World Health Organization. 2000. *The World Health Report 2000: Health Systems: Improving Performance*. Geneva: WHO.

Zach, Andra P., Patrick S. Romano, and Harold S. Luft. 1997. *Report on Heart Attack, 1991–1993, Volume 1: User's Guide*. Sacramento: California Office of Statewide Health Planning and Development.

2

Defining the Contents of the Data Set: The National Health Care Quality Framework

This chapter lays out the framework for the National Health Care Quality Report (also referred to as the Quality Report). The framework largely determines the contents of the National Health Care Quality Data Set and categories of measures. The framework proposed by the committee includes two major dimensions: (1) an assessment of the components of health care quality—*safety, effectiveness, "patient centeredness," and timeliness*—and (2) an assessment of how well the system responds to consumer perspectives on health care needs—*staying healthy, getting better, living with illness or disability, and coping with the end of life.* Some measures can be organized by specific condition (for example, diabetes), particularly for effectiveness. Equity can be assessed by analyzing quality of care across different groups of people.

RECOMMENDATION

RECOMMENDATION 1: The conceptual framework for the National Health Care Quality Report should address two dimensions: components of health care quality and consumer perspectives on health care needs. Components of health care quality—the first dimension—include safety, effectiveness, patient centeredness, and timeliness. Consumer perspectives on health care needs—the second dimension—reflect changing needs for care over the life cycle associated with staying healthy, getting better, living with illness or disability, and coping with the end of life. Quality can be examined

along both dimensions for health care in general or for specific conditions. The conceptual framework should also provide for the analysis of equity as an issue that cuts across both dimensions and is reflected in differences in the quality of care received by different groups of the population.

The four system components of health care quality are defined as follows:

1. *Safety* refers to "avoiding injuries or harm to patients from care that is intended to help them" (Institute of Medicine, 2001).
2. *Effectiveness* refers to "providing services based on scientific knowledge to all who could benefit, and refraining from providing services to those not likely to benefit (avoiding overuse and underuse)" (Institute of Medicine, 2001). Overuse occurs when "a health care service is provided under circumstances in which its potential for harm exceeds its potential benefit." Underuse "is the failure to provide a health care service when it would have produced a favorable outcome for a patient" (Chassin and Galvin, 1998:1002).
3. *Patient centeredness* refers to health care that establishes a partnership among practitioners, patients, and their families (when appropriate) to ensure that decisions respect patients' wants, needs, and preferences and that patients have the education and support they need to make decisions and participate in their own care.
4. *Timeliness* refers to obtaining needed care and minimizing unnecessary delays in getting that care.

The relative importance of the four components of health care quality may vary over time and for different providers and policy makers. These quality components apply across all health care settings—from institutionalized to in-patient and ambulatory care; from clinicians' offices to home health care and hospice care.

Consumers have several perspectives on health care. They want a system that will respond to their needs or reasons for seeking care, ranging from staying healthy to coping with the end of life. These needs vary over the life span and across groups of the population. Consumers would like to know about the overall quality of care, but they are particularly interested in care for specific conditions or situations that affect them or their families.

Equity in health care quality is considered an important cross-cutting issue. The framework allows for its consideration by comparing the quality of care for different groups of the population, across geographic areas and by condition, as appropriate.

Efficiency is not included in the committee's framework. Some aspects of efficiency are reflected in other components of quality. For example, errors in health care that result in additional procedures, hospitalizations, or other treatments are a form of waste or inefficiency. The provision of unnecessary services (that is, overuse or ineffectiveness) is another form of waste. Fragmentation of care and unnecessary waits and delays in service (that is, lack of timeliness) consume the patient's and the clinician's time and other resources that could be put to better use. One basic aspect of efficiency that is not reflected in the framework is the cost per unit of service (for example, cost per laboratory test), but this was viewed as falling outside the purview of a national report focusing on the quality of health care services.

IMPORTANCE OF THE FRAMEWORK

A framework serves several important purposes. The framework is a tool for organizing the way one thinks about health care quality. It provides a foundation for quality measurement, data collection, and subsequent reporting. A framework is a way of making explicit the aspects of health care that should be measured (Miles and Huberman, 1994) in order to assess quality and define policy accordingly. Given that quality is a multifaceted subject, the framework provides a way to organize the various elements of the National Health Care Quality Data Set and potential report contents.

A framework defines durable dimensions and categories of measurement that will outlast any specific measures used at particular times. In essence, it lays down an enduring way of specifying *what* should be measured while allowing for variation in *how* it is measured over time. For example, communication between clinicians and patients is an aspect of care that will always have to be measured. However, the ways that patients connect with their clinicians—ranging from office visits to electronic exchanges—will vary over time, and so will the corresponding measures (Balas et al., 1997). When a common framework is established internationally, it also allows for comparisons in the quality of care across countries. Although it will provide continuity for the Quality Report and the measures, the framework should be considered dynamic. In the long term, it may have to be adjusted in response to changes in the conceptualization of quality and/or significant changes in the nature of the U.S. health care system.

NATIONAL HEALTH CARE QUALITY FRAMEWORK

Overview

In order to develop a National Health Care Quality Framework, the committee examined many of the approaches available to analyze quality of care (see Appendix D). The framework proposed herein is based partially on elements from these other approaches. Its foundation ultimately derives from the purpose of the health care system, for which the committee endorses the following statement: "to continuously reduce the burden of illness, injury, and disability, and to improve the health and functioning of the people of the United States" (Advisory Commission on Consumer Protection and Quality in the Health Care Industry, 1998:2).

To assess whether the health care delivery system is making progress in achieving this purpose, the committee developed a framework with two major dimensions. The first dimension consists of the components of health care quality. Building on the work of the Institute of Medicine (IOM) Committee on the Quality of Health Care in America (Institute of Medicine, 2001), these components of quality are defined as *safety, effectiveness, patient centeredness,* and *timeliness.* The second dimension addresses the consumer perspective on health care needs, which reflects the life cycle of people's involvement with the health care system or their reasons for seeking care at any particular time. Building on the work of the Foundation for Accountability (FACCT), consumer perspectives on health care needs are defined as *staying healthy, getting better, living with illness or disability,* and *coping with the end of life* (Foundation for Accountability, 1997).

As the committee refined the framework, it kept in mind the audiences for this report. The framework can be used to encourage measurement and reporting in specific areas to inform national and state policy makers, purchasers, providers, and other specialized audiences. It can also be used to encourage measurement and reporting in areas that consumers and the media will find meaningful and important, including condition-specific care. Equity can be assessed by analyzing the quality of care received by different groups of the population. Defined in this manner, the framework can be used to guide policy and to inform relevant audiences.

Components of Health Care Quality

For each of the four components of quality—safety, effectiveness, patient centeredness, and timeliness—the committee defined a set of subcategories (Table 2.1) and specific examples of potential measures for the National Health Care Quality Report (Boxes 2.1 to 2.4).[1] The components of quality can be thought of as subsets of quality of care, but they are not completely independent of each other. There is some overlap at the boundaries.

---

[1] These measures are offered as examples and are in no way intended to represent the ideal measures or a comprehensive measure set. They are based on a limited review and evaluation of existing measures, leaving gaps with reference to the proposed framework. They do provide an appreciation of the type and range of measures that will be required for the Quality Report.

TABLE 2.1 Components of Health Care Quality and Their Subcategories

Safety	Effectiveness	Patient Centeredness	Timeliness
1. Diagnosis	1. Preventive care	1. Experience of care	1. Access to the system of care

2. Treatment
  a. Medication
  b. Follow-up
	2. Acute, chronic, and end-of-life care	2. Effective partnership	2. Timeliness in getting to care for a particular problem

3. Health care environment	3. Appropriateness of procedures		3. Timeliness within and across episodes of care

Safety refers to "avoiding injuries to patients from care that is intended to help them" (Institute of Medicine, 2001).

Safety

In operational terms, improving safety means designing and implementing health care processes to avoid, prevent, and ameliorate adverse outcomes or injuries that stem from the processes of health care itself (National Patient Safety Foundation, 2000). Safety is best understood in terms of injuries that occur to patients and the errors or latent failures that lead to these injuries or harm. Although both perspectives are essential in building a safer health care system, the overriding priority in the short term is the reduction of injuries or harm to patients. Assessing errors that lead to patient injuries or harm is one method for organizing a framework of measures that will define the safety of the health care system.

An error of execution is the failure of a planned action to be completed as intended, while an error of planning is the use of a wrong plan to achieve an aim (Reason, 1990). Errors have also been classified into errors of commission (doing unnecessary things or doing them wrongly) and errors of omission (failing to do necessary things) (Iezzoni, 1997; Leape et al., 1991). As a component of quality health care, safety problems or patient injuries have been found to occur along the continuum of clinical care functions and in the general environment of care (see examples of safety measures in Box 2.1). Errors in diagnosis, including misdiagnosis (wrong diagnosis) and missed diagnosis (failure to diagnose), are relatively

---

BOX 2.1 Examples of Areas in Which Measures of Safety May Be Applied and Selected Measures

Diagnosis
- Death within 30 days after elective outpatient cardiac stress test (e.g., treadmill, thallium, echocardiogram)
- Misdiagnosis rates based on autopsies
- Preoperative assessment of patients with chronic lung disease or cardiac disease before elective surgery
- Death within 30 days after elective outpatient colonoscopy
- Unplanned readmission after hospitalization at 1 day, 7 days (overall rate for both), and 30 days (diagnosis- or procedure-specific rate)

Treatment
- Death within 30 days after elective outpatient surgical procedures (e.g., cosmetic surgery such as liposuction, facelifts)
- Maternal death within seven days after delivery
- Neonatal death within seven days after birth (>2,500 grams, no congenital abnormalities)
- 30-day mortality following acute myocardial infarction or cardiac bypass surgery
- Deep surgical wound infection rates within 30 days of selected surgical procedures (e.g., cardiac bypass surgery, hip and knee replacement surgery)
- Surgical sentinel event (e.g., rates of wrong-site, wrong-organ, or wrong- patient surgery)
- Rate of inpatient transfusion reactions (overall rate and rate of death-related transfusion reactions)
- Rate of deep venous thrombosis after hip and knee replacement in patients younger than 50 years of age
- Rate of unplanned returns to the operating room within 24 hours for both inpatient and outpatient settings

Medication
- Rates of adverse drug events in diverse settings including inpatient (adult and pediatric), outpatient, and nursing home
- Rates of adverse drug events for specific drug classes

Follow-Up
- Lack of routine medication review for the elderly, the disabled, and patients with chronic illness
- Failure to follow up significant diagnostic abnormalities (e.g., Pap smears, breast biopsies, chest X-rays, HIV serology)
- Proportion of patients with do-not-resuscitate orders on admission who are subsequently intubated or resuscitated

Continued

BOX 2.1 *Continued*

Safety of the Environment
- Neonatal abduction or mixup after birth
- Patient falls (inpatient overall rate and rate with serious injury)
- Patient suicides within health care settings (e.g., inpatient or mental health care setting)
- Rate of hip fractures among nursing home patients
- Rate of restraint-related deaths in any health care setting
- Rate of inpatient nosocomial decubitus ulcers

SOURCES: Joint Commission on Accreditation of Healthcare Organizations, 2000 (see text and Appendix C for additional sources).

---

common (Leape et al., 1991). Their prevalence is estimated at 10 percent among hospital populations based on autopsy studies (Bordage, 1999) and even higher for patients in intensive care units (Mort and Teston, 1999). Treatment errors are problems related to planning, technical proficiency, or prescription practices. Lack of technical proficiency or competence in procedures such as colonoscopy (Miller, 1997) can lead to complications or nosocomial infections.

Medication-related adverse events are a subset of treatment errors that has been studied extensively (Institute of Medicine, 2000). It has been estimated that medication-related adverse drug events occur in nearly 10 percent of all hospital admissions (Leape et al., 1995). Errors can also occur in follow-up care (Christakis and Lamont, 2000). Finally, the safety of the overall health care environment (Gershon et al., 2000) is essential to avoid gross errors such as wrong-site surgery, patient suicide, homicide, and other sentinel events (Joint Commission on Accreditation of Healthcare Organizations, 2000a).

The site of care is one of several characteristics that can be used to further subclassify safety problems. This is an increasingly important aspect to document, given that much of health care, including surgery, is gradually moving away from the hospital to the ambulatory sector (Phillips et al., 1998; Quattrone, 2000). In order to ultimately improve patient safety in health care (as has occurred in high-reliability industries such as aerospace and nuclear power) safety has to be designed or built into the care system at all levels. The Quality Interagency Coordination Task Force (QuIC) has issued a report to the President defining needed actions to improve patient safety, which begins to address many of these issues (Quality Interagency Coordination Task Force, 2000). The Quality Report should include measures to assess the effects of some of these actions as they are implemented.

Effectiveness refers to "providing services based on scientific knowledge to all who could benefit, and refraining from providing services to those not likely to benefit (avoiding overuse and underuse)" (Institute of Medicine, 2001).

Effectiveness

Overuse occurs when "a health care service is provided under circumstances in which its potential for harm exceeds its potential benefit". Underuse "is the failure to provide a health care service when it would have produced a favorable outcome for a patient" (Chassin and Galvin, 1998:1002). Effectiveness is probably the component of health care quality most readily identified because ultimately it represents the "bottom line," that is, whether care leads to improved outcomes in terms of health status and quality of life for patients (Greenfield et al., 1994). People assume that care will be safe, but they want it to be effective as well. A growing body of evidence has documented problems of effectiveness with respect to the overuse of services that cannot help and may harm the patient, as well as problems arising from the underuse of care where benefit is likely to exceed harm (Chassin and Galvin, 1998). A number of studies have also documented the inappropriateness of specific procedures (McGlynn and Brook, 1996). These problems of effectiveness occur in all types of care and across sites.

Effectiveness should be distinguished from efficacy. The latter refers to the benefits achievable from a therapy or intervention under ideal conditions (such as a randomized controlled trial) while the former refers to the results of care in everyday clinical practice settings (Brook and Lohr, 1985). In evaluating the quality of the health care delivery system under actual operating conditions, it is effectiveness rather than efficacy that should be assessed. Effectiveness can be assessed according to the type of care (for example, preventive care, acute, chronic, and end-of-life care) or for specific conditions. The appropriateness of selected procedures is another subcategory of effectiveness (see examples of effectiveness measures in Box 2.2 and Appendix B).

The effectiveness of preventive care can be assessed comprehensively by examining the full spectrum of needs for a defined population or age group such as children or the elderly (see Appendix B). In this case, the services actually received by a specific group as reflected in medical records or a similar data source are compared to the services they should receive according to prevailing guidelines (U.S. Preventive Services Task Force, 1996). The effectiveness of preventive care can also be assessed selectively by examining screening and interventions for specific conditions or problems such as childhood immunizations (Centers for Disease Control and Prevention, 1999), prenatal care (Expert Panel on Prenatal Care, 1989; Genest, 1981; Grad and Hill, 1992), or cervical cancer screening (National Institutes of Health, 1996).

BOX 2.2 Examples of Areas in Which Measures of Effectiveness May Be Applied and Selected Measures

Preventive Care
- Advising smokers to quit
- Flu shots for adults over age 65
- Chlamydia screening
- Pap smears
- Childhood immunization rates
- Prenatal and postpartum care (includes timely initiation of prenatal care and checkups after delivery)
- Biennial mammography screening for women 52 to 69 years of age
- Screening for depression

Acute, Chronic, and End-of-Life Care

Asthma
- Appropriate medications for people with asthma
- Asthma-specific function as reported by the patient
- Asthma episodes of exacerbation
- Specific treatment such as appropriate inhaler use

Heart Disease
- Appropriate drug treatment for acute myocardial infarction (AMI) (e.g., beta-blockers, aspirin, angiotensin-converting enzyme [ACE] inhibitors)
- Use of alternate forms of vascularization for discrete indications
- 30-day mortality after AMI
- Cholesterol management after acute cardiovascular events
- Coronary artery bypass graft (CABG) mortality

Cancer (breast, prostate, colon)
Breast Cancer
- Biennial mammography screening
- Radiation therapy following breast conservation surgery
Prostate Cancer
- Patient-reported understanding of options
Colon Cancer
- Colon cancer screening tests beginning at age 40 for patients who have one or more first-degree relatives with colorectal cancer (fetal occult blood test every 2 years; Sigmoidoscopy every 5 years; colonoscopy every 10 years; double-contrast barium enema every 5 years)

HIV/AIDS
- Alternate regimens offered and used appropriately

Continued

BOX 2.2 *Continued*

Diabetes
Diabetes Quality Improvement (DQuIP) measure set including

- Percentage of patients with diabetes with blood pressure below 140/90 mmHg
- Percentage of patients with diabetes receiving a dilated eye exam in the past year (or two)
- Percentage of patients with diabetes with low-density lipoprotein (LDL) below 130 mg/dl
- Percentage of patients with diabetes receiving one or more hemoglobin A1c tests per year
- Hemoglobin A1c levels for people with diabetes

Depression
- Depression screening in primary care
- Percentage of patients with a current diagnosis of chronic, moderate, or severe depression (not in remission) receiving an antidepressant medication or electroconvulsive therapy
- Percentage of patients with a current diagnosis of depression with psychotic features (not in remission) receiving either a combination of an antidepressant medication and an antipsychotic medication or electroconvulsive therapy
- Percentage of patients with a current diagnosis of depression that is mild and not chronic (not in remission) receiving medication and/or psychotherapy

Hypertension
- Controlling high blood pressure
- Blood pressure levels

General
- Pain management at the end of life
- Proportion of nursing home residents with pressure ulcers at stage 2 or higher
- Inappropriate prescribing of antibiotics (e.g., for a cold)

Appropriateness of Procedures
- Procedures likely to be overused by 20 percent or more (e.g., carotid endarterectomy, coronary angiography, coronary angioplasty, tympanostomy tube insertion)

SOURCES: American Diabetes Association, 1998; Foundation for Accountability, 1996; Health Care Financing Administration, 2000; Joint Commission on Accreditation of Healthcare Organizations, 2000a; National Committee for Quality Assurance, 2000; Tuckson, 2000 (see text and Appendices B and C for additional sources).

Effectiveness can also be assessed by examining care for particular chronic or acute conditions as well as end-of-life care. For example, effective care for diabetes includes the reduction of potential complications through preventive retinal eye exams, monitoring of hemoglobin A_{1c}, and regular lipid profiles (American Diabetes Association, 1998; Health Care Financing Administration, 2000; National Committee for Quality Assurance, 2000). Care for selected types of cancer and terminal conditions includes appropriate pain management near the end of life (American Pain Society, 1995; Cherny and Catane, 1995; Wagner et al., 1996).

Much of the work on measures of quality of care has concentrated on effectiveness, usually based on practice guidelines for specific conditions (Medscape, 2000). Practice guidelines and well-tested quality measures are available for a variety of conditions including diabetes, acute myocardial infarction, heart failure, asthma, breast cancer, pneumonia, and stroke (Health Care Financing Administration, 2000; Jans et al., 2000; National Committee for Quality Assurance, 2000; Rolnick et al., 2000; Shiffman et al., 2000; Soumerai et al., 1998). However, well-defined measure sets that include both process and outcome measures and cover the entire spectrum of care are available for only a few conditions such as diabetes (American Diabetes Association, 1998; Health Care Financing Administration, 2000; Loeb, 2000; Tuckson, 2000).

In addition, effectiveness is reflected in the appropriateness with which selected surgical and diagnostic procedures are performed. One of the largest studies of overuse ever conducted found that 17 percent of coronary angiographies, 32 percent of carotid endarterectomies, and 17 percent of upper gastrointestinal tract endoscopies performed on Medicare beneficiaries were for inappropriate indications (Chassin et al., 1987). Overall, it is estimated that about one-third of the procedures performed in the United States are of questionable health benefit relative to their risks (McGlynn and Brook, 1996).

Patient Centeredness[2]

Patient centeredness is a characteristic of the relationship between clinician and patient (Charles et al., 1999a; Roter, 2000) and can be contrasted to disease-

> **Patient centeredness** refers to health care that establishes a partnership among practitioners, patients, and their families (when appropriate) to ensure that decisions respect patients' wants, needs, and preferences and that patients have the education and support they need to make decisions and participate in their own care.

[2] This topic is treated in depth in a paper commissioned by the committee from Christina Bethell on measures of patient centeredness for the National Health Care Quality Report (2000).

centered (Stewart et al., 1999b) and clinician-centered care (Byrne and Long, 1976). Patients of different races, cultures, genders, and ages have different preferences and beliefs that providers must take into account in order to achieve patient-centered care (Cooper-Patrick et al., 1997, 1999; Gostin, 1999; Ngo-Metzger et al., 2000; Stewart et al., 1999a). Patients vary in the degree of autonomy and involvement they want in health care decision making. Some prefer active self-management, while others prefer to rely completely on the clinician's recommendations (Arora and McHorney, 2000; Beisecker and Beisecker, 1990; Benbassat et al., 1998; Blackhall et al., 1995; Deber et al., 1996; Degner and Russell, 1988; Guadagnoli and Ward, 1998; Mazur et al., 1999; Wagner et al., 1995).

As shown in Table 2.1, the committee has defined two subcategories of patient centeredness that should be assessed in the National Health Care Quality Framework. They are the patient's experience of care and the presence of an effective partnership (for examples of measures of patient centeredness, see Box 2.3). The patient's experience of care refers to the caring (Scott et al., 1995), communication (Ong et al., 1995; Roter et al., 1997), and understanding that should characterize the clinician–patient relationship. The emphasis here is on the patient's report of her or his experience with specific aspects of care and goes beyond her or his general satisfaction or opinion regarding the adequacy of care.

An effective partnership should be the result of a clinical encounter shaped around the patient's needs and the context in which he or she lives (for example, his or her family relationships, job situation, and home life). It should increase understanding by both the clinician and the patient to enable the patient to act on the information provided (Bopp, 2000; Braddock et al., 1999; Maly et al., 1999; Mazur et al., 1999; Parrott, 1994). Creating effective partnerships means encouraging the kind of shared decision making and patient skills and knowledge needed for self-management of health conditions (Charles et al., 1999b). The degree of shared decision making is partly dependent on the clinician's participatory decision-making style (Brock, 1991; Emanuel and Emanuel, 1992; Kaplan et al., 1995; Kaplan et al., 1996; Szasz, 1956), the degree of trust established (Safran et al., 1998), the patient's desire to have a role in decisions (Mechanic and Meyer, 2000; Mechanic, 1998; Meehan et al., 1997; Pearson and Racke, 2000), and patient–clinician characteristics such as race (Cooper-Patrick et al., 1999), as has already been discussed.

An effective partnership also involves the opportunity for patient self-management or patient involvement in care for specific conditions (generally chronic problems), including self-monitoring and shared goal setting, so that a true partnership between the clinician and the patient and his or her family can be established (Center for the Advancement of Health and Milbank Memorial Fund, 1999). Through an effective partnership with their clinician, patients and their families obtain the skills and knowledge necessary for self-management and a sense of efficacy for managing their own conditions (Anderson et al.,

1995). Patient self-management, particularly for chronic diseases, has been found to be associated with improved health status (Lorig et al., 1999).

Finally, an effective partnership is facilitated by culturally competent health care. For example, patient centeredness can be furthered when patients receive information in their own language, when the clinicians have greater awareness of potential communication difficulties, and most importantly, when care is provided taking into account the context of the patient's cultural beliefs and practices (Chin, 2000; Langer, 1999; Rivadeneyra et al., 2000; Robins et al., 2001).

Patient centeredness, like other components of health care quality, can be measured. Research suggests that the trust established through the patient–provider relationship, the information exchanged between patient and provider, and the problem solving that occurs in the context of the patient-centered model of

---

BOX 2.3 Examples of Areas in Which Measures of Patient Centeredness May Be Applied and Selected Measures

Patient's Experience of Care
- Time spent with provider
- Patient's perception of the clinician's skills
- Patient's perception of being treated with respect and dignity
- Patient's perception of being listened to or having attention given to what he or she says
- Patient's perception of how much he or she was helped by the care he or she received
- Patient's ability to understand the clinician's explanations

Effective Provider–Patient Partnership
- Patient involvement in care in general
- Patient involvement in care for specific conditions (e.g., asthma, cancer, diabetes, depression)
- Patient offered choice of treatment
- Clinician's participatory decision-making style
- Frequency of self-monitoring by patient
- Patient involvement in decisionmaking
- Degree of patient self-management efficacy (patient's confidence in his/her ability to manage a specific condition)
- Cultural competence (e.g., clinician's sensitivity to cultural differences, patient reports that information was provided in his or her own language)

SOURCES: Agency for Health Care Policy and Research, 1998; Agency for Healthcare Research and Quality, 2001; Foundation for Accountability, 1996 (see Appendix C for additional sources).

care are the chief mechanisms that link patient-centered care to improved outcomes (Brody, 1989; DiMatteo et al., 1994; Prochaska, 1996; Seeman and Seeman, 1983; Von Korff et al., 1997).

Timeliness refers to obtaining needed care and minimizing unnecessary delays in getting that care.

Timeliness

Timeliness combines being able to obtain care and getting it promptly. It includes both access to care (people can get care when needed) (Aday and Anderson, 1975) and coordination of care (once under care, the system facilitates moving people across providers and through the stages of care) (Shortell, 1976).

As shown in Table 2.1, the committee has operationalized the concept of timeliness into three subcategories relative to the time elapsed until care is obtained. Timeliness requires access to the system of care, timeliness in getting to care for a particular problem, and timeliness within and across episodes of care (for examples of timeliness measures, see Box 2.4). Access to care is viewed as an aspect of timeliness and, ultimately, an antecedent to securing high-quality health care (Lave et al., 1979). It can be assessed from the patient's perspective or against absolute standards based on the clinical effects of delays in care.

Timeliness, as applied to general access to the health care system, is defined by the ability to obtain primary (Lambrew et al., 1996; Starfield, 1992; Starfield et al., 1998) and specialty care (Grumbach et al., 1999; Kassirer, 1994) when needed. Timeliness may also require access to special services, such as being able to obtain physical therapy for a disability or chronic condition and being able to obtain home health care when needed (Cheh and Phillips, 1993; Thomas and Payne, 1998). For example, access to home health care can affect the quality of end-of-life care since it influences the place of death and access to palliative home care (Grande et al., 1998).

The second subcategory of timeliness includes measures of whether people are actually able to obtain care for a specific problem once they have entered the system and how long it takes them to do so. It includes aspects such as delays and difficulties in getting a checkup, obtaining routine care, or obtaining urgent care (Bindman et al., 1991; Derlet and Hamilton, 1996). Delays in obtaining care can directly affect the effectiveness of care and health outcomes. In some cases, delays in care can endanger the life of the patient—for example, delays in receiving antibiotics for pneumonia (Centers for Disease Control and Prevention, 1995; Health Care Financing Administration, 2000; Meehan et al., 1997) or delays in reperfusion therapy after a heart attack (Brodie et al., 1998; Health

---

BOX 2.4 Examples of Areas in Which Measures of Timeliness May Be Applied and Selected Measures

Access to Care
- Able to get routine care when needed
- Able to get specialty care when needed

Timeliness in Getting Care Once Having Accessed the System
- Lead time or wait for appointment and/or care for checkup
- Lead time or wait for appointment and/or care for routine care
- Lead time or wait for appointment and/or care for urgent care
- Lead time or wait for appointment and/or care for specialty care
- Lead time for needed care for children with chronic conditions
- Time from diagnosis to first treatment for cancer (breast, colon)
- Initial antibiotic dose within eight hours after arrival at the hospital for pneumonia
- Time from admission for acute myocardial infarction (AMI) to administration of appropriate medications
- Timely reperfusion after AMI
- Stage of cancer at diagnosis (breast, colon) or proportion first detected at late stage
- Time to evaluation of special needs for children after first indications of need
- Time from request for hospice to admission
- Time from diagnosis of terminal illness to family counseling on terminal care

Timeliness for an Episode of Care
- Time waiting in clinician's office after scheduled appointment time
- Duration of wait in clinician's office between treatments during a visit
- Coordination between multiple providers for an episode of care

SOURCES: Agency for Health Care Policy and Research, 1998; Agency for Healthcare Research and Quality, 2001; Foundation for Accountability, 1996; Health Care Financing Administration, 2000; Joint Commission on Accreditation of Healthcare Organizations, 2000a; U.S. Department of Health and Human Services, 2000 (see text and Appendix C for additional sources).

Care Financing Administration, 2000; Marciniak et al., 1998; Ryan et al., 1999). Timeliness in getting to care can also be measured by the absence of administrative-based delays in care for specific conditions (for example, time from diagnosis to treatment for breast cancer).

The third subcategory of timeliness refers to timeliness within an episode of care and across multiple episodes of care for a single condition. It is characterized by smooth and continuous flow through the stages of care (Murray, 1998; Nolan et al., 1996) and by coordination across services and providers for a specific problem or for diverse problems (Starfield, 1998). It includes timeliness in starting care once a patient is at the provider site (for example, time in the waiting room); timeliness in moving through care for a specific problem (for example, time between evaluation, diagnosis, and treatment; between parts of the treatment; between different services at one visit or across separate visits) (Caplan and Helzlsouer, 1992; Mechanic et al., 2001; Meehan et al., 1997); and coordination of care across providers, for example, for children with special needs (Appleton et al., 1997).[3]

Consumer Perspectives on Health Care Needs

Systems of care and clinicians should provide high-quality health care for the different types of care sought by consumers. At one time or another, consumers may need such care to stay healthy, get better (or recover from a specific illness), live with an illness or disability, or cope with the end of life (Figure 2.1). Together, these consumer perspectives on health care needs represent the most important reasons why people seek care. They also reflect the life cycle of their involvement with the health care system.

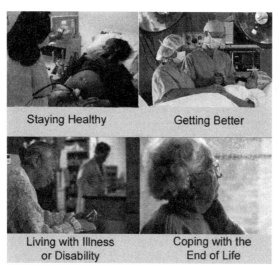

FIGURE 2.1 Consumer perspectives on health care needs.

---

[3] As mentioned earlier, the components of quality may overlap. Although coordination of care around the ensemble of needs for care of a particular person can also be regarded as an aspect of patient centeredness, the committee opted for including it in the framework as a subcategory of timeliness to emphasize the work flow aspects of coordination, that fit better

The relative importance of each of these health care needs changes over the life span of each individual from conception to death. For instance, "staying healthy" characterizes most of children's needs for care since they are generally healthy. At the other end of the spectrum, as an individual reaches an advanced age, the likelihood of dying increases and "coping with the end of life" becomes more of a concern. Furthermore, an individual may experience several health care needs simultaneously. For example, an elderly woman may seek care to get advice on managing her diabetes ("living with illness") and at the same time seek care to get a flu shot ("staying healthy").

The four categories of consumer perspectives on health care needs were adapted from FACCT's Consumer Information Framework (Foundation for Accountability, 1997) and correspond roughly to the clinical designations for different types of care.

Staying healthy refers to getting help to avoid illness and remain well.

To stay healthy, consumers need care that recognizes the importance of preventing conditions they may be at special risk of developing. To avoid illness, the health care system should encourage the development of healthy behaviors, facilitate early detection of illness, and educate consumers about how they can reduce health risks. From the point of view of clinicians, this category includes measures of preventive care.

Getting better refers to getting help to recover from an illness or injury.

If people develop an illness or injury, they need proper medical attention and follow-up care. In these situations, people seek care to help them recover and reestablish their daily activities as soon as possible. From the point of view of clinicians, this category includes measures of acute care.

---

with other system-related aspects affecting timeliness of care. Lack of coordination can also affect safety when there are problems with the flow of information.

Living with illness or disability refers to getting help with managing an ongoing, chronic condition or dealing with a disability that affects function.

If people develop an illness or disability that they must live with, they seek care to receive treatment based on the best evidence available. They also seek a health practitioner who will work with them to help them remain as healthy and active as possible. They want someone who will show them what they can do to take care of themselves, how to recognize warning signs, and how to avoid any related problems. From the point of view of clinicians, this category includes measures of chronic care and care for people with disabilities.

Coping with the end of life refers to getting help to deal with a terminal illness.

People and their families also seek care when needs change dramatically because of a terminal illness. A person facing death needs access to a wide range of services. She or he also needs a practitioner who will recommend and coordinate these services, including palliative treatment and caregiver support. From the point of view of clinicians, this category of care includes terminal and end-of-life care.

The committee chose to use modifications of the FACCT terminology rather than the more traditional, clinically focused terminology for three reasons. First, the FACCT terms have been shown to make more sense to consumers and policy makers (Foundation for Accountability, 1997). Second, they are worded in terms of the point of view of the consumer or patient rather than the clinician. Third, unlike clinical terminology, they are not directly linked to particular sites of care, encouraging a broader range of measures.

Consumer Perspectives on Health Care Needs as Reflected in Care for Specific Health Conditions

In addition to examining the quality of health care overall, presenting consumer perspectives on health care needs according to specific conditions will increase the usefulness of the National Health Care Quality Report and its policy relevance. In particular, it will increase understanding of the quality of care for

---

BOX 2.5 Sample Measures of Quality of Breast Cancer Care by Consumer Health Care Needs

Staying Healthy
- Biennial mammography screening
- Education on self-exam
- Estrogen replacement therapy
- Provision of informational materials in appropriate language for the patient

Getting Better
- Appropriateness of surgery
- Risk-adjusted five-year survival rates
- Postsurgical complication rate
- Proportion of early-stage detection (0–1) or proportion of late-stage detection

Living with Illness or Disability
- Follow-up care according to guidelines
- Patient experience regarding communication with clinician
- Frequency of routine checkups for breast cancer progression
- Patient involvement in care
- Patient involvement in treatment decisions, including radiation and type of surgery
- Rates of breast-conserving surgery at stages 1 and 2
- Radiation therapy following breast-conserving surgery

Coping with the End of Life
- Pain management
- Appropriate treatment at the end of life
- Shared decision making regarding terminal care
- Compliance with patients' advance directives
- Referral and access to a hospice

SOURCES: Foundation for Accountabilty, 1996; Health Care Financing Administration, 2000; Joint Commission on Accreditation of Healthcare Organizations, 2000b; Malin et al., 1999; Mandelblatt et al.,.1999; National Committee for Quality Assurance, 2000 (see text and Appendix C for additional sources).

---

particular health problems on the part of consumers and policy makers. Box 2.5 presents an example of how measures regarding care for breast cancer could be classified using the categories of consumer perspectives on health care needs.

A focus on selected conditions is in line with both consumer and policy-maker perspectives on care and consumers' interest in specific conditions that affect them and their families (Hibbard et al., 1996). Media coverage of health care issues also tends to focus on specific conditions, such as breast cancer, rather than generic aspects of health and health care.

In addition, a condition focus facilitates the study of the linkages between specific processes and outcomes of care for particular conditions. It would also allow an examination of care for specific conditions across health care settings (which may change over time), populations, and, in certain cases, stages of disease. For example, just as one might compare the quality of care received by low- and high-income people to examine equity, subanalyses of quality of care for people with heart disease versus those with diabetes might be used to compare achieved levels of quality of care by condition and corresponding clinical specialties. However, when comparing quality of care for different conditions it will be important to take into account possible confounding of the results by differences in the specific quality indicators used for each condition rather than true differences in the underlying quality of care.

The specific conditions or clinical areas that are the focus of the Quality Report can change from year to year, but they should be limited in number. Several methods are available for the prioritization of conditions (Siu et al., 1992). Two important national efforts have produced lists of priority conditions: *Healthy People 2010* (U.S. Department of Health and Human Services, 2000) and the Medical Expenditure Panel Survey (MEPS) (Agency for Healthcare Research and Quality, 2000a). Both used the importance of the problem, as defined by morbidity and mortality, as an essential criterion for defining disease priorities.

The 28 focus areas in *Healthy People 2010* represent the country's public health priorities and underwent extensive review and public comment (U.S. Department of Health and Human Services, 2000). Among these, 11 focus areas refer to conditions or health problems that may also be relevant to the National Health Care Quality Report (Table 2.2).[4] The Agency for Healthcare Research and Quality (AHRQ) has also produced a list of 15 priority conditions for the MEPS. Initially, the MEPS sample will be expanded to produce reliable estimates for seven of these conditions (Table 2.2) (Agency for Healthcare Research and Quality, 2000c; Cohen, 2000). Conditions can be used to examine quality across the two main dimensions of the framework (components of quality and health care needs) and, in certain cases, to prioritize measures. Although the conditions set forth in Table 2.2 would be a good starting point, a formal process

---

[4] Given the hoped-for policy focus on *Healthy People 2010* targets, it will also be important to assess whether quality improves more in focus or target areas than in non-target areas and to ensure that quality does not worsen in the latter due to a redirection of leadership and resources.

would be necessary to define the conditions for the National Health Care Quality Report, which could change periodically. Ideally, and in the long term, the Quality Report should expand to examine care comprehensively, and for the population as a whole, by selecting enough clinical areas to represent the majority of health care delivery, as discussed in Chapter 3.

TABLE 2.2 Comparison of Priority Conditions in MEPS and *Healthy People 2010*

MEPS[a]	Healthy People 2010[b]
Long Term, Life Threatening	Arthritis, osteoporosis, and chronic back
Cancer (any body part)	conditions
Diabetes	Cancer (lung, pharynx, breast, cervical,
Emphysema	colon, prostate, melanoma)
HIV/AIDS	Diabetes
Hypertension	Respiratory diseases (includes asthma,
High cholesterol	chronic obstructive pulmonary disease,
Ischemic heart disease	and sleep apnea)
Stroke	HIV
	Heart disease and stroke (includes blood
Chronic, Manageable Diseases	pressure and cholesterol)
Arthritis	Immunizations and infectious diseases
Asthma	Chronic kidney disease
Back problems	Mental health
Gall bladder disease	Overweight and obesity
Stomach ulcers	Sexually transmitted diseases
Mental Health Issues	
Alzheimer's and other dementias	
Depression and anxiety disorders	

[a] These are the conditions designated as "priority conditions" for MEPS sample expansion.
[b] This list includes only those *Healthy People 2010* focus areas that refer to health conditions.

SOURCES: Agency for Healthcare Research and Quality, 2000c; U.S. Department of Health and Human Services, 2000.

Using a Matrix to Portray the Framework

The framework provides a way of classifying possible measures for the National Health Care Quality Report. Measures included in the report should reflect the components of health care quality for one or more consumer perspectives on health care needs. Figure 2.2 shows the framework illustrated as a four-by-four matrix. The four consumer perspectives on health care needs—*staying healthy, getting better, living with illness or disability*, and *coping with the end of life*—are shown as rows, while the components of health care quality—*safety, effectiveness, patient centeredness,* and *timeliness*—are shown as columns.

Potential quality measures can be placed in one of the cells corresponding to the particular component of quality and the specific health care need it most reflects. For example, a measure of surgical errors would belong in the *safety–getting better* cell, whereas having an indication of egg sensitivity clearly noted in the medical record would be found in the *safety–staying healthy* cell. Likewise, waiting time for a well-baby visit would belong under *timeliness–staying healthy*, and waiting time for placement in a hospice would belong under *timeliness–coping with the end of life*. Some measures may appear in multiple rows, such as being able to understand your clinician (an aspect of patient centeredness), but the relative importance or salience given such measures may vary with the specific consumer perspective.

Consumer Perspectives on Health Care Needs	Components of Health Care Quality			
	Safety	Effectiveness	Patient Centeredness	Timeliness
Staying healthy				
Getting better				
Living with illness or disability				
Coping with the end-of-life				

FIGURE 2.2 Classification matrix for measures for the National Health Care Quality Report.

The matrix can be used to help define the type of measures that should go into the report, to categorize the measures, and to examine how various aspects of the framework may relate to each other. Every cell will not necessarily be of equal importance to policy makers and consumers, nor will all combinations of rows and columns be equally rich in data. When necessary and useful, the relative importance of each cell can be denoted by weights; however, the method used to arrive at these weights needs to be clearly explained and scientifically based. Ultimately, the matrix is intended only as a heuristic tool, rather than as a formulaic and inflexible template. It can be used when considering approaches to quality measurement to help visualize possible combinations of the two dimensions of the framework that could be used to evaluate quality.

The matrix should not be used as a template or checklist of measures for several reasons. First, it does not indicate the subcategories of measures for each core competency. For example, patient centeredness should be assessed using measures of both the patient's experience of care and the presence of an effective partnership, but this is not evident from the matrix. Second, measures may fit into more than one cell in the matrix. For example, measures for timeliness as the receipt of care when needed are relevant for all four consumer perspectives on health care needs. Third, the matrix format does not reflect the fact that some cells will provide more information than others. For example, although safety is important in all situations, instances in which safety is problematic or can be improved are more common when getting better or recuperating from acute illnesses that require hospitalization than in other situations. Finally, some cells in the matrix will not contain measures because the measures have not been developed yet. For example, very few measures exist for end-of-life care for any of the four components of quality. In this case, the matrix can serve to evaluate the extent to which indicators that are currently available through existing data sources provide some depth and breadth in capturing respective dimensions. Rather than being a drawback, the matrix can serve to point out areas of quality measurement that require further research.

Equity refers to providing care that does not vary in quality because of personal characteristics such as gender, ethnicity, geographic location, and socioeconomic status (Institute of Medicine, 2001).

Equity in Quality of Care as a Cross-Cutting Issue in the Framework

The committee recommends that equity be examined as an essential cross-cutting issue that may influence system performance and the quality of health care. Equity has to be assessed across all components of health care quality: safety, effectiveness, patient centeredness, and timeliness. Equity can also be assessed across consumer perspectives on health care needs and for specific conditions. Variations in the quality of care for any quality component may be analyzed by examining disparities among groups by race, ethnicity, gender, age, income, geographic location, or insurance status and other socioeconomic conditions. These are the factors that have to be considered within each cell of the classification matrix in order to examine equity or variations in quality of care for various subgroups (Figure 2.2). For example, to assess equity in the timeliness of care when patients seek to stay healthy, the waiting time for a well-baby visit for those living in rural areas can be compared to the waiting time for those living in urban areas. Such analyses would focus on the *nonclinical* sources of variations in quality and potential disparities in quality of care.[5]

The National Health Care Quality Report and Data Set should provide policy makers with the capability of examining issues of equity. Two aspects of quality are of particular interest: (1) differences in access to health care services by various subpopulations, and (2) differences in treatment received based on unrelated personal characteristics. The committee proposes that both of these aspects of equity be examined by conducting cross-cutting analyses.

A growing body of literature points to variations in access to health care services by several population characteristics (Ayanian et al., 2000; Fiscella et al., 2000). A recent article cited more than 100 studies indicating inequalities in access to care, utilization of services, treatment, and outcomes of care by race, ethnicity, age, insurance, and socioeconomic status, with a large number of these documenting differences between blacks and whites (Fiscella et al., 2000). The twenty-second report on the health status of the nation—*Health United States 1998*—documented inequalities in access to care and health status by income, education, gender, race, and Hispanic origin (National Center for Health Statistics, 1998). Other studies have shown that access to providers, use of services, and health outcomes are better for those with health insurance than for those without it, even after taking into account race and income (American College of Physicians–American Society of Internal Medicine, 1999). The National Health Care Quality Data Set and the Quality Report should permit identification of areas in which disparities are the greatest. They should also provide information on whether such disparities are getting larger or smaller over time in response to policy initiatives and/or general social and economic conditions.

A second aspect of equity has to do with the delivery of health care services to individuals. Recent studies, including the literature review by Fiscella and colleagues (2000) previously cited, raise concerns about whether treatment options identified, and the nature and quality of health care services provided, may vary by factors such as race, ethnicity, gender, age, income, or insurance status (Ayanian and Epstein, 1991; Ayanian et al., 1999; Bennett et al., 1991; Dedier et al., 1999; Gatsonis et al., 1995; Parham et al., 1997; Schulman et al., 1999). For example, studies have shown that African-American Medicare beneficiaries are less likely

---

[5] Nonclinical sources are those determined by social factors of both patients and providers and by geographical factors, rather than by the capabilities of the health care system in various clinical areas. Variations in quality may also be clinically driven, as is the case for variations in the quality of care across different chronic conditions, determined largely by the state of the science. Clinically driven variations are not the focus of this discussion because they are not indicators of equity; rather they are indicators of technological advances and of the extent of the evidence base regarding care for specific conditions.

than whites to receive many kinds of medical procedures, including cardiovascular procedures, orthopedic and back procedures, and several surgical procedures, and are more likely to die as a consequence of these procedures (McBean and Gornick, 1994). Others have shown that Hispanics are less likely than non-Hispanic whites to receive major inpatient therapeutic procedures for 24 of 63 conditions examined including coronary artery disease, several types of cancer (breast, colon, lung), most traumas, and several gastrointestinal conditions (Andrews and Elixhauser, 2000). Hispanics were more likely to receive major therapeutic procedures for four of the conditions examined including renal failure.

The committee views the lack of equity in access to care and medical treatment as a quality problem. Other things being equal, the presence of disparities may be an indication that quality is below the maximum obtainable level for some groups of the population given that others have attained higher levels. Current data collection and reporting systems are inadequate to examine disparities in quality of care (Eisenberg and Power, 2000; Fiscella et al., 2000). Given the U.S. Department of Health and Human Services' goal of eliminating disparities in health and health care within the next 10 years (U.S. Department of Health and Human Services, 2000), the importance of examining issues of equity in quality of care should not be underestimated. As mentioned in Chapter 1, the Quality Report, together with a planned report on disparities in health care delivery mandated by the same legislation, should help to remedy this situation (Healthcare Research and Quality Act, 1999:Sec. 902). One of the uses of the National Health Care Quality Report and Data Set should be to document and disseminate information on the equity of health care delivery for all the people of the United States. The Quality Report should be articulated with the planned "disparities report," which—according to the committee's understanding— would feature in-depth analyses of disparities in health care delivery by race and socioeconomic status.

What About Efficiency?[6]

As mentioned at the beginning of this chapter, the committee is aware of the economic size and importance of the health care industry and of the fact that quality is only one of several system goals. Efficiency, defined as "avoiding waste, including waste of equipment, supplies, ideas, and energy" by the IOM Committee on Quality of Health Care in America, is one of six health care system aims for quality improvement proposed by that same committee (Institute of Medicine, 2001). Health care systems and processes of care, in particular, can be

---

[6] This topic is treated in depth in a paper commissioned by the committee from Mark McClellan on measures of efficiency for the National Health Care Quality Report (2000).

BOX 2.6 Questions Addressed by the National Health Care Quality Report

Overall
- What do we know about the level of quality of care in the United States? Is quality improving, staying the same, or progressively worsening over time?

Components of Health Care Quality
- Is the system providing care safely and decreasing the rate of patient injuries and harm?
- Is the care provided effective and contributing to desired outcomes?
- Is care patient centered and tailored to the needs, values, and preferences of consumers?
- Is care provided in a timely manner?

Consumer Perspectives on Health Care Needs
- How well does the health care system help people maintain good health and avoid illness?
- How well does the system care for people when they become sick?
- How well does the system care for people with chronic conditions or people with disabilities?
- How well does the health care system help people to cope with the end of life?
- What is the quality of care for people with breast cancer, diabetes, or other specific conditions?

Equity
- What types of patients or consumers are receiving better quality of care? Who is better off? Who is worse off?
- Which states or regions of the country provide better care? Are differences in quality over time and between geographic regions getting smaller or larger?
- Are there unwarranted differences in the quality of care received by people of different races and ethnicities? Are there differences by age, gender, or other population characteristics? Are these differences increasing or decreasing over time? In which areas of quality of care are the differences the greatest? Which groups are the worst off?
- What is the quality of care for those without health insurance compared to those with insurance? If there is a difference, is it increasing or decreasing over time?

wasteful due to deficiencies in any of the four components of quality as defined in the framework. Quality measures related to safety, effectiveness, patient centeredness, or timeliness can indicate potential problems in the efficiency of production and/or the allocation of services. For example, lack of safety indicated by errors in health care that lead to avoidable complications can result in greater resource use. Efficiency is clearly related to the quality of care. For example, quality measures of specific aspects of effectiveness—particularly overuse and inappropriateness—may indicate potential problems of efficiency in service allocation. Ineffectiveness stemming from overuse or inappropriateness can result in wasted resources, as well as problems that include poor health associated with readmissions (Oddone et al., 1996) and lengthened hospital stays (Broderick et al., 1990). Ultimately, inefficiency is characterized by the use of resources that do not provide the best value in meeting people's health care needs.

Efficiency is clearly related to the quality of care. Many of the quality issues that will be presented in the Quality Report will require potential trade-offs. However, efficiency, particularly with regard to cost per unit of service, falls outside the scope of the Quality Report and will be better addressed by specific efforts designed to face the considerable methodological and measurement challenges involved (McClellan, 2000). Doing so will allow for examination of the value of health care as reflected in the relationship between quality and costs. It will also make possible the definition of appropriate policies to address each of these aspects of value separately.

SUMMARY

The National Health Care Quality Framework described in this chapter responds to a set of basic questions that together provide a picture of the quality of health care being delivered in this country over time. These questions refer to the components of health care quality and consumer perspectives on health care needs, including care for specific conditions. The measures included in the framework can be used to examine equity, or how certain groups of people fare compared to others, and to describe the evolution in the quality of care being delivered in the United States over time. Box 2.6 presents the list of basic questions that should be addressed by the Quality Report.

REFERENCES

Aday, Lu Ann, and Ronald M. Anderson. 1975. *Development of Indices of Access to Medical Care.* Ann Arbor, Mich.: Health Administration Press.
Advisory Commission on Consumer Protection and Quality in the Health Care Industry. 1998. *Quality First: Better Health Care for All Americans.* Washington, D.C.: U.S. Government Printing Office.
Agency for Health Care Policy and Research. 1998. *CAHPS 2.0 Questionnaires* [on-line]. Available at: http://www.ahrq.gov/qual/cahps/cahpques/htm [Feb. 18,. 2001].

Agency for Healthcare Research and Quality. 2000a. *Overview of MEPS* [on-line]. Available at: http://www.meps.ahrq.gov/WhatIsMEPS/Overview.htm [Jan. 3, 2001].

Agency for Healthcare Research and Quality. 2000b. *What Is MEPS?* [on-line]. Available at: http://www.meps.ahrq.gov/whatis/htm [Jan. 3, 2001].

Agency for Healthcare Research and Quality. 2000c. *MEPS HC-006R: 1996 Medical Conditions* [on-line]. Available at: http://www.meps.ahcpr.gov/pub doc/hc6rdoc.pdf [Feb.26, 2001].

Agency for Healthcare Research and Quality. 2001. *Survey Instruments and Associated Documentation* [on-line]. Available at: http://www.meps.ahrq. gov/survey.htm [Feb. 18, 2001].

American College of Physicians–American Society of Internal Medicine. 1999. *No Health Insurance? It's Enough to Make You Sick.* Philadelphia. Available at: http://www.acponline.org/uninsured/lack-contents.htm.

American Diabetes Association. 1998. *The Diabetes Quality Improvement Project* [on-line]. Available at: http://www.diabetes.org/dqip.asp [Jan. 12, 2001].

American Pain Society, Quality of Care Committee. 1995. Quality improvement guidelines for the treatment of acute pain and cancer pain. *Journal of the American Medical Association* 274:1874–1880.

Anderson, Robert, Martha M. Funell, Patricia M. Butler, Marilynn S. Arnold, James T. Fitzgerald, and Catherine C. Feste. 1995. Patient empowerment: Results of a randomized control trial. *Diabetes Care* 18(7):943–949.

Andrews, Roxanne M., and Anne Elixhauser. 2000. Use of major therapeutic procedures: Are Hispanics treated differently than non-Hispanic whites? *Ethnicity and Disease* 10:384–394.

Appleton, P. L., V. Boll, and J. M. Everett. 1997. Beyond child development centres: Care coordination for children with disabilities. *Child: Care, Health and Development* 23:29–40.

Arora, Neeraj K., and Colleen A. McHorney. 2000. Patient preferences for medical decision making: Who really wants to participate? *Medical Care* 38(3):335–341.

Ayanian, John Z., and Arnold M. Epstein. 1991. Differences in the use of procedures between women and men hospitalized for coronary heart disease. *New England Journal of Medicine* 325(4):221–225.

Ayanian, John Z., Joel S. Weissman, Scott Chasan-Taber, and Arnold M. Epstein. 1999. Quality of care by race and gender for congestive heart failure and pneumonia. *Medical Care* 37(12):1260–1269.

Ayanian, John Z., Joel S. Weissman, Eric C. Schneider, Jack A. Ginsburg, and Alan M. Zaslavsky. 2000. Unmet health needs of uninsured adults in the United States. *Journal of the American Medical Association* 284(16):2061–2069.

Balas, E. Andrew, Farah Jaffrey, Gilad J. Kuperman, Suzanne Austin Boren, Gordon D. Brown, Francesco Pinciroli, and Joyce A. Mitchell. 1997. Electronic communication with patients: Evaluation of distance medicine technology. *Journal of the American Medical Association* 278(2):152–159.

Beisecker, Analee E., and Thomas D. Beisecker. 1990. Patient information-seeking behaviors when communicating with doctors. *Medical Care* 28(1):19–28.

Benbassat, Jochanan, Dina Pilpel, and Meira Tidhar. 1998. Patients' preferences for participation in clinical decision making: A review of published surveys. *Behavioral Medicine* 24(2):81–88.

Bennett, Charles L., Sheldon Greenfield, Harriet Aronow, Patricia Ganz, Nicholas J. Vogelzang, and Robert M. Elashoff. 1991. Patterns of care related to age of men with prostate cancer. *Cancer* 67(10):2633–2641.

Bethell, Christina. 2000. Measuring Patient Centered Care Across Consumer Relevant Domains of Quality. Commissioned paper for the Institute of Medicine Committee on the National Quality Report on Health Care Delivery.

Bindman, Andrew B., Kevin Grumbach, Dennis Keane, Loren Rauch, and John Luce. 1991. Consequences of queing for care at a public hospital emergency department. *Journal of the American Medical Association* 266(8):1091–1096.

Blackhall, Leslie J., Sheila T. Murphy, Gelya Frank, Vicki Michel, and Stanley Azen. 1995. Ethnicity and attitudes toward patient autonomy. *Journal of the American Medical Association* 274(10):820–825.

Bopp, Kenneth D. 2000. Information services that make patients co-producers of quality health care. *Studies in Health Technology and Information* 76:93–106.

Bordage, Georges. 1999. Why did I miss the diagnosis? Some cognitive explanations and educational implications. *Academic Medicine* 74(10 (Supplement)):S138–S143.

Braddock, Clarence H. III, Kelly A. Edwards, Nicole M. Hasenberg, Tracy L. Laidley, and Wendy Levinson. 1999. Informed decision making in outpatient practice: Time to get back to basics. *Journal of the American Medical Association* 282(4): 2313–2320.

Brock, Dan W. 1991. The ideal of shared decision making between physicians and patients. *Kennedy Institute of Ethics Journal* 1(1):28–47.

Broderick, Ann, Motomi Mori, Mary D. Nettleman, Stephen A. Streed, and Richard P. Wenzel. 1990. Nosocomial infections: Validation of surveillance and computer modeling to identify patients at risk. *American Journal of Epidemiology* 131(4): 734–742.

Brodie, Mollyann, Lee Ann Brady, and Drew E. Altman. 1998. Media coverage of managed care: Is there a negative bias? *Health Affairs* 17(1):9–25.

Brody, Howard. 1989. Transparency. Informed consent in primary care. *Hastings Center Report* 19:5–9.

Brook, Robert H., and Kathleen Lohr. 1985. Efficacy, effectiveness, variations, and quality—Boundary-crossing research. *Medical Care* 23(5):710–722.

Byrne, Patrick S., and Barrie E.L. Long. 1976. *Doctors Talking to Patients. A Study of the Verbal Behavior of General Practitioners Consulting in Their Surgeries.* London: H.M.S.O.

Caplan, Lee S., and Kathy J. Helzlsouer. 1992. Delay in breast cancer: A review of the literature. *Public Health Review* 93(20):187–214.

Center for the Advancement of Health and Milbank Memorial Fund. 1999. *Patients as Effective Collaborators in Managing Chronic Conditions,* New York.

Centers for Disease Control and Prevention. 1995. Pneumonia and influenza death rates—United States, 1979–1994. *Morbidity and Mortality Weekly Report* 44:535–537.

Centers for Disease Control and Prevention. 1999. National vaccination coverage levels among children ages 19–35 months—United States, 1998. *Morbidity and Mortality Weekly Report* 48:829–830.

Charles, Cathy, Amiram Gafni, and Tim Whelan. 1999a. Decision-making in the physician–patient encounter: Revisiting the shared treatment decision-making model. *Social Science and Medicine* 49(5):651–661.

Charles, Cathy, Tim Whelan, and Amiram Gafni. 1999b. What do we mean by partnership in making decisions about treatment? *British Medical Journal* 319:780–782.

Chassin, Mark R., and Robert W. Galvin. 1998. The urgent need to improve health care quality: Institute of Medicine National Roundtable on Health Care Quality. *Journal of the American Medical Association* 280(11):1000–1005.

Chassin, Mark R., Jacqueline Kosecoff, Rolla E. Park, Constance M. Winslow, Katherine L. Kahn, Nancy J. Merrick, J. Keesy, Arlene Fink, David H. Solomon, and Robert H. Brook. 1987. Does inappropriate use explain geographic variations in the use of health services? A study of three procedures. *Journal of the American Medical Association* 258(18):2533–2537.

Cheh, Valerie, and Barbara Phillips. 1993. Adequate access to posthospital home health services: Differences between urban and rural areas. *Journal of Rural Health* 9(4): 262–269.

Cherny, Nathan I., and Raphael Catane. 1995. Professional negligence in the management of cancer pain: A case for urgent reforms. *Cancer* 76(11):2181–2185.

Chin, Jean Lau. 2000. Culturally competent health care. *Public Health Reports* 115(1): 25–33.

Christakis, Nicholas A., and Elizabeth B. Lamont. 2000. Extent and determinants of error in doctors' prognoses in terminally ill patients: Prospective cohort study. *British Medical Journal* 320(7233):469–473.

Cohen, Steven, 2000. Personal communication, October 5. Agency for Healthcare Research and Quality.

Cooper-Patrick, Lisa, Joseph L. Gallo, Junius J. Gonzales, Hong Thi Vu, Neil R. Powe, Christine Nelson, and Daniel E. Ford. 1999. Race, Gender, and Partnership in the Patient-Physician Relationship. *Journal of the American Medical Association* 282(6):583–589.

Cooper-Patrick, Lisa, Neil R. Powe, Mollie W. Jenckes, Junius J. Gonzales, David M. Levine, and Daniel E. Ford. 1997. Identification of patient attitudes and preferences regarding treatment of depression. *Journal of General Internal Medicine* 12(7):431–438.

Deber, Raisa B., Nancy Kraetschmer, and Jane Irvine. 1996. What role do patients wish to play in treatment decision making? *Archives of Internal Medicine* 156:1414–1420.

Dedier, Julien, Richard Penson, Winifred Williams, and Thomas Lynch, Jr. 1999. Race, ethnicity, and the patient–caregiver relationship. *Oncologist* 4(4):325–331.

Degner, Lesley F. and Cynthia A. Russell. 1988. Preferences for treatment control among adults with cancer. *Research in Nursing and Health* 11:367–374.

Derlet, Robert W., and Bridget Hamilton. 1996. The impact of health maintenance organization care authorization policy on an emergency department before California's new managed care law. *Academic Emergency Medicine* 3(4):338–344.

DiMatteo, M. Robin, Robert C. Reiter, and Joseph C. Gambone. 1994. Enhancing medication adherence through communication and informed collaborative choice. *Health Communication* 6(4):253–265.

Eisenberg, John M., and Elaine J. Power. 2000. Transforming insurance coverage into quality health care. *Journal of the American Medical Association* 284(16):2100–2107.

Emanuel, Ezekiel J., and Linda L. Emanuel. 1992. Four models of the physician–patient relationship. *Journal of the American Medical Association* 267(16):2221–2226.

Expert Panel on Prenatal Care. 1989. *Caring for Our Future: The Content of Prenatal Care.* Washington, D.C.: U.S. Public Health Service.

Fiscella, Kevin, Peter Franks, Marthe R. Gold, and Carolyn Clancy. 2000. Inequality in quality: Addressing socioeconomic, racial, and ethic disparities in health care. *Journal of the American Medical Association* 283(19):2579–2584.

Foundation for Accountability. 1996. *Measuring Quality* [on-line]. Available at: http://www.facct.org/measures.html.

Foundation for Accountability. 1997. *Reporting Quality Information to Consumers*, Portland, Ore.: FACCT.

Gatsonis, Constantine A., Arnold M. Epstein, Joseph P. Newhouse, Sharon-Lise T. Normand, and Barbara J. McNeil. 1995. Variations in the utilization of coronary angiography for elderly patients with an acute myocardial infarction. *Medical Care* 33(6):625–642.

Genest, M. 1981. Preparation for childbirth—Evidence for efficacy. A review. *Journal of Obstetric, Gynecologic, and Neonatal Nursing* 10(2):82–85.

Gershon, Robyn R., Christine D. Karkashian, James W. Grosch, Lawrence R. Murphy, Antonio Escamilla-Cejuso, Patricia A. Flanagan, Edward Bernacki, Christine Kastin, and Linda Martin. 2000. Hospital safety climate and its relationship with safe work practices and workplace exposure incidents. *American Journal of Infection Control* 28(3):211–221.

Gostin, Lawrence O. 1999. Informed consent, cultural sensitivity, and respect for persons. *Journal of the American Medical Association* 274(10):844–845.

Grad, Rae K., and Ian T. Hill. 1992. Financing maternal and child health care in the United States. Pp. 173–185 in *A Pound of Prevention: The Case for Universal Maternity Care in the U.S.* eds. Jonathan B. Kotch, Craig H. Blakely, Sarah S. Brown, and Frank Y. Wong. Washington, D.C.: American Public Health Association.

Grande, Gunn E., Julia M. Addington-Hall, and Chris J. Todd. 1998. Place of death and access to home care services: Are certain patient groups at a disadvantage? *Social Science and Medicine* 47(5):565–579.

Greenfield, Sheldon, Sherrie H. Silliman, Rebecca A. Kaplan, Lisa Sullivan, Willard Manning, Ralph D'Agostino, Daniel E. Singer, and David M. Nathan. 1994. The use of outcomes research for medical effectiveness, quality of care, and reimbursement in type II diabetes. *Diabetes Care* 17(Supplement 1):32–39.

Grumbach, Kevin, Joe V. Selby, Cheryl Damberg, Andrew B. Bindman, Charles Queensberry, Alison Truman, and Connie Uratsu. 1999. Resolving the gatekeeper conundrum: What patients value in primary care and referral to specialists. *Journal of the American Medical Association* 282(3):261–266.

Guadagnoli, Edward, and Patricia Ward. 1998. Patient participation in decision making. *Social Science and Medicine* 47(3):329–339.

Health Care Financing Administration. 2000. *Medicare Priorities*. Baltimore, Md.: U.S. Department of Health and Human Services.

Hibbard, Judith H., Shoshanna Sofaer, and Jacquelyn J. Jewett. 1996. Condition-specific performance information: Assessing salience, comprehension, and approaches for communicating quality. *Health Care Financing Review* 18(1):95–109.

Iezzoni, Lisa I. 1997. Assessing quality using administrative data. *Annals of Internal Medicine* 127(8):666–674.

Institute of Medicine. 2000. *To Err Is Human: Building a Safer Health System.* eds. Linda T. Kohn, Janet M. Corrigan, and Molla S. Donaldson. Washington, D.C.: National Academy Press.

Institute of Medicine. 2001. *Crossing the Quality Chasm: A New Health System for the 21st Century.* Washington, D.C.: National Academy Press.

Jans, Marielle P., Francois G. Schellevis, Wouter Van Hensbergen, and Jacques Th. van Eijk. 2000. Improving general practice care of patients with asthma or chronic obstructive pulmonary disease: Evaluation of a quality system. *Effective Clinical Practice* 3(1):16–24.

Joint Commission on Accreditation of Healthcare Organizations. 2000a. *Sentinel Event Statistics* [on-line]. Available at: http://www.jcaho.org/sentinel/se_ stats.html [Aug. 7, 2000].

Joint Commission on Accreditation of Healthcare Organizations. 2000b. *Joint Commission and Health Care Financing Administration Core Measure Crosswalks for Acute Myocardial Infarction, Heart Failure and Community Acquired Pneumonia* [on-line]. Available at: http://www.jcaho.org/ perfmeas/coremeas/letter.html [Feb. 19, 2001].

Kane, Beverley, and Daniel Z. Sands. 1998. Guidelines for the clinical use of electronic mail with patients. *Journal of the American Medical Informatics Association* 5(1): 104–111.

Kaplan, Sherrie H., Barbara Gandek, Sheldon Greenfield, William Rogers, and John E. Ware. 1995. Patient and visit characteristics related to physicians' participatory decision-making style: Results from the Medical Outcomes Study. *Medical Care* 33(12): 1176–1187.

Kaplan, Sherrie H., Sheldon Greenfield, Barbara Gandek, William H. Rogers, and John E. Ware. 1996. Characteristics of physicians with participatory decision-making styles. *Annals of Internal Medicine* 124(5):497–504.

Kassirer, Jerome P. 1994. Access to specialty care. *New England Journal of Medicine* 331(17):1151–1153.

Lambrew, Jeanne M., Gordon H. DeFriese, Timothy S. Carey, Thomas C. Ricketts, and Andrea K. Biddle. 1996. The effects of having a regular doctor on access to primary care. *Medical Care* 34(2):138–151.

Langer, N. 1999. Culturally competent professional in therapeutic alliances enhance patient compliance. *Journal of Health Care for the Poor and Underserved* 10(1): 19–26.

Lave, Judy R., Lester B. Lave, Samuel Leinhardt, and Daniel Nagin. 1979. Characteristics of individuals who identify a regular source of medical care. *American Journal of Public Health* 69(3):261–267.

Leape, Lucian L., Troyen A. Brennan, Nan Laird, Ann G. Lawthers, A. Russell Localio, Benjamin A. Barnes, Liesi Hebert, Joseph P. Newhouse, Paul C. Weiler, and Howard Hiatt. 1991. The nature of adverse events in hospitalized patients: results of the Harvard Medical Practice Study II. *New England Journal of Medicine* 324(6):377–384 .

Leape, Lucian, David Bates, David J. Cullen, Jeffrey Cooper, Harold J. Demonaco, Thersa Gallivan, Robert Hallisey, Jeanette Ives, Nan Laird, Glenn Laffel, Roberta Nemeskai, Laura A. Petersen, Kathy Porter, Deobrah Servi, Brian F. Shea, Stephen D. Small, Bobbie J. Sweitzer, B. Taylor Thompson, and Martha Vander Vliet. 1995. Systems analysis of adverse drug events. *Journal of the American Medical Association* 274(1):35–43.

Loeb, Jerod, 2000. Letter to Margarita Hurtado, July 13. Joint Commission on Accreditation of Healthcare Organizations

Lorig, Kate R., David S. Sobel, Anita L. Stewart, Byron William Jr. Brown, Albert Bandura, Phillip Ritter, Virginia M. Gonzalez, Diana D. Laurent, and Halsted R. Holman. 1999. Evidence suggesting that a chronic disease self-management program can improve health status while reducing hospitalization. *Medical Care* 37(1):5–14.

Malin, Jennifer L., Steven M. Asch, Eve A. Kerr, and Elizabeth A. McGlynn. 1999. Evaluating the quality of cancer care: Development of cancer quality indicators for a global quality assessment tool. *Cancer* 88(3):701–707.

Maly, Rose C., Linda B. Bourque, and Rita F. Engelhardt. 1999. A randomized controlled trial of facilitating information given to patients with chronic medical conditions. *Journal of Family Practice* 48(5):356–363.

Mandelblatt, Jeanne S., Patricia A. Ganz, and Katherine L. Kahn. 1999. Proposed agenda for the measurement of quality-of-care outcomes in oncology practice. *Journal of Clinical Oncology* 17(8):2614–2622.

Marciniak, Thomas A., Edward F. Ellerbeck, Martha J. Radford, Timothy F. Kresowik, Jay A. Gold, Harlan M. Krumholz, Catarina I. Kiefe, Richard M. Allman, Robert A. Vogel, and Stephen F. Jencks. 1998. Improving the quality of care for Medicare patients with acute myocardial infarction. *Journal of the American Medical Association* 279(17):1351–1357.

Mazur, Dennis J., David H. Hickham, and M. D. Mazur. 1999. How patients' preferences for risk information influence treatment choice in a case of high risk and high therapeutic uncertainty: Asymptomatic localized prostate cancer. *Medical Decision Making* 19(4):394–398.

McBean, A. M., and M. Gornick. 1994. Differences by race in the rates of procedures performed in hospitals for Medicare beneficiaries. *Health Care Financing Review* 15(4):77–90.

McClellan, Mark. 2000. Potential Efficiency Measures for the National Quality Report on Health Care. Commissioned paper for the Institute of Medicine Committee on the National Quality Report on Health Care Delivery.

McGlynn, Elizabeth A., and Robert H. Brook. 1996. Ensuring Quality of Care. *Beyond Health Care Reform: Key Issues in Policy and Management*. eds. R.J. Anderson, T.H. Rice, and G.F. Kominski. San Francisco, Calif.: Jossey-Bass.

Mechanic, David. 1998. The functions and limitations of trust in the provision of medical care. *Journal of Health Politics, Policy and Law* 23(4):661–686.

Mechanic, David, Donna D. McAlpin, and Marsha Rosenthal. 2001. Are patients' office visits with physicians getting shorter? *New England Journal of Medicine* 344(2): 190–204.

Mechanic, David, and Sharon Meyer. 2000. Concepts of trust among patients with serious illness. *Social Science and Medicine* 51(5):657–658.

Medscape. 2000. *Medscape Multispecialty Practice Guidelines* [on-line]. Available at: http://www.medscape.com/Home/Topics/multispecialty/directories/dir-MULT. PracticeGuide.html [Oct. 15, 2000].

Meehan, Thomas P., Michael J. Fine, Harlan M. Krumholz, Jeanne D. Scinto, Deron H. Galusha, Joyce T. Mockalis, Georgina F. Weber, Marcia K. Petrillo, Peter M. Houck, and Jonathan M. Fine. 1997. Quality of care, process, and outcomes in elderly patients with pneumonia. *Journal of the American Medical Association* 278(23):2080–2084.

Miles, Matthew B., and A. Michael Huberman. 1994. *Qualitative Data Analysis*. Thousand Oaks, Calif.: Sage.

Miller, M. D. 1997. Office procedures. Education, training, and proficiency of procedural skills. *Primary Care* 24(2):231–240.

Mort, T. C., and N. S. Teston. 1999. The relationship of pre-mortem diagnoses and post-mortem findings in a surgical intensive care unit. *Critical Care Medicine* 27(2): 299–303.

Murray, Mark, and Catherine Tantau. 1998. Must patients wait? *Joint Commission Journal on Quality Improvement* 24(80):423–425.

National Center for Health Statistics. 1998. *Health, United States, 1998: Socioeconomic Status and Health Chartbook*, Hyattsville, Md.: U.S. Government Printing Office.

National Committee for Quality Assurance. 2000. *HEDIS 2001*, Vol. 1. Washington, D.C.: NCQA.

National Institutes of Health. 1996. Cervical Cancer. NIH Consensus Statement. 14(1):1–38.

National Patient Safety Foundation. 2000. *Agenda for Research and Development in Patient Safety* [on-line]. Available at: www.npsf.org.

Ngo-Metzger, Q., M. P. Massaglu, B. Clarridge, M. Manocchia, R. B. Davis, L. I. Iezzoni, and R. S. Phillips. 2000. Patient-centered quality measures for Asian Americans: Research in progress. *American Journal of Medical Quality* 15(4):167–173.

Nolan, Thomas W., and Marie W. Schall. 1996. *Reducing Delays and Waiting Times Throughout the Healthcare System*. Boston, Mass.: Institute for Healthcare Improvement.

Oddone, Eugene Z., Morris Weinberger, Maria Horner, Charles Mengel, Francis Goldstein, Paulette Ginier, David Smith, James Huey, Neil J. Farber, David A. Asch, Lawrence Loo, Edward Mack, Anita G. Hurder, William G. Henderson, and John R. Feussner. 1996. Classifying general medicine readmissions. Are they preventable? Veterans Affairs Cooperative Studies in Health Services Group on Primary Care and Hospital Readmissions. *Journal of General Internal Medicine* 11(10):597–607.

Ong, L. M., J. C. de Haes, A. M. Hoos, and F. B. Lammes. 1995. Doctor–patient communication: A review of the literature. *Social Science and Medicine* 40(7):903–918.

Parham, G., J. L. Phillips, and M. L. Hicks. 1997. The National Cancer Data Base report on malignant epithelial ovarian carcinoma in African-American women. *Cancer* 80:816–826.

Parrott, Roxanne. 1994. Exploring family practitioners' and patients' information exchange about prescribed medications: Implications for practitioners' interviewing and patients' understanding. *Health Communication* 6(4):267–280.

Pearson, Steven D., and Lisa H. Racke. 2000. Patients' trust in physicians: many theories, few measures, and little data. *Journal of General Internal Medicine* 15(7):509–513.

Phillips, David P., Nicholas Christenfeld, and Laura M. Glynn. 1998. Increase in U.S. medication-error deaths between 1983 and 1993. *Lancet* 351:643–644.

Prochaska, James O. 1996. A revolution in health promotion: Smoking less as a case study. *Health Psychology Through the Lifespan: Practice and Research*. eds. Robert J. Resnick and Ronald H. Rozensky. Washington, D.C.: American Psychological Association.

Quality Interagency Coordination Task Force. 2000. Doing What Counts for Patient Safety: Federal Actions to Reduce Medical Errors and Their Impact. *Report of the Quality Interagency Coordination Task Force to the President*, Rockville, Md.

Quattrone, M. S. 2000. Is the physician office the wild, wild west of health care? *Journal of Ambulatory Care Management* 23(2):64–73.

Reason, James T. 1990. *Human Error*. New York: Cambridge University Press.

Rivadeneyra, R., V. Elderkin-Thompson, R. C. Silver, and H. Waitzkin. 2000. Patient centeredness in medical encounters requiring an interpreter. *American Journal of Medicine* 108(6):470–474.

Robins, Lynne S., Casey B. White, Gwen L. Alexander, Larry D. Gruppen, and Cyril M. Grum. 2001. Assessing medical students' awareness of a sensitivity to diverse health beliefs using a standardized patient station. *Academic Medicine* 76(1):76–80.

Rolnick, S. J., S. K. Flores, A. M. O'Fallon, and N. R. Vanderburg. 2000. The implementation of clinical guidelines in a managed care setting: Implications for children with special health care needs. *Managed Care Quarterly* 8(2):29–38.

Roter, Debra L. 2000. The enduring and evolving nature of the patient–physician relationship. *Patient Education and Counseling* 39(1):5–15.

Roter, Debra L., Moira Stewart, Samuel M. Putnam, Mack Lipkin Jr., William Stiles, and Thomas S. Inui. 1997. Communication patterns of primary care physicians. *Journal of the American Medical Association* 277(4):350–356.

Ryan, Thomas J., Elliott M. Antman, N. H. Brooks, Robert M. Califf, L. David Hillis, Loren F. Hiratzka, Elliot Rapaport, Barbara Riegel, Richard O. Russell, Earl E. Smith III, and W. Douglas Weaver. 1999. *ACC/AHA Guidelines for the Management of Patients with Acute Myocardial Infarction: 1999 Update: A Report of the American College of Cardiology/ American Heart Association Task Force on Practice Guidelines (Committee on Management of Acute Myocardial Infarction)* [online]. Available: http://www. acc.org/ clinical/guidelines/nov96/1999/amipdf99.pdf [Jan. 17, 2001].

Safran, Dana G., Deborah A. Taira, William H. Rogers, Mark Kosinski, John E. Ware, and Alvin R. Tarlov. 1998. Linking primary care performance to outcomes of care. *Journal of Family Practice* 47(3):213–220.

Schulman, Kevin A., Jesse A. Berlin, William Harless, Jon F. Kerner, Shyrl Sistrunk, Bernard J. Gersh, Ross Dube, Christopher K. Taleghani, Jennifer E. Burke, Sankey Williams, John M. Eisenberg, and Jose J. Escarce. 1999. The effect of race and sex on physicians' recommendations for cardiac catheterization. *New England Journal of Medicine* 340(8):618–626.

Scott, Robert A., Linda H. Aiken, David Mechanic, and Julius Moravcsik. 1995. Organizational aspects of caring . *Milbank Quarterly* 73(1):77–95.

Seeman, Melvin, and Teresa E. Seeman. 1983, Health behavior and personal autonomy: A longitudinal study of the sense of control in illness. *Journal of Health and Social Behavior* 24:144–160.

Shiffman, Richard N., Kimberly A. Fredigman, Cynthia A. Brandt, Yischon Liaw, and Deborah D. Navedo. 2000. A guideline implementation system using handheld computers for office management of asthma: Effects on adherence and patient outcome. *Pediatrics* 105(4 Pt. 1):767–773.

Shortell, Stephen. 1976. Continuity of medical care: Conceptualization and measurement. *Medical Care* 14:377–391.

Siu, Albert L., Elizabeth A. McGlynn, Hal Morgenstern, Mark H. Beers, David M. Carlisle, Emmett B. Keeler, Jerome Beloff, Kathleen Curtin, Jennifer Leaning, Bruce C. Perry, Harry P. Selker, Andrew Weisenthal, and Robert H. Brook. 1992. Choosing quality of care measures based on the expected impact of improved care on health. *Health Services Research* 27(5):619–650.

Soumerai, Stephen B., Thomas J. McLauglin, Jerry H. Gurwitz, Edward Guadagnoli, Paul J. Hauptman, Catherine Borbas, Nora Morris, Barbara McLaughlin, Xiaoming Gao, Donald J. Willison, Richard Assinger, and Fredarick Gobel. 1998. Effect of local medical opinion leaders on quality of care for acute myocardial infarction: a randomized controlled trial. *Journal of the American Medical Association* 279(17): 1358–1363.

Starfield, Barbara. 1992. *Primary Care: Concept, Evaluation, and Policy.* New York: Oxford University Press.

Starfield, Barbara. 1998. *Primary Care: Balancing Health Needs, Services, and Technology.* New York: Oxford University Press.

Starfield, Barbara, Charlyn Cassady, Joy Nanda, Christopher B. Forrest, and Ronald Berk. 1998. Consumer experiences and provider perceptions of the quality of primary care: Implications for managed care. *Journal of Family Practice* 46(3):216–226.

Stewart, Anita L., Anna Napoles-Springer, and Eliseo Perez-Stable. 1999a. Interpersonal processes of care in diverse populations. *Milbank Quarterly* 77(3):305–339.

Stewart, M., J. B. Brown, H. Boon, J. Galajda, L. Meredith, and M. Sangster. 1999b. Evidence on patient-doctor communication. *Cancer Prevention and Control* 3(1): 25–30.

Szasz, Thomas. 1956. The basic models of the doctor–patient relationship. *Archives of Internal Medicine* 97:585–592.

Thomas, C. P., and S. M. Payne. 1998. Home alone: Unmet need for formal support services among home health clients. *Home Health Care Services Quarterly* 17(2): 1–20.

Tuckson, Reed, 2000. Letter to Margarita Hurtado, July 25. American Medical Association.

U.S. Department of Health and Human Services. 2000. *Healthy People 2010,* Washington, D.C.: U.S. Government Printing Office.

U.S. Preventive Services Task Force. 1996. *Guide to Clinical Preventive Services,* 2nd ed. Baltimore, Md.:Williams and Wilkins.

Von Korff, Michael, Jessie Gruman, Judith Schaefer, Susan J. Curry, and Edward H. Wagner. 1997. Collaborative management of chronic illness: Essential elements. *Annals of Internal Medicine* 127(12):1097–1102.

Wagner, A. M., M. Baker, and B. Campbell. 1996. *Pain Prevalence and Pain Treatments for Residents in Oregon's Long-Term Care Facilities.* State of Oregon Senior and Disabled Services Division, Client Care Monitoring Unit.

Wagner, Edward H., Paul Barrett, and Michael J. Barry. 1995. The effect of a shared decisionmaking program on rates of surgery for benign prostatic hyperplasia. Pilot results. *Medical Care* 33:765–770.

3

Selecting Measures for the
National Health Care Quality Data Set

The committee proposes two basic guidelines for defining the content of the National Health Care Quality Data Set that will be used to produce the National Health Care Quality Report (also referred to as the Quality Report). The first one is the framework (Chapter 2), which indicates the aspects or domains of health care quality that should be measured. The second involves criteria for the selection of measures, which are discussed in this chapter. The criteria indicate the desirable characteristics of individual measures and the measure set as a whole. They can be used to help assess candidate measures and potential measure sets. This chapter presents the criteria proposed by the committee, as well as diverse aspects related to the definition of the measures and of measurement in general. Although the measures may and should change over time, the framework and the criteria for measure selection, as set forth here, should remain relatively constant.

RECOMMENDATIONS

RECOMMENDATION 2: The Agency for Healthcare Research and Quality should apply a uniform set of criteria describing desirable attributes to assess potential individual measures and measure sets for the content areas defined by the framework. For individual measures, the committee proposes ten criteria grouped into the three following sets: (1) the overall importance of the aspects of quality being measured, (2) the scientific soundness of the mea-

sures, and (3) the feasibility of the measures. For the measure set as a whole, the committee proposes three additional criteria: balance, comprehensiveness, and robustness.

Among the ten specific criteria for selecting individual measures for the National Health Care Quality Data Set, three refer to the importance of the subject of measurement: (1) its impact on health, (2) its meaningfulness, and (3) its susceptibility to being influenced by the health care system. Three other criteria pertain to the scientific soundness of the measure: (4) its validity, and (5) its reliability, and (6) the explicitness of the evidence base for the measure. The last four criteria relate to the feasibility of using the measure: (7) the availability of measure prototypes, (8) the availability of required data across the system, (9) the appropriateness of the cost or burden of measurement, and (10) the capacity of data and measure to support subgroup analysis to compare across populations and states.

The measure set as a whole should also fulfill three separate criteria. It has to be balanced so that it includes both positive and negative aspects of the quality of care; it should be comprehensive so that it will represent the majority of care; and finally, it should be robust to minor changes in the measures or in the sample so that it reflects only significant changes in the underlying quality of care.

These are ideal criteria and should not be interpreted as strict requirements for potential measures. In the short term, all criteria referring to feasibility and/or scientific soundness may not always be fulfilled. The evaluation of measures based on the proposed criteria can be used to pinpoint areas for improvement in measure development.

RECOMMENDATION 3: The Agency for Healthcare Research and Quality should have an ongoing independent committee or advisory body to help assess and guide improvements over time in the National Health Care Quality Report.

Measure selection is a complex process that includes several steps ranging from identifying a set of candidate measures to updating these measures. Activities relating to the definition of the measure set, the reporting of measures, and the eventual interpretation of the findings in the National Health Care Quality Report all require expert input. The committee recommends that the Agency for Healthcare Research and Quality obtain the collaboration of an independent advisory body with broad-based representation in this process. The advisory body should include major interested parties from both the private and the public sectors with technical expertise in measure development and reporting. It should also include representatives from labor unions and organizations of purchasers, consumers, providers, insurers, state policy makers, and academia. It should include both national- and state-level representatives. The body could be analo-gous to the National Committee on Vital and Health Statistics (NCVHS) or the National Quality Forum (NQF) (Kizer, 2000; National Quality Forum, 2000; Stead, 1998) and should fulfill technical, representative, and interpretive func-tions.

RECOMMENDATION 4: The Agency for Healthcare Research and Quality should set the long-term goal of using a comprehensive approach to the assessment and measurement of quality of care as a basis for the National Health Care Quality Data Set.

A comprehensive system is one in which the majority of care for a given population is assessed using a large number of measures representing the many components of health care quality and consumer perspectives on health care needs in an integrated manner and spanning a variety of health care settings and conditions. This approach should result in a more complete and accurate picture of the state of quality in the nation than is now available. To this end, the Agency for Healthcare Research and Quality should evaluate current efforts to develop comprehensive quality measurement systems (for example, in the area of effectiveness) and examine how they may be used and expanded.

The committee agreed that a comprehensive approach to measurement is ideal for the National Health Care Quality Data Set on which the Quality Report will be based. A limited set of measures would be insufficient to capture the four components of quality and the diverse consumer perspectives on health care needs. Therefore, conceptually, the National Health Care Quality Data Set should be as comprehensive as possible, but by necessity, reporting will be se-lective (see Chapter 5 for further discussion of the Quality Report).

Experience with comprehensive systems of health care quality measurement is limited. The RAND QA Tools system (McGlynn, 2000), although still under development, shows promise as a means to assess effectiveness. QA Tools could be expanded to examine limited aspects of "patient centeredness," timeliness, and safety, but complementary data collection and reporting systems may be have to be developed and expanded in order to cover all four components of quality in a comprehensive manner.

RECOMMENDATION 5: When possible and appropriate, and to enhance robustness, facilitate detection of trends, and simplify presentation of the measures in the National Health Care Quality Report, the Agency for Healthcare Research and Quality (AHRQ) should consider combining related individual measures into sum-mary measures of specific aspects of quality. AHRQ should also make available to the public information on the individual mea-

sures included in any summary measure, as well as the procedures used to construct them.

Summary measures combining several individual measures have an important but selective, role in the National Health Care Quality Report. Carefully crafted and thoroughly evaluated summary measures should be used when it seems sensible and where it will facilitate understanding. They should not be overemphasized. Despite the challenges in the design and validation of summary measures in the area of health care quality, they may be useful in summarizing broad trends in quality of care, such as for each of the components of quality or their subcategories. Summary measures are clearer when presented along with a corresponding reference point or benchmark (for example, past performance, desirable performance).

The highest level of aggregation should be the major categories of the framework. In general, it is better to combine only measures for the same quality component or consumer health care need (or one of its subcategories). For example, diverse measures of safety could be aggregated across health care needs. Using a matrix to classify the measures, in which components of health care quality are represented as columns and consumer perspectives on health care needs as rows, a summary measure could aggregate measures within a cell or measures across cells in the same column or row of the matrix (see Figure 2.2). In either case, it will be necessary to determine if all component measures should or should not be weighted equally. An overall summary measure of health care quality across the components of quality (that is, safety, effectiveness, patient centeredness, and timeliness) is problematic and not feasible at this time. Regardless of the number and nature of summary measures that are defined for the Quality Report, information on individual measures that make up the summary measure should also be made available. This will allow interested parties to examine how the summary measures were constructed.

RECOMMENDATION 6: The National Health Care Quality Data Set should reflect a balance of outcome-validated process measures and condition- or procedure-specific outcome measures. Given the weak links between most structures and outcomes of care and the interests of consumers and providers in processes or practice-related aspects as well as outcome measures, structural measures should be avoided.

The National Health Care Quality Report and Data Set should rely on a balanced set of process and outcome measures and should avoid structural measures. A combination of process and outcome measures will satisfy the needs of policy makers, clinicians, and consumers. The committee recognizes that clinical processes change. Any measures for the National Health Care

Quality Report and Data Set should not stifle innovation by institutionalizing specific processes or structures that can soon become outdated.

EXAMINING POTENTIAL MEASURE SELECTION CRITERIA

Many potential measures of health care quality have been developed. The number and nature of the measures vary according to the area of quality being considered. Sound criteria are needed for the selection of individual measures, as well as for the definition of the measure set for the National Health Care Quality Data Set. As a starting point in its efforts to define the criteria to select measures for the data set, the committee reviewed criteria defined by other groups involved in similar efforts (see Appendix E) (Advisory Commission on Consumer Protection and Quality in the Health Care Industry, 1998; Department of Health, 1999; Donabedian, 1982; Foundation for Accountability, 1999a; Institute of Medicine, 1999; National Committee for Quality Assurance, 2000; National Research Council, 1999). The committee also examined the preliminary criteria proposed by the Department of Health and Human Services (DHHS) working group on the National Health Care Quality Report, led by the Agency for Healthcare Research and Quality. The most common selection criteria among those examined were relevance, meaningfulness, scientific or clinical evidence, reliability, feasibility, validity, and health importance (Table 3.1). The relevance of the aspect being measured was the only criterion present in all of the sets of criteria examined. After relevance, the most commonly cited criteria were meaningfulness (considered an aspect of relevance by some) and the availability of scientific or clinical evidence for the measure.

The number of criteria for measure selection ranged from 6 for the Child and Adolescent Health Measurement Initiative of the Foundation for Accountability (FACCT) (Foundation for Accountability, 1999a) to 19 for the HEDIS (Health Plan Employer Data and Information Set) measures developed by the National Committee for Quality Assurance (NCQA) (National Committee for Quality Assurance, 2000). As might be expected, sets with fewer criteria usually had more inclusive definitions, whereas those with more criteria were more specific.

CRITERIA FOR SELECTING INDIVIDUAL MEASURES FOR THE NATIONAL HEALTH CARE QUALITY DATA SET

Major Aspects to Consider

For purposes of the National Health Care Quality Data Set, the committee proposed two levels of measure criteria classification: (1) a higher level of major categories to group similar criteria and, (2) a lower level of specific, individual criteria.

TABLE 3.1 Most Common Criteria for Measure Selection Proposed by Other Groups [a,b]

Criterion	Explanation
Relevance [c]	The measure should address features of the health care system applicable to health professionals, policy makers, and consumers.
Meaningfulness or interpretability	The measure should be understandable to at least one of the audiences. It should help inform them about important issues or concerns.
Scientific or clinical evidence	The measure should be based on evidence documenting the links between the interventions, clinical processes, and/ or outcomes it addresses.
Reliability or reproducibility	The measure should produce the same results when repeated in the same population and setting.
Feasibility [c]	The measure should be specified precisely. Collection of data for the measure should be inexpensive and logistically feasible.
Validity	The measure should make sense (face validity); correlate well with other measures of the same aspects of care (construct validity); and capture meaningful aspects of care (content validity).
Health importance	The measure should include the prevalence of the health condition to which it applies and the seriousness of the health outcomes affected.

[a] Criteria are listed in order of frequency, with the one mentioned most often listed first.
[b] The same label for a criterion can have different meanings depending on the framework because the criteria are not standardized. The definitions, rather than the labels, were used to construct this table.
[c] This term was used as a category covering several criteria in some of the frameworks and as a single criterion in others.

SOURCES: This table is based on the analysis of measure selection criteria from frameworks used to study health care quality and health status (see Appendix E). Parts of this table were adapted from NCQA's list of desirable attributes for HEDIS measures (National Committee for Quality Assurance, 2000).

The individual measure criteria are grouped into three major categories—importance, scientific soundness, and feasibility (Box 3.1). Each of these categories refers to different aspects of the process for measure selection. *Importance*, the first category, groups criteria having to do with selecting the areas or subjects of measurement. Together with the framework, the importance criteria can be used to define the content areas of the report, in other words, *what* will be measured. *Scientific soundness*, the second category of criteria, refers to the characteristics of the measures themselves. It groups criteria describing the properties of the measure and the available evidence on the soundness of the measure being considered. The criteria for scientific soundness are used to define *how* to measure or, more precisely, which specific measures are best suited to evaluating the areas under consideration. *Feasibility,* the third and last category, refers to the ease of actually using the measures being considered. In other words, once what to measure and alternative ways of measuring it have been determined, the likelihood of success in actually using the measures proposed must to be examined.

Specific Aspects to Consider When Selecting Measures

Having defined the three major categories of criteria—importance, scientific soundness, and feasibility—that should be taken into account when examining possible measures for the National Health Care Quality Data Set, the committee then determined the specific criteria under each of these categories. In doing so, the committee aimed to capture the essential attributes of the final measures with as parsimonious a set of criteria as possible. After extensive discussion, the committee agreed on 10 criteria across the three major categories, as defined below.[1]

Criteria Regarding Importance

This category of criteria refers to whether the area under consideration should be measured at all or whether it is important in a clinical care sense, important to the general population, or important to improve the quality of health care delivery. The subject of measurement can refer to a health condition or to an organizational aspect of the health care system that influences quality of care. Importance criteria answer the following questions:

- What is the impact on health associated with this problem?
- Are policy makers and consumers concerned about this area?
- Can the health care system meaningfully address this aspect or problem?

Each of the criteria for importance is defined more precisely below.

---

[1] Definitions of criteria are based on the committee's understanding of them but draw on previous work, particularly the criteria for HEDIS measures defined by the National Committee for Quality Assurance (2000).

BOX 3.1 Desirable Characteristics of Measures for the National Health Care Quality Report

To be selected as a measure for the Quality Report, the measure or area it represents should rate highly in terms of the following:

1. *Importance* of what is being measured
- *Impact on health.* What is the impact on health associated with this problem?
- *Meaningfulness.* Are policy makers and consumers concerned about this area?
- *Susceptibility to being influenced by the health care system.* Can the health care system meaningfully address this aspect or problem?

2. *Scientific soundness* of the measure
- *Validity.* Does the measure actually measure what it is intended to measure?
- *Reliability.* Does the measure provide stable results across various populations and circumstances?
- *Explicitness of the evidence base.* Is there scientific evidence available to support the measure?

3. *Feasibility* of using the measure
- *Existence of prototypes.* Is the measure in use?
- *Availability of required data across the system.* Can information needed for the measure be collected in the scale and time frame required?
- *Cost or burden of measurement.* How much will it cost to collect the data needed for the measure?
- *Capacity of data and measure to support subgroup analyses.* Can the measure be used to compare different groups of the population?

---

1. *Impact on health.* The measure should address important health priorities, such as issues related to care or specific conditions. They should represent problems that significantly affect morbidity, disability, functional status, mortality, or overall health. Preferably, the measure will address areas in which there is a clear gap between the actual and potential levels of health that can be influenced by improvements in the quality of care. Areas in which there is a large degree of unexplained variation in health status, death rates, or disease rates can also be the subject of measurement when there is reason to believe that quality of care influences the variation (Wennberg and Gittelsohn, 1973). Many of the health priorities for the next decade spelled out in *Healthy People 2010* could apply here (U.S. Department of Health and Human Services, 2000b). However, while the first focuses on specific measures of health status (for example, the incidence of heart attack in a specific population), the second will

focus on measures of the quality of care for specific conditions (for example, the administration of aspirin after a heart attack and related outcomes).

2. *Meaningfulness to policy makers and consumers.* The measure should be easily understood by policy makers and individual consumers and should refer to something that matters to them or should matter to them. A meaningful measure represents an aspect that is relevant to the intended audience and can be communicated easily to that audience (the latter is also called interpretability). Consumers should be able to understand the significance of differences in quality of care that the measure conveys. Policy makers should be able to interpret easily the meaning of changes that the measure tracks, across population groups or from one period to the next—for example, changes in therapy for heart attack that lead to reduced death rates. If a measure is meaningful to key stakeholders, it is usually easier to obtain their support.

3. *Susceptibility to influence by the health care system.* The measure should reflect an aspect of care that can be influenced by the health care system as it exists or as it is envisioned. That is, policy makers can take specific actions (generally at the structural or process level) to improve health care in that area and, ultimately, health status. Injuries caused by automobile accidents, for example, are the leading cause of death among young adults, but most remedies (for example, changing car design or reducing the speed limit) lie outside the influence of the health care sector (National Center for Health Statistics, 2000:Table 33). The time period for the measure should also capture events that have an impact on clinical outcomes and reflect the time horizon over which the quality of the health care system can be measured. For example, while better nutritional counseling may lead to less osteoporosis and bone fractures, the lead time is too long for it to be used as a measure of quality of care.

Criteria Regarding Scientific Soundness

The second category of criteria is the scientific soundness of the measure. These criteria refer to properties of the measure that often have to be assessed formally by researchers. They largely determine the credibility of the measure, particularly among health care practitioners. These criteria answer the following questions:

- Does the measure actually measure what it is intended to measure?
- Does the measure provide stable results across various populations and circumstances?
- Is there scientific evidence available to support the measure?

Each of the criteria for scientific soundness is defined as follows:

1. *Validity.* The measure should make sense logically and clinically (face validity); it should correlate well with other measures of the same aspects of the quality of care (construct validity) and should capture meaningful aspects of the quality of care (content validity) (Carmines and Zeller, 1991; Nunnally, 1978). In general, measures should be linked to significant processes or outcomes of care as demonstrated by scientific studies. For example, the provision of selected screening tests in a timely manner is a process measure of quality that has construct validity when the screening is linked to earlier detection of disease and a better prognosis or outcome. Outcome measures should be examined for validity in a similar manner.

2. *Reliability.* The measure should produce consistent results when repeated in the same populations and settings, even when assessed by different people or at different times. Measure variability should be result from changes in the subject of measurement rather than from artifacts of measurement (for example, a change in the definition of the measure or, for rare events, restricted sample size or small numbers of cases) (Carmines and Zeller, 1991; Nunnally, 1978). This aspect is particularly important for periodic data collection. Most measures will have to be repeated every year, and any changes in the measure should reflect a true change in quality.

3. *Expliciness of the evidence base.* There should be a clearly documented scientific foundation for the measure as demonstrated in the literature. An explicit evidence base could also mean that there is some other specific, formal process by which the measure has been accepted as a valid marker for quality, such as review by an expert panel (Brook, 1994). This criterion should not be interpreted as a strict requirement for evidence from randomized clinical trials only. Scientific evidence for the measure can also include observational studies since they are often complementary approaches (Black, 1996).

Criteria Regarding Feasibility

The third category of criteria refers to the feasibility of implementing the selected measures: that is, once it has been decided what to measure and how to measure it, one must examine whether it can actually be measured. The criteria for feasibility answer the following set of questions:

- Is the measure in use?
- Can the information needed for the measure be collected in the scale and time frame required?
- How much will it cost to collect the data needed for the measure?
- Can the measure be used to compare different groups of the population?

The criteria for feasibility are defined in more detail below:

1. *Existence of measure prototypes.* The availability of a prototype means that the measure has already been tested and applied, so it can be used by others and incorporated into a national data set. Evidence should be available that data for the measure have been collected in a variety of settings. In other words, the measure should currently be operational. In addition, it is precisely defined, and specifications have been field tested. Documentation for the measure should include clear and understandable statements of the requirements for data collection and the definition and computation of the value of the measure (Joint Commission on Accreditation of Health Care Organizations, 1999).

2. *Availability of required data across the system.* Data required for the measure should generally be available for the nation as a whole and available during the period allowed for data collection. Information for the measure should be anticipated from an established data source on a regular basis. Selecting measures for which several sources of data are available can increase the validity of the information when this facilitates the use of multiple measures of the same concept. This process can provide a more complete and valid picture of quality (Kvale, 1995).

3. *Cost or burden of measurement.* Collecting the information for the measure should not impose an excessive burden on the health care system or on national data collection systems. The cost of data collection and reporting should be justified by potential improvements in quality and outcomes that could result from the act of measurement. This criterion also means that measures that will be examined at the population subgroup or state level should not require sample sizes so large as to be virtually impractical.

4. *Capacity of data and measure to support subgroup analyses.* Since equity and medical conditions will be examined in the Quality Report, measures should be available for relevant groups of the population (for example, by race and ethnicity, level of income, insurance status) and by condition (for example, diabetes, breast cancer, asthma) when applicable and feasible. Although the report is national in scope, it should be possible to use the measures to drill down to the state level.[2] To make meaningful comparisons across groups, the measure should not be appreciably affected by variables beyond the control of the health care system. For example, time from the occurrence of a heart attack to admission to the emergency department is crucial to survival, but it can be influenced more heavily by transportation issues than by quality of health care. Extraneous factors should be known and measurable so that the necessary data can be collected and their effects assessed. Well-described methods for taking these factors into account should be used. These include stratification to examine quality of care separately for each group of interest and case-mix or risk adjustment methods using validated statistical models to control for these factors (Greenfield, in

---

[2] This aspect is discussed in more detail in Chapter 4 as it relates to the criteria for selecting data sources.

press; Greenfield et al., 1993; McGlynn and Asch, 1998; Romano, 2000; Wang et al., 2000; Zaslavsky et al., 2000). When measures are affected by outside factors and the required information to account formally for these is not available, data should still be reported for the unadjusted measures. Researchers can subsequently perform the statistical analyses required to adjust the data.

Evaluating Individual Measures According to the Criteria

Each of the criteria described above is a desirable attribute of the measures selected for the report, but not an absolute requirement. That is, a measure does not have to fulfill all 10 criteria to be part of the National Health Care Quality Data Set, but measures in the final set should be those that satisfy the greatest number of criteria. In addition, there is a hierarchy among criteria categories. Measures should be evaluated first for importance and scientific soundness and then for feasibility. Measures that address important areas and are scientifically sound, but are not feasible in the immediate future, deserve potential inclusion in the data set and further consideration. However, measures that are scientifically sound and feasible, but do not address an important problem area, would not qualify for the report regardless of the degree of feasibility or scientific soundness.

The level of scientific evidence available will vary by measure and by subject. Several rating scales have been proposed to evaluate the quality of the studies or level of evidence (Clark and Oxman. 2000; Lohr and Carey, 1999). In some instances, the level of evidence for the measures will not be as high as desired, while in others, new measures will have to be developed. Rather than ignore such areas of quality of care, measures should be included if they fit the framework and meet other criteria while additional evidence is being developed to assess them.

The committee's vision for the Quality Report has not been limited by the fact that it might not be possible at present to fulfill all of the desired criteria. The feasibility criteria do not mean that only easily available measures should be used. In order to define needed measures, it may be desirable to relax the requirement for feasibility to go beyond existing measures for evaluating the quality of care. Previous experience with the definition and production of *Healthy People 2000* has shown that feasibility can be constructed over time. In 1990, approximately one-third of the original *Healthy People 2000* objectives were not measurable and were labeled "developmental objectives." By the end of the decade, data were available for most of these objectives. Including them in the agenda led to data generation (U.S. Department of Health and Human Services, 2000b).

EVALUATION CRITERIA FOR THE NATIONAL
HEALTH CARE QUALITY MEASURE SET

The committee discussed several aspects that should characterize the complete set of measures for the National Health Care Quality Data Set. Three criteria are basic for the measurement set: *balance, comprehensiveness*, and *robustness.*

Balance

First, the set of measures should be characterized by *balance.* Collectively, the measures should be useful for examining areas in which the quality of health care delivery is usually satisfactory or outstanding and areas in which it is often deficient. The set of measures should be representative of the entire range of experiences with care and not be limited to just the negative or positive aspects of the current health care quality landscape. There should be balance across components of quality and health care needs. The number of measures in each category (for example, safety versus effectiveness) does not have to be the same, but it should be sufficient to adequately measure the area of interest, rather than just one narrow aspect. For example, several measures of safety focusing only on surgical operations might be balanced by measures of medication errors and certain sentinel events. The number of measures will also be determined partly by a combination of the degree of differentiation of the area of measurement, the generality of the measures available, and the number of measures available.

Comprehensiveness

Comprehensiveness is a second criterion for the measure set related to balance. The measurement set should present a complete and thorough picture of the quality of care being delivered in the United States; it should reflect the spectrum of care for the population. The measures should be representative of different elements of the health care system, as well as of how they interact (Sofaer, 1995). There should be measures representing safety, effectiveness, patient centeredness, and timeliness for the various health care needs—staying healthy, getting better, living with illness or disability, and coping with the end of life. This means that there should be a reasonable distribution of measures across categories, rather than only in areas where data are presently available. Measures should also cover different health care settings, from hospital to home, drawing on measures of quality of care in both ambulatory and inpatient settings. In addition, the measure set should address the problems of diverse groups of the population over the entire life span.

To examine potential inequities in the quality of care, it will also be important that the measure set include information on health conditions or clinical areas more prevalent among certain vulnerable populations, such as lower-income groups. For example, to examine equity, the report should include measures of the quality of care for people with tuberculosis (more prevalent among the poor) (Bock et al., 1998), as well as those receiving infertility treatment (more prevalent among higher-income people) (Stephen and Chandra, 2000).

It is important to distinguish between the number of measures that will be included in the National Health Care Quality Data Set and the number of measures in the National Health Care Quality Report. Given that one can rarely generalize from the quality of care for one condition to the quality of care for another (Brook et al., 1996), the number of measures in the data set will have to be quite large in order to fulfill the criteria. In contrast, as discussed in Chapter 5, the number of measures in any specific year's Quality Report will be more limited and much smaller than the number of measures included in the data set to facilitate understanding of the report.

Robustness

Robustness is the third criterion for the measure set. A robust measure set is stable over time and reflects only true changes in the quality of care. Information drawn from the measure set should not be extremely sensitive to minor changes in the organization, financing, or delivery of health care services because these factors are not, in themselves, changes in the quality of care. The measure set should retain its value as processes of care evolve or the implementation of particular measures changes. For example, if data on the quality of medical care are being drawn from prescribing patterns, it would not be good to focus on medications that shift from prescription to over-the-counter drugs since this change would affect interpretation of the results. Rather, changes in the measures should reflect meaningful changes in the overall quality of health care delivered.

Measures included in the set should represent a cross section of care so that if one aspect of the quality of care changes, it does not unduly affect the total picture of quality captured by the measure set. In this sense, robustness is related to the comprehensiveness of the measure set because the larger and more varied the number of measures, the more likely is the set to be both comprehensive and robust. In general, it is better to have multiple measures for each category and subcategory of the framework, even if some measures might be used for more than one category. The measure set should not be unduly affected by minor changes in component measures. For example, the appraisal of safety of care in a given year should not change just because a new measure was added to the data set. Robustness means that changes in the measure set reflect true changes in the quality of care over time and that the measure set can be used over time. In order to do so, it would be appropriate to update the measure set to conform to evolving practice guidelines and standards of quality of care, as discussed below.

MEASURE SELECTION PROCESS

Steps in the Process of Measure Selection

Measure selection lies at the heart of the National Health Care Quality Report and the data set from which it will draw. To decide *what* to measure, the Agency for Healthcare Research and Quality should identify areas for measurement based on the framework and their importance. To decide *how* to measure quality, AHRQ should evaluate competing measures and determine the measure set for the report. These actions, in turn, involve several steps (Box 3.2).

More specifically, to identify areas for measurement, AHRQ should examine the framework to identify the categories of measurement for the Quality Report and areas that should be included in the data set. The components of quality offer ready-made measurement categories: safety, effectiveness, patient centeredness, and timeliness. AHRQ should next evaluate specific areas for measurement within the framework, applying the criteria for importance presented earlier in this chapter. In other words, areas for measurement should have an impact on health status, be meaningful to policy makers and consumers, and be under the influence of the health care system. If national goals and standards for the quality of health care delivery based on the framework have been defined, AHRQ should include measures to evaluate progress in meeting them.

To identify a set of candidate measures, AHRQ should first define a pool of available measures. For example, to select measures for timeliness, AHRQ should identify possible data sources and existing databases such as HEDIS, the Consumer Assessment of Health Plans Survey (CAHPS), and measures proposed by FACCT, the Picker Institute, and others. AHRQ can examine the examples proposed by the IOM committee for general guidance on measures that may be more appropriate than others (Boxes 2.1 to 2.5, Chapter 2) (Agency for Healthcare Research and Quality, 2000; Foundation for Accountability, 1999c; National Committee for Quality Assurance, 2000a; Picker Institute, 2001). The agency should also consult provider and patient groups, and other interested parties, for feedback on candidate measures. After casting this broad net, AHRQ should identify those areas in which measures are lacking and should be developed.

To actually select individual measures for the data set, AHRQ should evaluate competing measures by examining evidence of their scientific soundness—or their validity, reliability, and explicit evidence base. In the long term, it should also assess their feasibility or the existence of measure prototypes; the cost or burden of measurement; the availability of requisite data across the system; and the capacity of the data and the measure to allow comparisons by populations or subpopulations.

BOX 3.2 Steps in the Process of Defining the National Health Care Quality Measure Set

1. Identify the areas for measurement.

- Examine the framework for the National Health Care Quality Data Set to identify the categories of measurement.
- Evaluate specific areas for measurement within categories, applying the *importance* criteria.
- If available, examine these areas against goals or standards for quality of health care delivery.

2. Identify candidate measures for the National Health Care Quality Data Set.

- Examine existing databases.
- Consider sample measures proposed by the Institute of Medicine committee.
- Seek input on particular measures from provider and patient groups and others.
- Identify gap areas (areas where measures are lacking) for future development.
- Define a pool of available measures.

3. Evaluate competing measures.

- Examine the evidence for the measures.
- Apply predefined selection criteria for individual measures.
- Select individual measures.

4. Determine the measure set for the National Health Care Quality Data Set.

- Evaluate the potential measure set using predefined criteria.
- Define weights for summary measures, if necessary.
- Have the measures vetted by the public.
- Finalize the measure set.

5. Test and evaluate the measure set.

- Periodically review the measures included in the data set.
- Examine available and needed data sources.
- Update and change measures as necessary.

Thus, to determine the final set of measures, AHRQ should evaluate individual potential measures and the resulting measure set according to the criteria outlined above. AHRQ should also arrange to have the measures reviewed by the public. In doing so, the agency could learn of concerns it had not anticipated or gather other information that might be valuable. In addition, the agency may learn of possible objections to the report that it should be prepared to effectively address. The measure set will have to be revisited periodically in response to changes in the availability of data, the evaluation of the measure set, the development of new measures, and potential changes in the framework. Other aspects related to measure selection are addressed below.

Role of an Advisory Body

Although responsibility for producing the National Health Care Quality Data Set rests with AHRQ (Healthcare Research and Quality Act, 1999), the committee believes that the agency should establish a mechanism to solicit input from major stakeholders and technical experts engaged in health care quality improvement, measurement, and reporting. These should include representatives from the public- and private-sectors at both the national and the state levels, such as public and private purchasers, labor unions, consumer groups, providers, insurers, federal and state health policy makers, national accrediting organizations, and academia. The advisory body would provide a common venue for public and private sector health care quality measurement, quality improvement, and oversight organizations to coordinate and collaborate on the most important national quality measurement and reporting activity. In parallel, AHRQ should continue to sponsor a specific group within the agency, or within DHHS, that will ultimately be responsible for the design and production of the Quality Report.

The activities of the external advisory body would range from providing advice on measure selection to report production and eventual updates. This body could also play a role in setting national goals and standards for health care quality so as to facilitate quality measurement and reporting. It could also provide insights into the interpretation of any findings and the formulation of potential policy solutions. Another activity of the advisory body could be to promote research on new measures, the definition of summary measures, and other areas needed to update and improve the Quality Report.

Establishing an advisory body can be accomplished through a variety of alternative mechanisms. One avenue would be to build on the collaborative working relationship already in place between AHRQ and other organizations that serve this purpose, such as the National Quality Forum (Foster et al., 1999; Miller and Leatherman, 1999; National Quality Forum, 2000). Another would be for AHRQ to establish a body analogous to the National Committee on Vital and Health Statistics (NCVHS), which provides advice to DHHS in areas related to health data (U.S. Department of Health and Human Services, 2000a).

Reviewing and Updating the Measure Set

Once the initial set of measures has been defined, there will be a need for periodic review and updating. This could be one of the functions of the advisory body recommended by the committee. At defined intervals, it will be necessary to examine whether any changes are needed in what is measured or in the way it is measured. Changes in measures should be considered if new evidence becomes available on aspects being measured, if a new priority has to be reflected, if new and relevant data become available, or if specific measures are improved. For example, the Consumer Price Index (CPI) produced by the Bureau of Labor Statistics is based on a market basket of goods and services that is updated periodically according to changes in consumption patterns (Bureau of Labor Statistics, 2000).

This periodic review of measures may also be useful to obtain support from key stakeholders. After an initial period of development, testing, and improvement, updating should tend to be conservative given the extensive process undertaken to define the initial measure set. In addition, only by keeping most measures the same from year to year will it be possible to analyze potential changes over time in the aspects being measured. The frequency of review and updating is also likely to decrease over time as the process of measure selection, the data set, and the report become established.

MEASURING HEALTH CARE QUALITY COMPREHENSIVELY

A selective approach to measuring quality relies on a limited number of measures thought to be representative of the general state of quality. The alternative is a comprehensive approach based on a large number of measures to assess the quality of the majority of care across both dimensions of the framework. Such an approach is necessary to examine the quality of care for most populations and problems ranging from the delivery of care to children with complex conditions to mental health care for the vulnerable elderly. The main advantage of a selective rather than a comprehensive approach to measurement is its economy. A smaller number of key indicators can be understood easily by a broader audience. The selective approach also tends to be more appealing to policy makers, who have limited time and resources.

Advocates of a comprehensive approach point to the great variability in the practice of medicine and argue that a limited set of measures cannot accurately reflect the wide differences in health care across conditions. A more comprehensive approach is also seen as less likely to be biased because the measures included would be more representative of the totality of care. The amount of information from the hundreds of indicators included can be made more manageable by combining them into a limited number of summary measures for reporting purposes, as discussed below.

Although no comprehensive group of measures is available that would cover all quality components and consumer health care needs at this time, the committee recommends that this be the ultimate goal of the National Health Care Quality Data Set. Measurement systems for particular components of quality are now being developed that exemplify the potential of a comprehensive approach. One of these efforts is RAND's QA Tools system developed to measure the effectiveness of health care for populations across the most common conditions and clinical areas. Data are drawn from patient records on more than 1,000 indicators, which are combined into summary measures of compliance with guidelines for recommended care (see Appendix B). Evaluating the suitability of RAND's QA Tools is beyond the scope of the committee's work. However, AHRQ should examine this and other promising initiatives more closely to determine if they could be used as the basis for a more comprehensive measure set and reporting system on the quality of health care in the United States.

To be truly comprehensive, the Quality Report should also address the quality of health care delivery not just in the traditional settings of hospitals and clinician's offices but also in a growing number of other settings—patient's homes, hospices, nursing homes, and community health centers—where care is also being provided in increasing numbers. Strategies for improving measurement and data collection systems for many of these settings will have to be defined by AHRQ. The relative importance of each of these settings for improving health care delivery will also have to be examined.

TYPES OF MEASURES

Role of Summary Measures

Deciding whether or not the National Health Care Quality Report should feature summary measures as well as discrete individual measures is one of the most important measurement-related issues. This is a common dilemma that confronts those presenting data on complex subjects such as health care quality. In most cases, the objective will be to strike a balance between the two. It will also be necessary to determine if all individual measures that make up the summary measure are equally important and should therefore be weighted equally. The committee recommends that once individual measures for the data set have been defined AHRQ consider the possibility of defining and testing alternative summary measures for each of the components of health care quality (and other major categories and subcategories in the framework) when appropriate. It should, however, avoid using an overall summary measure of quality of care.

Admittedly, an overall summary measure would provide a single number representing the quality of health care delivery in the United States. Summary measures are generally easier for the public to grasp. However, summary measures can mask important differences and relationships among the individual measures included in them and may make it difficult to identify which parts of the health care system contributed most to quality (Mulligan et al., 2000). For example, the quality score for a year when safety was extremely deficient, but other quality components were above expectations, would be about equal to the score for a year when all four quality components were average.

Adding the measures across the four components of quality for a single overall summary measure of quality or for a quality index is clearly problematic. Summary measures are useful only when measures using the same metric (that is, the same unit of measurement and the same denominator) or measures within a single category or subcategory can be combined in meaningful ways. Such summary measures would allow for an examination of high-level trends regarding each of the components of quality or their subcategories, for example, the safety of surgery or the quality of care for diabetes. Summary measures are also more understandable when they are presented with a benchmark or standard as a reference point.

Even when summary measures are not possible, the Quality Report should include sets of individual measures based on data from similarly defined populations. Including measures that share a common denominator (for example, rates of services per 1,000 persons per year) can facilitate comparisons across different aspects of the quality of care.

Individual measures provide more detailed information for policy action than summary measures, but relying exclusively on individual measures for the Quality Report would make it unmanageable. Many would be needed to convey important aspects of a complex topic such as health care quality. The sheer number of measures overwhelms even policy specialists, leading them to take cognitive shortcuts, such as emphasizing the importance of just one factor (Hibbard, 1998).

Therefore, well-tested summary measures, along with well-tested individual measures, are needed for the Quality Report. England's set of high-level indicators of the performance of the National Health Service (NHS) includes mostly individual measures along with a few summary measures. For example, it combines individual measures of cervical and breast cancer screening coverage into a summary indicator for early detection of cancer (Department of Health, 2000).

Transparency is essential when summary measures are used. Otherwise, the use of summary measures can potentially detract from the impact and credibility of the Quality Report (Kingdon, 1995). To reduce the possibility of misinterpretation and dispel any apparent arbitrariness, the way in which summary measures have been constructed should be explained clearly, and the information and data for the individual measures that make up a summary measure should be made available as well.

Measures of the Structure, Processes, and Outcomes of Health Care

Donabedian's framework for quality assessment (1966) retains viability as a major way to classify quality indicators because it parallels clinical and organizational perspectives on care. Structure, process, and outcome measures each provide a different piece of the quality picture. However, given the present limitations of each of these types of measures and the generally weak links among them, the committee recommends that the National Health Care Quality Data Set include a balance of outcome-validated process measures and disease-specific or procedure-specific outcome measures. It should include structural measures only rarely.

Providers tend to focus on measures of processes of care because processes are actionable. They are the ones most closely linked to health care delivery and reflect the actual practice of health care as it takes place. This is most evident in measures of compliance with practice guidelines; for example, effective care for diabetics includes measuring blood sugar levels at specific intervals, which is a process measure (Greenfield, in press). However, many different process measures are necessary to comprehensively assess quality and guide specific improvements (Palmer, 1997).

One of the main problems with process measures is that they are not always directly linked to a significant health-related outcome that is of interest to the policy community (Welch et al., 2000). This is due to several factors. Process measures are usually studied independently of the total context of care. Even when processes have a direct and important impact on outcomes (for example, immunizations, beta-blockers for a heart attack), their effect on routine practice may not be as strong as that recorded in clinical trials. For example, studies have shown that mortality following a heart attack is similar for patients under the care of generalists and patients under the care of cardiologists, despite the fact that the latter perform more of the processes that have been shown to reduce mortality in randomized clinical trials (Ayanian et al., 1997). In the field, factors such as competing diseases and patient characteristics can dilute the effect of specific processes on health (Greenfield et al., 1993).

Many process measures refer to diagnostic tests, such as performing a Pap smear. Although important, correct diagnoses do not necessarily lead to proper treatment. Over time, some process measures can stifle innovation because they may focus attention on processes that quickly become obsolete or they become the maximum required, rather than the minimum standard that is acceptable. For example, a guideline for diabetes care that calls for an annual eye exam by an ophthalmologist could retard the use of digital computerized interpretation of fundal pictures because ophthalmologists are written into the process. These caveats should be considered when analyzing potential quality measures based on processes of care.

Outcome measures are used to examine the levels of health and disability in the population that are associated with the quality of health care delivery. Consumers often relate more to outcome than to process measures, although they are interested in both. Outcome measures are very important, but data are limited and they are often expensive to produce. Outcome measures should be used as quality measures when they refer to specific conditions or procedures so that the link between processes and outcomes can be established more clearly. In addition, they should be used when there are good statistical adjustment models, when stratification or other ways can be used to address population differences, when the time intervals between treatment and outcome are not too long, and when the events are not too rare. Unlike process and structural measures, outcome measures can foster innovation.

Structural measures reflect the organizational, technological, and human resources infrastructure of the system necessary for high-quality care (Donabedian, 1966). For example, the use of computerized order entry systems by hospitals is a structural aspect that may foster safety in prescription practices and reduce errors that could result in injury or death (Bates et al., 1998). However, the committee recommends measuring outcomes (in this case, adverse drug events and deaths due to prescribing errors) or processes (medication error rates) rather than structure because of the weak links between structure and processes and between structure and outcomes of care (Evans et al., 1998). Using structural measures of technology could stifle innovation by "locking in" any structures sanctioned for use in the National Health Care Quality Report.

Recent research has attempted to relate the volume of certain procedures—another structural measure—to outcomes. In a review of the literature on the subject, the authors concluded that "there can be little doubt that for a wide variety of medical conditions and surgical procedures, patients treated at higher volume hospitals or by higher volume physicians experience on average lower mortality rates than those treated by low-volume hospitals and physicians" (Halm et al., 2000:31). However, others have pointed out that at least at this time, volume cannot be used as an independent measure of quality of care because it appears to be a proxy for more direct indicators of quality of care, such as the use of appropriate procedures, that require further study to be defined and should be used instead (Institute of Medicine, 2000).

Given the limitations of structural measures, the committee recommends that when available, outcome-validated process measures and disease- or process-specific outcome measures be used rather than structural measures. Ultimately, the number and type of measures will depend partly on the aspect of quality of care being examined and the information available. Regardless, process measures (and any structural ones) will have to be revised as medical technology advances and practice guidelines are updated.

BOX 3.3 Toward an Ideal Measure Set

• An external advisory body provides counsel on measure selection, updates, and report production.
• The individual measures and measure set meet the specified criteria.
• The data set is based on a comprehensive approach to measurement rather than on a small number of leading indicators.
• The measure set includes a balanced mix of process and outcome measures of quality of care.
• Summary measures of the components of quality or health care needs (or some of their subcategories) are included when appropriate. Summary measures refer to the same subject, are based on the same metric, and are used only when they will increase understanding by the public.

SUMMARY

This chapter has set forth the committee's ten criteria for the selection of measures for the National Health Care Quality Data Set. Some of the criteria apply to the area of measurement and others to the measures themselves. The chapter also describes selection criteria for the measure set and the steps in the process of measure selection. These are criteria for the ideal measures and measure set. The committee is aware that many existing measures will not fulfill them, but this is what AHRQ should strive to achieve. As the examples proposed by the committee in Chapter 2 indicate, new measures of both processes and outcomes of care will have to be developed, and others will have to be improved, in order to assess quality in all of the dimensions proposed in the framework. For example, new measures will be necessary to assess the quality of care for children with special needs.

The chapter closes with a discussion of other measurement-related aspects that should be considered by AHRQ for the Quality Report. These include the role of an advisory body, revisions to the measure set, measuring quality comprehensively, the role of summary measures, and the use of measures of the structure, processes, and outcomes of care. These are all complex issues, and most do not have clear-cut answers.

The advisory body will have a very important role in measure selection and revision and in any eventual reassessment of the framework. The composition and adequate functioning of the advisory body will be determining factors in the success of the Quality Report. In the short term, a comprehensive approach to measurement as proposed by the committee will not be feasible, but study and further development of existing efforts in the area of effectiveness can make it a reality. AHRQ will have to weigh the advantages and disadvantages of using summary measures in the Quality Report. When these are used, they should refer to the same subject, be based on the same metric, and increase understanding by the public. The committee recommends against the use of a single quality index or summary measure. At the risk of oversimplification, Box 3.3 lists factors that should be considered in moving toward an ideal measure set. This chapter opens with a set of recommendations that should facilitate reaching that ideal.

REFERENCES

Advisory Commission on Consumer Protection and Quality in the Health Care Industry. 1998. *Quality First: Better Health Care for All Americans.* Washington, D.C.: U.S. Government Printing Office.

Ayanian, John Z., Edward Guadagnoli, Barbara J. McNeil, and Paul D. Cleary. 1997. Treatment and outcomes of acute myocardial infarction among patients of cardiologists and generalist physicians. *Archives of Internal Medicine* 157(22):2570–2576.

Bates, David W., Lucien L. Leape, David J. Cullen, Nan Laird, Laura A. Petersen, Jonathan M. Teich, Elizabeth Burdick, Mairead Hickey, Sharon Kleefield, Brian Shea, Martha Vander Vliet, and Diane L. Seger. 1998. Effect of a computerized physician order entry and a team intervention on prevention of serious medication errors. *Journal of the American Medical Association* 280(15):1311–1316.

Black, Nick. 1996. Why we need observational studies to evaluate the effectiveness of health care. *British Medical Journal* 312:1215–1218.

Bock, N. N., Jr. J. E. McGowan, and H. M. Blumberg. 1998. Few opportunities found for tuberculosis prevention among the urban poor. *International Journal of Tuberculosis and Lung Disease* 2(2):124–129.

Brook, Robert H. The RAND/UCLA Appropriateness Method. 1994. *Clinical Practice Guideline Development: Methodology Perspectives.* Rockville, Md.: U.S. Department of Health and Human Services, Agency for Health Care Policy and Research.

Brook, Robert H., Elizabeth A. McGlynn, and Paul D. Cleary. 1996. Quality of health care. Part 2: Measuring quality of care. *New England Journal of Medicine* 335(13):966–969.

Bureau of Labor Statistics. 2000. *Consumer Price Indexes* [on-line]. Available at: http://stats. bls.gov/cpihome.htm [Dec. 5, 2000].

Carmines, Edward G., and Richard A. Zeller. 1991. *Reliability and Validity Assessment.* Newbury Park, Calif.: Sage Publications.

Clarke, Mike and Oxman, Andrew, eds. 2000. Cochrane Reviewers' Handbook 4.1 [updated June 2000]. In: Review Manager (RevMan) [computer program]. Ver. 4.1. Oxford, England: The Cochrane Collaboration. Available at: http://www.cochrane. dk/cochrane/handbook/handbook.htm.

Department of Health. 1999. *Quality and Performance in the NHS: High Level Performance Indicators.* London: NHS Executive. Available at: www.doh.gov.uk/ nhshlpi.htm.

Department of Health. 2000. *NHS Performance Indicators.* Leeds, England: NHS Executive. Available at: http://www.doh.gov.uk/nhsperformanceindicators.

Donabedian, Avedis. 1966. Evaluating the quality of medical care. *Milbank Memorial Fund Quarterly* 44:166–203.

Donabedian, Avedis. 1966. Evaluating the quality of medical care. *Milbank Memorial Fund Quarterly* 44:166–203.

Donabedian, Avedis. 1982. *The Criteria and Standards of Quality.* Ann Arbor, Mich.: Health Administration Press.

Evans, R. Scott, Stanley L. Pestotnik, David C. Classen, Terry P. Clemmer, Lindell K. Weaver, James F. Orme, James F. Lloyd, and John P. Burke. 1998. A computer-assisted management program for antibiotics and other antiinfective agents. *New England Journal of Medicine* 338(4):232–238.

Foster, Nancy S., Anthony D. So, and John M. Eisenberg. 1999. *Improving the Nation's Health Care Quality: The President's Quality Commission Report, the Quality Forum and the Quality Interagency Task Force.* U.S. Department of Health and Human Services. Unpublished.

Foundation for Accountability. 1999a. *Key Questions and Decision Making Criteria, Child and Adolescent Health Measurement Initiative.* Living with Illness Task Force Meeting. Portland, Ore.

Foundation for Accountability. 1999b. *Sharing the Quality Message with Consumers,* Portland, Ore.: FACCT.

Foundation for Accountability. 1999c. *FACCT/ONE* [on-line]. Available at: http://www.facct.org/measures/Develop/FACCTONE.htm [Mar. 13, 2001].

Greenfield, Sheldon, Giovanni Apolone, Barbara J. McNeil, and Paul D. Cleary. 1993. The importance of co-existent disease in the occurrence of postoperative complications and one-year recovery in patients undergoing total hip replacement. Comorbidity and outcomes after hip replacement. *Medical Care* 31(2):141–154.

Greenfield, Sheldon, Richard Kahn, Sherrie H. Kaplan, John Nonomiya, and John Griffith. In press. Evaluating practice differences in the delivery of diabetes care: Effects of specialty, patient characteristics and individual practice variation. *Annals of Internal Medicine.*

Halm, Ethan A., Clara Lee, and Mark R. Chassin. 2000. Commissioned paper for the Institute of Medicine Committee on the Quality of Health Care in America and the National Cancer Policy Board. Unpublished.

Healthcare Research and Quality Act. 1999. Vol. 113, Sec. 1653. *Statutes at Large.*

Hibbard, Judith H. 1998. Use of outcome data by purchasers and consumers: new strategies and new dilemmas. *International Journal for Quality in Health Care* 10(6):503–508.

Institute of Medicine. 1999. *Leading Health Indicators for Healthy People 2010.* eds. Carole A. Chrvala and Roger J. Bulger. Washington, D.C.: National Academy Press.

Institute of Medicine. 2000. *Interpreting the Volume–Outcome Relationship in the Context of Health Care Quality: Workshop Summary.* ed. Maria Hewitt. Washington, D.C.: National Academy Press.

Joint Commission on Accreditation of Health Care Organizations. 1999. *Facts about ORYX: The Next Evolution in Accreditation* [on-line]. Available at: http://www.jcaho.org/perfmeas/nextevol.html [Dec. 7, 2000].

Kingdon, John W. 1995. *Agendas, Alternatives, and Public Policies.* New York: Harper Collins.

Kizer, Kenneth W. 2000. The National Quality Forum enters the game. *International Journal for Quality in Health Care* 12(2):85–87.

Kvale, Steinar. 1995. The social construction of validity. *Qualitative Inquiry* 1(1):19–40.

Lohr, Kathleen N., and Timothy S. Carey. 1999. Assessing "best evidence": Issues in grading the quality of studies for systematic reviews. *Joint Commission Journal on Quality Improvement* 25(9):470–479.

McGlynn, Elizabeth A. 2000. QA Tools and the National Quality Report. Presentation to the Institute of Medicine Committee on the National Quality Report on Health Care Delivery, Oakland, Calif., August 18.

McGlynn, Elizabeth A., and Steven M. Asch. 1998. Developing a clinical performance measure. *American Journal of Preventive Medicine* 14(3S):14–21.

Miller, Tracy, and Sheila Leatherman. 1999. The National Quality Forum: A 'me-too' or a breakthrough in quality measurement and reporting. *Health Affairs* 18(6):233–237.

Mulligan, Jo, John Appleby, and Anthony Harrison. 2000. Measuring the performance of health systems. *British Medical Journal* 321:191–192.

National Center for Education Statistics. 2000. *The Nation's Report Card: National Assessment of Educational Progress* [on-line]. Available at: http://nces.ed.gov/ nationsreportcard/site/home.asp [Dec. 8, 2000].

National Center for Health Statistics. 2000. *Health, United States, 2000 with Adolescent Health Chartbook*, Hyattsville, Md.: U.S. Government Printing Office.

National Committee for Quality Assurance. 2000. *HEDIS 2001*, Vol. 1. Washington, D.C.: NCQA.

National Committee for Quality Assurance. 2000a. *Quality Compass 2000*. Washington, D.C.: NCQA.

National Quality Forum. 2000. *National Quality Forum Mission* [on-line]. Available at: http://www.qualityforum.org/mission/home.htm [Jul. 10, 2000].

National Research Council. 1999. *Health Performance Measurement in the Public Sector: Principles and Policies for Implementing an Information Network*. eds. Edward B. Perrin, Jane S. Durch, and Susan M. Skillman. Washington, D.C.: National Academy Press.

Nunnally, J. C. 1978. *Psychometric Theory*. 2nd ed. New York: McGraw-Hill.

Palmer, R. Heather. 1997. Quality of care. *Journal of the American Medical Association* 277(23):1896–1897.

Picker Institute. 2001. Research Services [on-line]. Available at: http://www.picker.org/ Research/Default.htm [Mar. 13, 2001].

Romano, Patrick S. 2000. Should health plan quality measures be adjusted for case mix? *Medical Care* 38(10):977–980.

Schuster, Mark A., Elizabeth A. McGlynn, Cung B. Pham, Myles D. Spar, and Robert H. Brook. 2001. The quality of health care in the United States: A review of articles since 1987. *Crossing the Quality Chasm: A New Health System for the 21st Century*, Appendix A. Washington, D.C.: National Academy Press.

Sofaer, Shoshanna. 1995. *Performance Indicators: A Commentary from the Perspective of an Expanded View of Health*. Washington, D.C.: Center for the Advancement of Health. Available at: http://www.cfah.org/website2/16.htm.

Stead, William W. 1998. *Issues Related to Patient Medical Record Information: Testimony to National Committee on Vital and Health Statistics, Subcommittee on Standards and Security* [on-line]. Available at: http://www.mc.vanderbilt.edu/ infocntr/stead/med-rec.html [Nov. 9, 2000].

Stephen, E. H., and A. Chandra. 2000. Use of infertility services in the United States: 1995. *Family Planning Perspectives* 32(3):132–137.

U.S. Department of Health and Human Services. 2000a. *NCVHS Charter 1999* [on-line]. Available at: http://ncvhs.hhs.gov/99charter.htm [Dec. 6, 2000a].

U.S. Department of Health and Human Services. 2000b. *Healthy People 2010*, Washington, D.C.: U.S. Government Printing Office.

Wang, P. S., A. Walker, M. Tsuang, E. J. Orav, R. Levin, and J. Avorn. 2000. Strategies for improving comorbidity measures based on Medicare and Medicaid claims data. *Journal of Clinical Epidemiology* 53(6):571–578.

Welch, H. Gilbert, Lisa M. Schwartz, and Steven Woloshin. 2000. Are increasing 5-year survival rates evidence of success against cancer? *Journal of the American Medical Association* 283(22):2975–2978.

Wennberg, John, and Alan Gittelsohn. 1973. Small area variations in health care delivery. *Science* 182(117):1102–1108.

Zaslavsky, Alan M., John N. Hocheimer, Eric C. Schneider, Paul D. Cleary, Joshua J. Seidman, Elizabeth A. McGlynn, Joseph W. Thompson, Cary Sennett, and Arnold M. Epstein. 2000. Impact of sociodemographic case mix on the HEDIS measures of health plan quality. *Medical Care* 38(10):981–992.

4
Data Sources for the National Health Care Quality Report[1]

To be a reliable and authoritative source of information on the quality of health care in the United States, the National Health Care Quality Report (also referred to as the Quality Report) must draw from a set of data sources adequate to support measures on the components of health care quality—safety, effectiveness, "patient centeredness," and timeliness. The set of sources must also be able to support consumer perspectives on health care needs, which include staying healthy, getting better, living with illness or disability, and coping with the end of life as they apply to each quality component.

This chapter presents the major criteria that the sources for the National Health Care Quality Data Set should meet, followed by a preliminary examination of how several leading public and private data sources compare on these criteria. As discussed, the Agency for Healthcare Research and Quality (AHRQ) should pursue parallel short-term and long-term strategies in defining and using the National Health Care Quality Data Set to report on health care quality. For the next decade or so, AHRQ will have to rely mostly on current approaches to collecting data. The Medical Expenditure Panel Survey (MEPS), coupled with a Consumer Assessment of Health Plans Survey (CAHPS) component, has the potential to support measures of patient centeredness and timeliness. To support measures of effectiveness and safety, AHRQ should draw from a combination of public and private data sources such as claims and other administrative data, sur-

---

[1] Sections of this chapter are drawn from a paper on data sources for the National Health Care Quality Report commissioned by the committee from Marsha Gold (2000).

veys, and medical records. At the same time, AHRQ should encourage research and demonstration projects that will lead to the implementation of a robust health information infrastructure as is being assessed by the National Committee on Vital and Health Statistics (NCVHS) (U.S Department of Health and Human Services, 1999). Over the long term, fulfilling the committee's vision of a comprehensive Quality Report will be facilitated by the development of electronic clinical data systems integrated with the care process itself. In addition, the data system should permit the aggregation of individual records for the purpose of examining quality of care overall and for specific population subgroups, as well as disaggregation for the purpose of examining reasons behind potential disparities. These kind of data will be available only if significant progress is made toward development of a health information infrastructure. It is imperative that efforts be made to encourage electronic access to standardized clinical data, including patient history and diagnosis, medication and ancillary service orders and results, procedures performed, and patient outcomes, in both inpatient and outpatient settings. Means of capturing community-level information on the experience of care (most commonly through surveys) will also be necessary.

RECOMMENDATIONS

RECOMMENDATION 7: Potential data sources for the National Health Care Quality Data Set should be assessed according to the following criteria: credibility and validity of the data, national scope and potential to provide state-level detail, availability and consistency of the data over time and across sources, timeliness of the data, ability to support population subgroup and condition-specific analyses, and public accessibility of the data. In addition, in order to support the framework, the ensemble of data sources defined for the National Health Care Quality Data Set should be comprehensive.

The data sources that are intended to support the long-term goal of a National Health Care Quality Data Set must meet certain high standards to support analysis of the state of health care quality in the United States. Although these criteria are not exhaustive, they do include the essential ideal features that should characterize data sources for the Quality Report in the future. When current data collection efforts do not fulfill these criteria, AHRQ should explore ways to enhance existent data sources and establish new data collection and reporting systems that exhibit these characteristics, in collaboration with the appropriate entities in the public and private sectors.

RECOMMENDATION 8: The Agency for Healthcare Research and Quality will have to draw on a mosaic of public and private

data sources for the National Health Care Quality Data Set. Existent data sources will have to be complemented by the development of new ones in order to address all of the aspects included in the proposed framework and resulting measure set. Over the coming decade, the evolution of a comprehensive health information infrastructure including standardized, electronic clinical data systems will greatly facilitate the definition of an integrated and comprehensive data set for the Quality Report.

Elsewhere, the committee has recommended the definition of a wide-ranging set of measures for the National Health Care Quality Data Set based on the proposed framework and specified criteria (see Recommendations 1, 2 and 4.) To create the data set, the Agency for Healthcare Research and Quality will have to rely on a number of data sources. A formal and exhaustive review of data sources based on the suggested criteria (see Recommendation 7) will be needed. This process will be used to determine how presently available data sources can best be used and which others will have to be developed (particularly for the framework elements of safety and coping with the end of life).

A preliminary and limited evaluation of several candidate data sources suggests that a combination of MEPS and CAHPS may have the best potential to supply data for measures of patient centeredness and aspects of timeliness. However, the CAHPS component presently planned for MEPS will have to include additional questions in order to meet the data requirements for these two components of quality and related consumer perspectives on health care needs. To assess effectiveness and safety and relevant health care needs, a combination of public and private data sources should be used, including MEPS, other population surveys, claims and other administrative data, medical record abstraction, and new data sources that will have to be developed.

Administrative data, such as Medicare claims, represent one of the most practical and cost-effective data sources on selected components of health care quality available today. Although they may have important limitations, they can be used to identify areas that require closer study through other means such as surveys and medical record abstraction.

Whenever possible, AHRQ should pursue data strategies that encourage the collection of standardized clinical data in electronic form as a part of the care process. Although there are many clinical and administrative reasons for using this type of information, in the long run it will also provide the best data on components of quality and consumer health care needs allowing for a more textured picture of quality.

RECOMMENDATION 9: The data for the National Health Care Quality Report should be both nationally representative and, in the long term, reportable at the state level.

By measuring health care quality at the national and state levels, the National Health Care Quality Report would provide benchmarks to judge how well health care delivery systems are performing at the state level in comparison to the nation as a whole. The ability to examine certain quality measures across states would substantially enhance the policy relevance, visibility, and usefulness of the report. In some cases, the available data will yield estimates that may be fairly precise for larger states, but not as precise for smaller states. In such instances, data for smaller states might be aggregated over several years before being reported. States should also be allowed to supplement the sample size called for by federal reporting requirements and fund additional data collection efforts to produce more detailed estimates.

Local-level identifiers such as zip codes can be used to examine specific subpopulations when needed. Since health care is inherently a local phenomenon, further detail on the quality of care for geographic units smaller than states is usually required to address potential problems at the provider and organizational levels. However, this level of detail should generally correspond to other regional or specialized reports since the purpose of the National Health Care Quality Report is to examine the quality of care provided by the system as a whole, not by individual providers, localities, or health plans.

DATA SOURCE SELECTION CRITERIA

It is not surprising that national health care quality measurement demands much from potential data sources, given the fact that quality of care is a complex topic. The six criteria listed in Box 4.1 help to specify and clarify what the data source needs are. These represent the combination of characteristics of an ideal data source. It is unlikely that every potential data source will meet all of them, and a data source does not have to do so in order to qualify for the National Health Care Quality Data Set. The criteria are listed in Box 4.1 in approximate order of importance.

BOX 4.1 Desirable Attributes for Sources for the National Health Care Quality Data Set

1. Credibility and validity of the data
2. National scope and potential to provide state-level detail
3. Availability and consistency of the data over time and across sources
4. Timeliness of the data
5. Ability to support subgroup- and condition-specific analyses
6. Public accessibility of the data

Credibility and Validity of the Data

The value of the Quality Report will largely reflect the credibility of the measures and the corresponding data sources. Two important determinants of credibility are the underlying validity and reliability of the data. This means that sources that meet established professional standards for data are likely to be more credible than those that do not. Factors that should be considered in evaluating the quality of potential sources of data include their prior use in research, the availability of good documentation, and review by researchers and others of their suitability for use in the Quality Report.

National Scope and Potential to Provide State-Level Detail

Data for the Quality Report should cover the nation and should be collected using methods that limit the bias that would otherwise exist if particular populations or geographical locales were systematically excluded or underrepresented in the sample. This means that data available nationally or from all states are more desirable than those covering only a subset of states. In addition, it is recommended that quality data be reportable at the individual state level in the long term; therefore, data sources that provide this level of detail—or have the potential to do so—should be preferred. Also, data sources (in particular, those based on population surveys) that cover all of the people in the United States are better than those that leave out subsets of the population (for example, the homeless, the uninsured, or immigrants) or particular health care settings (for example, nursing homes). Such omissions present problems for the representativeness of the data, especially when sources of comparable data for those excluded do not exist.

In general, it is desirable to collect national information that is sufficiently detailed to support estimates for states and for subgroups in states that are defined by demographic variables (such as race or income) and health conditions. However, the sample sizes required to support state estimates are obviously much larger than those required to support a single national estimate or even a national estimate together with a few broad regional or subgroup comparisons. For example, a common sample size for a survey might be 1,000 respondents for each reportable domain; a measure that might feasibly be collected by a national survey could be very expensive at the state level. Even if a survey is large enough to support estimates at the state level for some general measures, it might not do so for measures that apply only to subpopulations such as those with specific health care needs. Therefore, states should be given the opportunity to supplement sample size to produce reliable state-level estimates. Although the ability to collect state-level estimates is preferable, a measure of an important aspect of health care should not be rejected because it is not available at the state level.

Availability and Consistency of the Data Over Time and Across Sources

The Quality Report must track the quality of health care and identify areas for improvement over time. Data sources that are collected on an ongoing basis are more useful for this purpose than those that are produced occasionally or at irregular intervals. Data sources based on similarly defined populations are preferable because they can be used to construct uniform denominators across measures and over time that will allow for valid comparisons. Consistency can be fostered by selecting or developing data sources where data are gathered in a standardized fashion based on uniform definitions and denominators. The National Committee on Vital and Health Statistics is addressing many of these key health data issues (U.S. Department of Health and Human Services, 1999).

As a practical matter, however, the way data elements are defined may change or be improved over time, potentially enriching the content of the Quality Report but jeopardizing the ability to compare quality from one period to the next. Whenever possible, maintaining the continuity of data sources over time and across sources ought to be an important objective. One can reconcile the need for available data, the value of improved data, and the need for consistent data over time by giving preference to data sources in which changes are well documented, systematically introduced, and thoughtfully made. Although stable and consistent data sources are ideal and needed to track changes in quality over time, cross-sectional data from occasional data sources are also important. They will be useful for examining specific topics and, in the short term, may be the only way to obtain information for some of the measures.

Timeliness of the Data

Data available on a reasonably timely basis should be favored over data for which the lag between collection and availability is substantial. A reasonably timely basis can amount to as much as a three-year time lag, but a year or less would be better since the data would be more valuable to policy makers in assessing the effects of innovations.[2] Further, more timely data provide feedback on the current system, rather than on the system as it existed several years ago. The report should also include measures that reflect any recent systemwide interventions for quality improvement that require assessment.

---

[2] This criterion applies to the data source as a whole and not to individual measures or indicators. Some data sources will include measures for which yearly data collection is impractical or unnecessary. However, the data source should preferably be available every year even if all the data elements are not updated yearly.

Ability to Support Subgroup- and Condition-Specific Analyses

Because equity in the quality of care for different population groups and quality of care for specific health conditions should be examined in the Quality Report, data sources must allow the definition of consistent estimates for various subgroups of the population such as children, the poor, minorities, the uninsured, and other vulnerable populations, as well as people with specific health conditions. In many cases, it will be necessary to oversample population subgroups of interest in order to obtain reliable estimates. This makes both the content and the sample design (if relevant) of data sources important to an assessment of data quality. For example, data sources that capture sociodemographic characteristics and specific health conditions and that include adequate numbers of these subpopulations should be stronger contenders for inclusion than those that do not. Similarly, individual-level or discrete data that can be used to generate diverse estimates are more suitable than sources that provide only aggregate measures.

Public Accessibility of the Data

As mentioned in the discussion of credibility, data for the Quality Report should be widely accepted and respected. One way to achieve this is to focus on data in the public domain, either because they are drawn from a public data source or because they are drawn from a private data source that is routinely available to public agencies. Some data from private sources may be made available to public agencies under strict procedures to ensure patient or respondent confidentiality. In some instances, organizational confidentiality may be ensured (for example, hospital reports on adverse drug events), even though state estimates may be made public. Regardless of the source, there should be a reasonable guarantee of availability to the public and of predictability in the cost of acquiring the data for the report. In some cases, part or all of the data will be made available only to researchers. This is also acceptable but public accessibility is more desirable. For example, AHRQ has recently opened the CCFS Data Center, which allows researchers access to MEPS data files not available for public use (Agency for Healthcare Research and Quality, 2001).

POTENTIAL DATA SOURCES

The criteria for discrete data sources and the requirement of comprehensiveness for the entire set of data sources can be used to assess candidate sources for the report. This holds true for both the short and the long term. As noted, in the short term, a mosaic of data sources will make up the National Health Care Quality Data Set. The criteria will help to rule out some sources and to clarify the strengths and weaknesses of others. In addition, the criteria indicate how the data sources used initially can be improved to provide better, more complete information. In the long term, however, the development of electronic clinical data systems will support data that more adequately meet the criteria of comprehensiveness, as well as national- and state-level coverage, availability and consistency over time, timeliness, support for subgroup- and condition-specific analyses, and public accessibility.

The following is a description of potential public and private data sources that can be used in the National Health Care Quality Data Set in the next several years. It should be noted that the distinction between public and private data sources is not always a clear one. Although data sources may be produced by public entities such as federal and state governments, this does not necessarily mean that they can be accessed easily and used without restriction. For example, those that contain information on health care for individuals generate confidentiality concerns that can strictly limit their use. Private data sources run the gamut from those that have minor restrictions to those that are proprietary. Generally, proprietary sources can be used only for a fee or by meeting other requirements such as organizational membership.

Public Data Sources

There are several kinds of public data sources, including population-based health surveys and payer and provider data. Most of these data sources can provide only national or regional estimates. Some, however, include state-level detail. This section contains a brief overview of some of the public data sources that could be used in the National Health Care Quality Data Set. This is followed by a discussion of how these sources fulfill the criteria proposed by the committee and how they cover specific components of quality. They are listed alphabetically.

Behavioral Risk Factor Surveillance Survey

The Behavioral Risk Factor Surveillance Survey (BRFSS) is a state-administered survey. It is designed for telephone administration, and it has core sections and optional modules. Topics for the core section include health status, health care access, demographics, particular diseases, and risk factors. Topics for the optional module include health care coverage and utilization, health care satisfaction, preventive behavior and practices, and other diseases and risk factors. In addition, states can add their own questions on matters of particular local interest, as Oklahoma did when it examined stress and other health issues following the 1995 bombing in Oklahoma City. Sample size varies across states and ranges from 1,800 to 7,500 people per year depending on the state (Centers for Disease Control and Prevention, 2000a; Powell-Griner, 2000).

Consumer Assessment of Health Plans Survey

The Consumer Assessment of Health Plans Survey is a survey and reporting tool. CAHPS is actually a family of surveys and consists of several core questionnaires that can be combined with supplements on special topics (Agency for Healthcare Research and Quality, 2000a). The core questionnaires include the adult core questionnaire, the Medicaid managed care questionnaire, the child core questionnaire, the child Medicaid managed care questionnaire, and the Medicare managed care questionnaire. Supplements include those on mental health care, prescription medicine, and communication with providers.

CAHPS is used by more than 20 states, 10 employer groups, the National Committee on Quality Assurance (NCQA), the Agency for Healthcare Research and Quality, the Health Care Financing Administration (HCFA) for Medicare, the Federal Employees Health Benefits Program (FEHBP), the Ford Motor Company, and a number of health plans (Agency for Healthcare Research and Quality, 2000a). Only recently have selected items in CAHPS been administered by AHRQ within MEPS.

The National CAHPS Benchmarking Database, funded by AHRQ, publishes CAHPS data yearly in each of the three major sectors (commercial, Medicare, and Medicaid) (Agency for Healthcare Research and Quality, 2000b). CAHPS data are also released annually by NCQA, by HCFA for Medicare, and by state Medicaid programs.

Healthcare Cost and Utilization Project

The Healthcare Cost and Utilization Project (HCUP) is a family of databases created from data in the Nationwide Inpatient Sample (NIS) and from the State Inpatient Databases (SID). The Nationwide Inpatient Sample is based on a national sample of more than 1,000 hospitals. State Inpatient Databases consist of inpatient data collected voluntarily by community hospitals for use in HCUP and now cover 31 states (Agency for Healthcare Research and Quality, 2000c).

HCUP quality indicators (QIs) are a set of 33 clinical performance measures drawn from HCUP databases. The measures concern the quality of inpatient care and access to primary care. The measure set is currently being revised and expanded (Agency for Healthcare Research and Quality, 2000c).

HCUP QIs involve three dimensions of care. First, there are adverse hospital outcomes, which include inpatient mortality rates among low-risk patients who have common elective procedures and complication rates related to events that occur during hospitalization. The second dimension is potentially inappropriate use of hospital procedures, which include utilization rates for procedures identified as overused or underused. Third, there are potentially avoidable hospital admissions, which are indirect measures of access to—and appropriateness of—primary care (Agency for Healthcare Research and Quality, 2000c).

Medical Expenditure Panel Survey

The Medical Expenditure Panel Survey is a nationally representative survey of health care utilization, spending, insurance coverage, and other data elements. It applies mainly to noninstitutionalized civilians, although there is also a MEPS survey of nursing home residents. Since 1997, MEPS has been conducted annually, with the National Health Interview Survey (NHIS) national core sample as the sampling frame. It contains cross-sectional and longitudinal data.

The main component of MEPS is a household survey of noninstitutionalized civilians (roughly 10,000 families and 24,000 individuals) that yields data at the household and individual levels. It can be used to produce estimates at the national and regional levels, but not at the state level. It asks respondents about their health conditions, status, access to care, use of various care settings, prescribed and over-the-counter medicines, and medical expenses for the prior two years (Agency for Healthcare Research and Quality, 2000d). Other core components are followback surveys of insurers and providers, including physicians, hospitals, and pharmacies. Followback surveys are used to validate and supplement information provided in the household component and to support analyses of individual behavior and choices (Agency for Healthcare Research and Quality, 2000e).

The Healthcare Research and Quality Act of 1999 calls for MEPS to be expanded in several ways to improve its capacity as a major data source on the quality of care. These include the collection of data needed "to study the relationships between health care quality, outcomes, access, use, and cost, measure changes over time, and monitor the overall national impact of Federal and State policy changes on health care," as well as "the quality of care and patient outcomes for frequently occurring clinical conditions for a nationally representative sample of the population including rural residents" (Healthcare Research and Quality Act, 1999).

In response to the Healthcare Research and Quality Act, AHRQ is planning changes for MEPS that may include expanding the survey's coverage of such topics as preventive care and the treatment of particular medical conditions. AHRQ is also planning to incorporate some measures of patient experience with care borrowed from CAHPS, including consumer satisfaction, patient centeredness, and timeliness (Lefkowitz, 2000).

Medicare Claims or Payer Data

HCFA has developed extensive databases that feature claims-based information from intermediaries and carriers on inpatient and outpatient services for which it has paid under coverage provided by Medicare Part A (called hospital insurance) and Part B (called medical insurance) (Health Care Financing Administration, 2000b). As of 1998, about 39 million people, or 95 percent of those

65 years of age or older were covered by Medicare Part A, Medicare Part B, or both (Health Care Financing Administration, 1999).

Claims data can be linked to enrollment data to provide information on providers, up to nine patient diagnoses during an inpatient stay, medical treatment, some medical services, demographics, and mortality (Eggers, 2000; Health Care Financing Administration, 2000a). Such data could be used to target surveys of patients with specific conditions or treatments to complete the picture of their care. They have been used to make risk-adjusted outcome comparisons among states (Peterson et al., 1998) and to estimate the rate of complications following procedures (Lu-Yao et al., 1994).

Claims data, however, omit care that is not covered by Medicare Parts A or B. Claims data do not reflect care that is paid by supplemental medical coverage, nor do they reflect care in the form of laboratory services, even if covered by Medicare. These data provide information on insurance claims for the approximately 85 percent of beneficiaries who are enrolled in fee-for-service Medicare, but not for the remaining beneficiaries who are enrolled in Medicare managed care (Eggers, 2000; Hannan et al., 1997).

Medicare Current Beneficiary Survey

The Medicare Current Beneficiary Survey (MCBS) is an ongoing longitudinal panel survey of 12,000 Medicare beneficiaries, drawn from Medicare enrollment files. It includes the institutionalized and noninstitutionalized Medicare population. Data collection covers a three-year period. The survey includes information on health care utilization, expenditures, insurance coverage, and health status, resulting in measures similar in some ways to those in MEPS. Medicare links survey data with claims data from Medicare files, but to date, the linked data have included only beneficiaries in fee-for-service arrangements. This design has complicated efforts to develop common measures of utilization by type of plan (Health Care Financing Administration, 2000a).

Medicare Quality Data

HCFA collects a range of other data that specifically support quality measurement, such as the Medicare Health Plan Employer Data and Information Set/Consumer Assessment of Health Plans Survey (HEDIS/CAHPS). As of 2000, most Medicare managed care organizations must use performance measures based on HEDIS, which includes the Medicare Health Outcomes Survey (HOS). Medicare CAHPS also provides information on consumer experience with Medicare managed care plans. Examples of CAHPS measures include those on effectiveness of care for specific conditions, access to or availability of care, and utilization of services. Beginning in 2001, health plans will report data in different ways. As in previous years, most will continue to report on the area they contract with HCFA to cover. Five states—California, Florida, New York, Ohio, and Texas—will each be divided into two geographical units, and plans will issue reports based on these units. Plans in states that have more than 5,000 members and that operate in both units will issue two reports (Elstein, 2000).

In addition, beginning in 2000, HCFA collected data for a CAHPS survey aimed at those in Medicare fee-for-service insurance. Reporting is scheduled to begin in 2001. Initially, information will be reported on 50 states, the District of Columbia, and Puerto Rico. Findings are based on a survey of 168,000 people (Sekscenski, 2000).

National Ambulatory Medical Care Survey and National Hospital Ambulatory Medical Care Survey

The main surveys on ambulatory care are the National Ambulatory Medical Care Survey (NAMCS), which collects data on a sample of visits to physicians' offices, and the related National Hospital Ambulatory Medical Care Survey (NHAMCS), which collects data on a sample of visits to hospital outpatient and emergency departments. Both surveys collect data on patient characteristics and care, including diagnostic and screening services, diagnoses, procedures, therapeutic services, medications, disposition, and causes of injury where applicable. The surveys can be used to produce national estimates. They cannot be used to produce meaningful state-level estimates (National Center for Health Statistics, 2000a).

National Health and Nutrition Examination Survey

The National Health and Nutrition Examination Survey (NHANES) uses a combination of interviews, direct physical examinations, and medical tests and procedures to collect information on a nationally representative sample of the U.S. population. Sample size consists of about 5,000 people per year, including children and adults. NHANES focuses on health status rather than health care services. The survey allows monitoring of national trends in diabetes, nutritional status, osteoporosis, physical activity, and respiratory health and disease. Since 1999, NHANES has been conducted continuously and annually, replacing earlier versions that were conducted over several years with larger samples. It can be linked to the NHIS and, beginning in 2001, to the U.S. Department of Agriculture's Continuing Survey of Food Intakes by Individuals (CSFII) (National Center for Health Statistics, 2000b).

National Health Interview Survey

The National Health Interview Survey is an annual cross-sectional survey of more than 40,000 households that include more than 100,000 people, selected to represent the civilian noninstitutionalized population of the United States. The NHIS is the main source of national data on the incidence of acute illness, prevalence of chronic conditions and impairments, extent of disability, and use of health services. Questions about preventive services have been expanded and asked more routinely in recent years. The NHIS includes basic information collected annually, other items collected on a periodic basis, and topical items collected on a one-time basis as special supplements (National Center for Health Statistics, 2000c).

National Immunization Survey and State and Local Area
Integrated Telephone Survey

Unlike most federal surveys, the National Immunization Survey (NIS) and the State and Local Area Integrated Telephone Survey (SLAITS) are conducted by telephone. NIS is a survey of both households and health care providers. For NIS, immunization data are obtained on children 19 to 35 months of age, who are located in 78 nonoverlapping geographic units across the nation. The survey includes telephone screening of 800,000 households annually to identify 32,000 households with children of the target age. The survey also collects data from 30,000 providers who have administered immunizations to survey participants. SLAITS is a special-purpose survey that includes questions from NIS and provides state-based estimates of health insurance coverage, utilization, and access. It also provides feedback on various policies and programs (for example, the effect of welfare reform). In addition, SLAITS includes special surveys of families with young children, children with special needs, and a pilot on testing for human immunodeficiency virus (HIV) and sexually transmitted disease (STD) risk behaviors. Measures of the quality of care for disabled children are being developed in collaboration with staff from the Foundation for Accountability (FACCT) (Blumberg, 2000; Centers for Disease Control and Prevention 2000b; National Center for Health Statistics, 2000d).

National Vital Statistics System

As its name indicates, the National Vital Statistics System (NVSS) records all vital statistics including births and deaths (National Center for Health Statistics, 1999, 2000e). As such, it is the most complete data source on infant mortality and general mortality by cause of death and several population characteristics. It has the potential to provide nationwide, continuous, and uniform baseline data on adverse health outcomes, complications (including drug complications), and misadventures to patients as a result of or during surgical and medical care when these are part of the International Classification of Diseases, particularly the External Causes of Death Codes, or E Codes (National Center for Health Statistics, 1995). The data can be classified by specific population subgroups defined by age, race, Hispanic origin, sex, place of birth, and place of occurrence, among others. Several specific programs and surveys are associated with the NVSS. These include the Linked Birth and Infant Death Data Set, the National Maternal and Infant Health Survey, the National Mortality Followback Survey, the National Survey of Family Growth, and the National Death Index. Each of these provides more detail regarding recorded births and deaths, including information on access to prenatal care, behavioral risk factors, maternal characteristics, and others. The main limitation of these associated sources is that they do not have a defined periodicity, so it would not be possible to use them to regularly examine trends.

Surveillance, Epidemiology, and End Results Program

The Surveillance, Epidemiology, and End Results (SEER) Program of the National Cancer Institute is one of the nation's two main national cancer registries (for information on the other registry, see a description of the National Cancer Data Base below). Cancer registries collect data on such items as cancer type, stage of cancer at diagnosis, course of treatment, and patient characteristics (Institute of Medicine and National Research Council, 1999). SEER is the only registry that contains data on the stage of cancer when diagnosed and the rates of survival for a stage. SEER began to ascertain cases in 1971. Currently, it collects data on patients drawn from five states, several metropolitan areas, and other localities, who make up 14 percent of the population. Compared to the population of the United States as a whole, the sample is more urban, has a greater proportion of the foreign born, but has similar levels of poverty and education (Hankey et al., 1999; Institute of Medicine and National Research Council, 2000).

Private Data Sources

As mentioned in Chapter 1, the committee held a call for measures for the National Health Care Quality Report and requested submissions from the private sector.[3] The 138 measures submitted covered most of the components of quality and consumer perspectives on health care needs set forth in the framework. However, many of the measures were not part of regular data collection efforts (see Appendix C for the list of measures submitted).

There are many kinds of private data sources, including private insurance plans, accrediting organizations, providers, and vendors. The following is a brief overview of some that could be used for the National Health Care Quality Data

---

[3]AHRQ planned and held a subsequent call for measures for the Quality Report among federal agencies after the committee had concluded its deliberations.

Set in the short term. In the long term, electronic data systems in combination with selected surveys would be preferred, as has been discussed.

National Cancer Data Base

In addition to the National Cancer Institute's SEER Program (see above), the National Cancer Data Base (NCDB) is one of the nation's two main cancer registries. It is sponsored by the American College of Surgeons' Commission on Cancer and the American Cancer Society. Initiated in 1989, it contains data reported by 1,600 hospitals, with the number of reporting hospitals slated for expansion. Hospitals report all new cases seen in a data year, which include 600,000 new cases of cancer annually, or 58 percent of all new cases in the nation. Patient background, cancer characteristics, first course of treatment, and treatment follow-up are among the items of information collected. Hospitals that have a computerized cancer registry seem more likely to report to the NCDB (Institute of Medicine and National Research Council, 2000).

ORYX

The Joint Commission on Accreditation of Healthcare Organizations (JCAHO) is an independent, nonprofit entity that accredits nearly 19,000 health care organizations and programs (Joint Commission on Accreditation of Healthcare Organizations, 2000a). To advance the use of quality improvement measures in the accreditation process, JCAHO launched the ORYX initiative in 1997. It is currently being implemented in the accreditation process for hospital, long-term care, home care, network, laboratory, and behavioral health care organizations. JCAHO also plans to implement it for ambulatory care and long-term care pharmacy organizations.

In 2000, JCAHO's board approved a set of 25 common measures for ORYX distributed across five core measurement sets: acute myocardial infarction (AMI), heart disease, surgical procedures and complications, pregnancy and related conditions, and community-acquired pneumonia. Hospitals will be required to select some of these common core measures for data collection activity starting in January 2002 and to submit the initial information no later than July 2002. The measurement sets were developed by expert advisory panels, with extensive input from interested parties. The initial set of ORYX measures on pneumonia, AMI, and heart failure includes 17 that are from the sixth contract cycle for HCFA peer review organizations (PROs) (see section that follows). These measures will be refined to reflect the fact that patient data will not be restricted to the Medicare population. JCAHO initially focused on acute care and the five conditions listed here, but it plans to expand ORYX to other conditions and to add measures relevant to long-term care. However, JCAHO will limit the frequency of change and the ultimate size of the measurement (Joint

Commission on Accreditation of Healthcare Organizations, 2000b). Eventually, JCAHO plans to publicly release comparative information on organizational performance that will include risk-adjusted core measurement data. Raw data on organizations will be kept confidential (Schyve, 2000).

Peer Review Organization Data

HCFA collects a range of quality care data through its peer review organizations. PROs are private organizations that contract with HCFA to provide a variety of services, including evaluation of the quality of medical services provided to Medicare beneficiaries and funded by Medicare. Under their current contract with HCFA (the sixth contract cycle, which includes the sixth scope of work) to provide services to Medicare, PROs monitor certain clinical practices, including six condition-related services relevant to health care quality: care for AMI, heart failure, stroke or atrial fibrillation, pneumonia or influenza, breast cancer, and diabetes (Elstein, 2000).

Quality Compass

Quality Compass is a database on managed care information produced by the National Committee on Quality Assurance. As explained in Chapter 1, the NCQA is a private, nonprofit organization that accredits managed care organizations. For accreditation, it requires managed care organizations to report on selected measures from HEDIS including consumer survey results. By 2001, all managed care organizations will be required to report measurement results publicly as a condition of accreditation (National Committee for Quality Assurance, 2000).

Quality Compass contains the data supporting HEDIS, which features more than 50 measures across eight domains of care: effectiveness of care, access to or availability of care, satisfaction with the experience of care, health plan stability, use of services, cost of care, informed health care choices, and health plan descriptive information. In addition, Quality Compass contains the data for HEDIS/CAHPS, which features measures drawn from adult CAHPS measures regarding consumer satisfaction and experience with health care, including aspects of timeliness and patient centeredness (Schilling, 2000).

EVALUATING DATA SOURCES FOR THE
NATIONAL HEALTH CARE QUALITY DATA SET
IN THE SHORT TERM

Applying the criteria described at the beginning of the chapter to individual public and private data sources helps to clarify their relative advantages and disadvantages. However, choosing a set of data sources for the Quality Report for the short term will involve more than applying the criteria and evaluating which sources meet more criteria than others. Not only can the criteria be weighted differently, but there are also many practical considerations, such as a sponsoring organization's capacity to field a suitable survey and adequate budgetary support for necessary changes. It should be noted that this evaluation is only preliminary. AHRQ and other agencies and offices in the Department of Health and Human Services (DHHS) are better suited to perform the kind of thorough analysis that this activity requires.[4]

Table 4.1 presents an evaluation of some major public data sources by the data source selection criteria described above. Because all of the public and private data sources analyzed here are reasonably credible and valid, evaluation of these criteria is not included in the table. Although comprehensiveness is a criterion that the set of data sources taken together should meet, Table 4.1 contains an evaluation of the comprehensiveness of each individual data source, with respect to the components of quality and consumer perspectives on health care needs covered by each data source.

As Table 4.1 shows, public data sources are similar in the extent to which they meet many of the criteria. However, they differ in other ways. For example, whereas MEPS and NHIS use nationally representative samples, HCUP's State Inpatient Databases currently draw from a nonrandom sample of 31 states (Agency for Healthcare Research and Quality, 2000c). MCBS and Medicare claims data concern only beneficiaries in fee-for-service Medicare and exclude the approximately 15 percent of beneficiaries enrolled in managed care plans (Health Care Financing Administration, 2000a).

Public data sources also differ in the comprehensiveness of coverage regarding components of quality and consumer perspectives on health care needs (discussed later in this chapter). MEPS contains the broadest coverage with respect to these two components of quality. In addition, it includes information that allows analysis of equity, but certain groups may have to be oversampled. Since it shares a sampling frame with NHIS and NHANES, it can be linked to them to provide other needed data (Agency for Healthcare Research and Quality, 2000f). That MEPS compares favorably with other data sources is due in part to enhancements to the survey that have been or will be implemented by AHRQ in response to the Healthcare Research and Quality Act (Lefkowitz, 2000).

Table 4.2 presents an evaluation of major private data sources by the same criteria used for public sources. Again, because all of the data sources are reasonably credible and valid, evaluation of these criteria is not included. In addition, this table evaluates the coverage or comprehensiveness of a single data source with respect to measures of health care quality components and consumer perspectives on health care needs.

---

[4] See Cohen (2000) and Arispe (2000) for other data source analyses.

TABLE 4.1 Preliminary Evaluation of Public Data Sources on Health Care Quality

| Type and Name of Source | Comprehensiveness | | | Consumer Perspectives on Health Care Needs[b] |
	Condition-Specific Data	Links to Clinical Information	Components of Health Care Quality[a]	
BRFSS[c]	No	No	2, 4	1
CAHPS[d]	No	No	3, 4	1–3
HCUP	Yes	Yes	2–4	2, 3
MCBS[f]	Yes[e]	Yes[e]	2–4	1–3
Medicare Claims Data[f]	Yes	Yes	2, 4	1–4
MEPS[g]	Yes	No[h]	2, 4	1–4
NAMCS/NHAMCS	Yes	No	2	1–3
NHANES	Yes	No	4	1–3
NHIS	No	Yes[e]	3, 4	1–3
NIS/SLAITS[f]	No	No	2, 4	1, 2
NVSS[j]	Yes	Yes[e]	1, 2	1–3
SEER[f]	Yes	Yes	No	No

NOTE: Evaluations were conducted of individual sources only, not of sources to which they could be linked. BRFSS, Behavioral Risk Factor Surveillance System; CAHPS, Consumer Assessment of Health Plans Survey; HCUP, Healthcare Cost and Utilization Project; MCBS, Medicare Current Beneficiary Survey; MEPS, Medical Expenditure Panel Survey; NAMCS, National Ambulatory Medical Care Survey; NHAMCS, National Hospital Ambulatory Medical Care Survey; NHANES, National Health and Nutrition Examination Survey; NHIS, National Health Interview Survey; NIS, National Immunization Survey; NVSS, National Vital Statistics System; SEER, Surveillance, Epidemiology, and End Results; SLAITS, State and Local Area Integrated Telephone Survey.

[a] 1 = safety, 2 = effectiveness, 3 = patient centeredness, 4 = timeliness.

[b] 1 = staying healthy, 2 = getting better, 3 = living with illness or disability, 4 = coping with the end of life.

[c] State administered with considerable variability across states. However, there is a core set of questions that is used by all states.

	Scope		Other Data Source Criteria			
National Coverage	State or Regional Coverage	Released Annually	Timely Availability of Data	Consistency of Content over Time	Supports Population Sub-Group Analysis	Publicly Accessible Data
Yes	Yes	Yes	5 months	Yes	No	Yes
Yes	Yes[e]	Yes[e]	6 months	Yes	Yes	Yes
No	No	Yes	2 years	Yes	Yes	Yes
Yes	No	Yes	1 year	Yes	Yes	Yes
Yes	Yes	Yes	6–18 months	Yes	Yes	Yes[e]
Yes	No	Yes	18 months	Yes	Yes	Yes
Yes	No	Yes	1 year	Yes	Yes	Yes
Yes	No	Yes[i]	3 years	Yes	Yes	Yes
Yes	Yes[e]	Yes	18 months	Yes[e]	Yes	Yes
Yes	No	No	6 months	No	Yes	Yes
Yes	Yes	Yes	Continuous	Yes	Yes	Yes
No	No	Yes	8 months	Yes	Yes	Yes

[d] Evaluation includes both core and supplemental items of CAHPS 2.0 for both child and adult versions.

[e] With limitations.

[f] Targeted eligibility criteria for inclusions. Medicare claims data applies only to beneficiaries in fee-for-service Medicare. MCBS is administered to Medicare beneficiaries. The NIS is a screening survey for children 19–35 months and is by telephone so it excludes those without phones. SEER is limited to those with cancer. SLAITS is being piloted in some states.

[g] Evaluation of version of MEPS containing enhancements planned by AHRQ (Lefkowitz, 2000).

[h] Athough MEPS contains followback surveys with providers, individual survey data cannot at this time be linked to clinical records.

[i] Annual since 1999.

[j] Birth and death data only, not related surveys.

SOURCES: Arispe, 2000a; Cynamon, 2000; Darby, 2001; Dickey, 2000; Elixhauser, 2000; Eppig, 2000; Johnson, 2000; Powell-Griner, 2000; Schappert, 2000; Yang, 2000 (see text for additional sources).

TABLE 4.2 Preliminary Evaluation of Private Data Sources on Health Care Quality

| Type and Name of Source | Comprehensiveness | | | |
	Condition-Specific Data	Links to Clinical Information	Components of Health Care Quality[a]	Consumer Perspectives on Health Care Needs[b]
HCFA Peer Review Organizations (PROs) (sixth contract cycle)[c]	Yes	Yes	2, 4	1–3
National Cancer Data Base (NCDB)[c]	Yes	Yes	2, 4	2, 3
ORYX (JCAHO)[c]	Yes	Yes	2, 4	1–3
Quality Compass (NCQA)[c]	Yes	Yes	2–4	1–3

NOTES: Evaluations were conducted of the individual sources only, not of other sources to which they could be linked. NA=not applicable. HCFA, Health Care Financing Administration; JCAHO, Joint Commission on Accreditation of Healthcare Organizations; NCQA, National Committee for Quality Assurance.

[a] 1 = safety, 2 = effectiveness, 3 = patient centeredness, and 4 = timeliness.

[b] 1 = staying healthy, 2 = getting better, 3 = living with illness or disability, and 4 = coping with the end of life.

[c] Targeted eligibility criteria for inclusions. The NCDB covers data on patients with cancer as reported by 1,600 hospitals nationwide. ORYX covers those health care organizations accredited by JCAHO. The HCFA PROs sixth contract cycle covers quality measurement of care for Medicare beneficiaries. Quality Compass includes data from those managed care organizations accredited by NCQA

Scope			Other Data Source Criteria			
National Coverage	State or Regional Coverage	Released Annually	Timely Availability of Data	Consistency of Content over Time	Supports Population Subgroup Analysis	Publicly Accessible Data
Yes	Yes	NA[d]	1 year	No[d]	Yes	Yes
Yes	Yes	Yes	1 year	Yes	Yes	Yes[c]
Yes	Yes	Yes	3 months	Yes	Yes	No
Yes	Yes	Yes	1 year	Yes	Yes	No[e]

[d] HCFA PROs have contracts in a given contract cycle for 3 years. In addition, the 3-year periods are staggered. This means that PRO X could still be reporting under one contract while PRO Y could be reporting under a more recent contract. Also, the set of data collected by the PROs can differ by contract cycle.

[e] Quality Compass data can be reported publicly only by organizations licensed to do so. By 2001, all managed care organizations accredited by NCQA must permit their performance measures to be reported publicly.

SOURCES: Elstein, 2000; Hankey, 1999; Institute of Medicine and National Research Council, 2000; National Committee for Quality Assurance, 2000; Schilling, 2000; Schyve, 2000. See text for additional sources.

As Table 4.2 shows, there are important limitations in the use of these private databases. First, the data sources evaluated here contain data on subpopulations rather than data from representative national samples. In addition, the subpopulations themselves are often not well-defined subsets. Currently, Quality Compass data are collected from those managed care organizations accredited by NCQA that have agreed to public reporting of performance measurement results, which in turn represent a subset of the approximately 50 percent of managed care organizations in the nation that are accredited by NCQA (Schilling, 2000). The National Cancer Data Base is drawn from data from 1,600 hospitals, which tend to be those with computerized cancer registries (Institute of Medicine and National Research Council, 2000).

Second, consistent availability of the data over time can be an issue. Specifically, the three-year contract cycles under which HCFA PROs report contain different measurements, limiting the ability to capture change in specific areas of health care quality over time. Also, different PROs begin and end a contract cycle at staggered times, reducing the potential of using these data to draw conclusions about performance during a period of time. There has been some overlap in the conditions targeted for special attention in each cycle. For example, AMI was targeted in both the fifth and the sixth contract cycles. However, continuity is not an objective, and overlap has been the exception (Elstein, 2000).

Third, much of the data are not publicly accessible. Although some data from the Quality Compass are reported publicly, this generally occurs only at the aggregate level and only by those licensed by NCQA (National Committee for Quality Assurance, 2000). In the case of JCAHO, there are plans to make organizational-level ORYX data publicly available, but organizationally identifiable raw data will not be released publicly either (Schyve, 2000).

This is not to say that these limitations rule out the potential use of private data sources as elements in the National Health Care Quality Data Set. For example, data reported by PROs have often been used to gauge health care quality (Dartmouth Medical School, Center for the Evaluative Clinical Sciences, 1998; Jencks et al., 2000). In addition, PRO data have the particular potential to supplement public data sources on the health care quality aspect of effectiveness, at least for a given contract cycle or annual edition of the Quality Report.

Coverage of Health Care Quality Components

This section looks more closely at the coverage that public and private data sources offer for the components of quality and consumer perspectives on health care needs included in the framework. As shown below, MEPS supports measures on several of the components of health care quality, but not all. In addition, its support is uneven. Even with the addition of a CAHPS component and other enhancements planned by AHRQ, MEPS will have to be supplemented with other data sources, particularly in the quality components of safety and effectiveness.

Safety

In the framework, safety is defined as "avoiding injuries to patients from care that is intended to help them" (Institute of Medicine, 2001). Chapter 2 explains how safety can be analyzed along the continuum of care of diagnosis, treatment, including medication, and follow-up. Safety also involves the total health care environment. At present, the public and private databases evaluated in Tables 4.1 and 4.2 contain few questions that speak directly to safety. This gap is not unusual—safety is an aspect of health care quality in which measurement is particularly underdeveloped relative to other components of quality (Institute of Medicine, 2000).

In the short term, this gap could be filled by the use of safety measures suggested in Chapter 3, such as selected sentinel events (for example, wrong-site surgery) reported to JCAHO; data on hospital-acquired infections collected by the Centers for Disease Control and Prevention's (CDC's) National Nosocomial Infections Surveillance System; and selected adverse hospital outcomes tracked by HCUP (Agency for Healthcare Research and Quality, 2000c; Centers for Disease Control and Prevention, 2000c; Joint Commission on the Accreditation of Healthcare Organizations, 2000c). However, these data provide a very limited and highly fragmented view of the safety of health care. They do not address important safety issues such as errors of omission, failure to diagnose or delay in diagnosis, or patient injuries related to an unsafe environment, and they do not include data for the corresponding measures such as restraint-related deaths and medication-related deaths or disability (Institute of Medicine, 2000). As a result, these data can yield a potentially misleading picture of safety, for example, by underestimating the extent to which patient injuries or harm occur or accounting for safety only in hospital settings.

In the future, much more research will be needed on valid and reliable measures of health care safety to provide a more complete picture of this component of quality. AHRQ should aggressively foster new studies on this important and underdeveloped area. This research will be a necessary prerequisite for the further development of safety measures within existing data sources, as well as the further development of new data sources such as electronic clinical information (Quality Interagency Coordination Task Force, 2000). Surveys of patients after they have been discharged from the hospital represent another potential source of safety information regarding, for example, hospital-acquired infections or unwanted side effects after surgery.

Effectiveness

Effectiveness refers to "providing services based on scientific knowledge to all who could benefit, and refraining from providing services to those not likely to benefit (avoiding overuse and underuse)" (Institute of Medicine, 2001). As also explained in Chapter 2, it includes (1) effectiveness of preventive care;

(2) effectiveness of acute, chronic, and end-of-life care (usually with respect to specific conditions); and (3) appropriateness of the procedures. As such, effectiveness is integrally related to the health care needs of staying healthy, getting better, living with illness, and coping with the end of life.

As the definition suggests, to measure effectiveness it is especially important to probe whether people with specific health conditions are receiving needed care. Public and private data sources have offered coverage of condition-related treatment. For example, up to the present, MEPS data on conditions have been generated by survey questions that have asked respondents to recall provider appointments, hospital stays, emergency room visits, or other events; the treatments they received; and the conditions to which these events and treatments are tied. MEPS data generated by questions on prevention are more explicitly linked to conditions. For example, the alternative and preventive care sections of the household component contain questions on blood pressure and cholesterol-level checks, flu shots, prostate exams, and Pap smears, among other practices (Agency for Healthcare Research and Quality, 2000d). Data on effective treatment for certain conditions might be less reliable than data on prevention since they were generated with catch-all questions used by MEPS, which ask respondents to recall conditions and treatments over a two-year period. Followback surveys with providers and insurers may not be sufficient to fill in all of the needed information.

This situation is likely to change soon, given that the Healthcare Research and Quality Act calls for improved MEPS coverage of condition-based treatment (Healthcare Research and Quality Act, 1999). In keeping with the act and addressing the issue raised above, AHRQ has identified 15 priority conditions, with an initial focus on increases in sample size for 7 conditions: arthritis, asthma, chronic obstructive pulmonary disease (COPD), coronary heart disease, diabetes, hypertension, and stroke (as discussed in Chapter 2). Future versions of MEPS include screener questions to identify patients with these conditions. For some, there could be questions that probe appropriate treatments of household members depending on the condition. For example, MEPS will borrow several questions from the Diabetes Quality Improvement Project (DQuIP) to measure quality of care for diabetes, including aspects such as foot and eye exams and insulin injections (Lefkowitz, 2000).

MEPS could also serve as a "platform" for patient-approved review of medical records to examine more clinically specific measures of effectiveness that rely on the findings of various laboratory tests and clinical diagnoses. To a limited extent, this is already done. However, collecting such data on a larger scale is costly and would require significant additional resources to achieve meaningful sample sizes.

AHRQ could further supplement its coverage of specific conditions by drawing from other public and private data sources. Both Medicare claims data and particular HCFA contract cycles with PROs provide data with which to measure a range of issues in effectiveness. Specifically, they could be used to examine the underuse and overuse of effective medical care for particular conditions, as well as different stages of care (or health care needs) such as getting better or coping with the end of life, and the appropriateness of procedures (Dartmouth Medical School, Center for the Evaluative Clinical Sciences, 1998).

Patient Centeredness

Patient centeredness refers to health care that establishes a partnership among practitioners, patients, and their families (when appropriate) to ensure that decisions respect patients' wants, needs, and preferences and that patients have the education and support they need to make decisions and participate in their own care. As discussed in Chapter 2, patient centeredness addresses two aspects: (1) the patient's experience of care, and (2) the establishment of an effective partnership between patients and providers. These two aspects of patient centeredness are relevant across all of the consumer perspectives on health care needs.

In general, MEPS does a better job of providing data on the patient's experience of care than on effective partnerships. The household component contains several MEPS questions that address the first dimension. For example, questions in the section on access to care ask respondents whether their providers listen to them and supply needed information. In addition, a question in the section on medical provider visits probes how much time providers have spent with their patients. However, respondents are not asked whether they felt the time was sufficient. Proposed questions drawn from CAHPS will help to provide more data on the experience of care. They ask respondents whether their clinicians or their children's clinicians listened to them, explained things in ways they could understand, and showed them respect (Lefkowitz, 2000).

However, even if the proposed questions are added, this leaves at best minimal coverage of effective partnerships. The Quality Report should identify sources that include questions on important aspects of effective partnerships, such as the degree of cultural competence (essential to customize health care for an increasingly diverse population) (Waidmann and Rajan, 2000). It should also survey efforts to educate patients about health care, as opposed to merely attempting to inform them about certain facts. Given the substantial proportion of Americans who now have access to the Internet (Economic and Statistics Administration and National Telecommunications and Information Administration, 2000), there should also be questions on efforts to use this medium to educate patients, communicate with providers, and support self-management (Balas et al, 1997; Kinsella, 1998).

Timeliness

Chapter 2 defines timeliness as obtaining needed care and minimizing unnecessary delays in getting that care. Specifically, timeliness includes (1) access to the system of care; (2) timeliness in obtaining care for a particular problem; and (3) timeliness within and across episodes of care.

Access to the system of care coincides with one of the chief data collection objectives of the MEPS survey. The household component of MEPS contains several sections that directly or indirectly examine issues of access. For example, there is a series of questions on the regular place to which household members go for health care including specific questions that probe reasons for not having a regular place of care or for preferring to use places such as emergency rooms for care. Additional MEPS questions that are being proposed would also focus on access to care (Agency for Healthcare Research and Quality, 2000f).

MEPS also contains data on the ability of household members to obtain care for a particular problem—another aspect of timeliness. For example, in the section on access to care there are questions on transportation, convenience of office hours, ease of getting appointments, and telephone access. Several questions drawn from CAHPS are also being proposed (Lefkowitz, 2000). Aside from two questions related to diabetes, they are general and not tied to specific problems or conditions. Instead, they involve individual visits and solicit responses on the ease of obtaining care as soon as it was wanted as soon as respondents or their doctors thought it necessary (Lefkowitz, 2000). It should be noted that not all condition-specific data require condition-specific questions. For example, one could assess responses to questions on timeliness from patients who are seen for chronic illnesses versus those who are seen just for preventive care or acute problems.

Currently, MEPS does not have questions that specifically address timeliness within and across episodes of care. The sixth contract cycle for the HCFA PROs contains data related to timeliness within and across episodes of care that could be used as a supplement. For example, for pneumonia, there are data indicating whether and when Medicare patients received antibiotics, blood cultures, and other appropriate treatments. The same holds true for timeliness in the episode of care with respect to AMI (Jencks, 2000). However, because contract cycles target particular conditions and aspects of quality of care that can vary from cycle to cycle, relying on supplemental data from PROs can be only a very short-term strategy for supplementation. Medicare claims data could also be used to examine timeliness within and across episodes of care for Medicare beneficiaries. Although claims data have well-documented drawbacks (Fowles et al., 1995; Jollis et al., 1993; Lohr, 1990; Romano et al., 1994; Weintraub et al., 1999), they could be used to examine such dimensions as dates of diagnoses and treatments billed to Medicare, as well as some patient and provider characteristics.

DATA SOURCES FOR THE
NATIONAL HEALTH CARE QUALITY REPORT

In the short term, a mosaic of existent data sources will be used to create the National Health Care Quality Data Set, which in turn will be used to examine a number of areas in health care quality as discussed in Chapters 2 and 3. However, given the many gaps in the presently available data sources on effectiveness and timeliness, AHRQ should supplement these sources with targeted medical record abstraction. To more adequately address these gaps, AHRQ should work to further the development and implementation of electronic data systems, including electronic medical records. In the long term, standardized electronic clinical information holds the key to providing data that will meet the criteria already presented in this chapter.

Data Sources in the Short Term

The *Dartmouth Atlas of Health Care in the United States* is an example of an annual report that uses the variety of existent public and private data sources to examine aspects of health care quality, including effectiveness (Dartmouth Medical School, Center for the Evaluative Clinical Sciences, 1998). In particular, the atlas makes extensive use of Medicare claims data to analyze whether beneficiaries received treatments, services, or drugs that have been proven effective or are believed to be so. For example, for the populations measured, the evidence suggests national underuse of immunization for pneumonia, certain tests and drugs for diabetes, and certain treatments for heart attacks. The atlas also presents benchmarks generated by the use of private data sources such as Kaiser-Permanente to make quality performance comparisons across the nation on a range of treatments, including those for heart attack and diabetes.

AHRQ could make similar use of public and private data sources to produce useful findings on timeliness and effectiveness in the National Health Care Quality Report. In addition, it will have to use different types of data in order to cover all aspects of the framework. For example, patient surveys are usually needed to examine patient centeredness and aspects of timeliness, while claims data for billing purposes have greater potential to capture information regarding safety and effectiveness. However, data drawn from administrative records present problems as well. For example, in addition to the limits on Medicare claims data previously described, certain kinds of conditions and services tend to be underreported. Other limits include the difficulty of performing risk adjustment on claims data because necessary information is not available (Iezzoni, 1997; Institute of Medicine and National Research Council, 1999; Malin et al., 2000). The development of standardized electronic information systems to capture clinical data will be necessary to efficiently obtain detailed data on effectiveness and safety on a wide scale.

As explained above, current administrative sources also provide inadequate data on safety, for different reasons. At present, safety reporting by providers and health care organizations is limited, which lessens the amount of data on safety that is available for analysis. Current reporting tends to be voluntary, confidential, and nonstandardized (Institute of Medicine, 2000). AHRQ, as part of the Quality Interagency Coordination Task Force (QuIC), is working to address issues related to patient safety, including issues that limit reporting (Quality Interagency Coordination Task Force, 2000). Until these issues are resolved and new data sources are developed, data on safety will be relatively sparse and incapable of supporting useful measurement.

After existent data sources have been used to identify areas of effectiveness and timeliness in which closer study is needed, AHRQ could turn to targeted medical record abstraction, at least in the short term, given that electronic clinical data are not available. Information supplied by medical records includes medical history; diagnostic data such as information from the physical examination performed; presence of other diseases or comorbidities; clinical information such as the results of laboratory tests; and description of the treatment plan (Institute of Medicine and National Research Council, 1999). Compared to other administrative sources such as claims data, data from medical records tend to have greater clinical detail. For example, according to one study, medical records more clearly differentiate complications and comorbidities than do administrative data (Hannan et al., 1995). They may also include information on outcomes. In addition, they can supply information that is often needed to perform risk adjustment. For inpatient care, they differentiate between a person's condition before hospitalization and a new condition that might have arisen during hospitalization, which claims data often do not (Iezzoni, 1997; Institute of Medicine and National Research Council, 2000).

RAND's QA Tools system is a data source in development that provides an example of medical record abstraction as a means of supplementing administrative data. Medical records abstracted for QA Tools supply data that can be used primarily to support measures of effectiveness, although they can also support some measures of safety, patient centeredness, and timeliness. They can also support the health care needs—staying healthy, getting better, living with illness or disability, and coping with the end of life (see Appendix B) (McGlynn, 2000).

Collecting data from paper medical records can also be problematical (Institute of Medicine, 1997; Institute of Medicine, 2001; Institute of Medicine and National Research Council, 2000; McDonald et al., 1997; Palmer, 1997). Locating and abstracting physical records take time and labor, and abstracted data will likely contain some errors. However, the kind of information collected from medical records makes it easier to measure health care quality comprehensively, across components of health care quality and consumer perspectives on health care needs. It also facilitates examination of the quality of care for specific health conditions. For example, to measure effectiveness, inpatient medical records make it possible to assess whether people received prescriptions for appropriate medications given their medical profiles. To measure timeliness, inpatient medical records make it possible to identify the time at which a particular drug was administered, which a patient may not be able to recall accurately. Medical records are useful to examine certain safety problems. However, because patient injuries occur relatively infrequently, administrative files are usually necessary to target the search. The long-term solution to the need for accessible data on these aspects of health care quality lies in electronic clinical data systems that span health care settings. This would greatly facilitate access to information currently registered in paper medical records and should be part of a new health information infrastructure that contributes to quality reporting and improvement.

Another short-term challenge with data sources should be acknowledged: it is especially difficult to obtain population-based measures for processes of care that affect relatively small populations. Examples would include those that refer to a particular chronic condition that is not very common, or to a specific procedure. A survey such as the expanded MEPS or a population-based medical record review will usually not have large enough samples of patients from such subpopulations to measure the quality of their care adequately. Typically, such measures are targeted to the appropriate subpopulation by using administrative record systems (such as claims databases) to find eligible patients and then conducting medical record reviews for those patients. Although this approach may be adequate for measures applied to members of specific health plans or being treated at specific hospitals, at this time there is no corresponding universal database that can serve as a sampling frame for collecting such data for measures of an entire population.

Encouraging the Long-Term Development of
Electronic Clinical Data Systems

Compared to paper records, electronic clinical data systems would offer several clear advantages in promoting health care quality. For example, they could provide linkages to clinical knowledge bases needed to support health care decision making. Electronic clinical data systems would facilitate quality reporting by making it more feasible to collect more comprehensive information. Depending on how standardized they become across health care settings, they could also make it easier to produce the kind of universal database needed to support a sampling frame for measures of processes that affect small populations. Currently, the availability of medical records is a significant issue. According to a study by the General Accounting Office, one hospital it examined was not able to find the proper records 30 percent of the time (1991). According to other studies, lost, misplaced, and inaccessible paper records are not uncommon (Institute of Medicine, 1997).

For the Agency for Healthcare Research and Quality to take an active role in fostering the development and implementation of electronic data systems is consistent with the Healthcare Research and Quality Act of 1999. The act calls for the agency to promote a range of innovations in health information, including the "use of computer-based health records in all settings for the development of personal health records for individual health assessment and maintenance, and for monitoring public health and outcomes of care within populations" (Healthcare Research and Quality Act, 1999:Sec. 914). Experts in the field of information technology have advocated a diverse set of solutions to encourage the development of electronic clinical data systems (Institute of Medicine, 1997; Stead, 1998; Stead et al., 2000). These include the definition of uniform data standards, the development of standard software architectures, and the use of emerging e-commerce technologies to support patient (as contrasted to facility) ownership of the record. NCVHS recently issued a report to the Secretary of Health and Human Services with recommendations for the definition of uniform data standards for the electronic exchange of patient medical record information (National Committee on Vital and Health Statistics, 2000). The implementation of these standards should facilitate the development of a health information infrastructure that could support the type of Quality Report recommended by this committee.

The development and implementation of electronic clinical data systems in health care will also require several long-term strategies. These include support for medical informatics research, support for demonstration projects, and incentives for the use of electronic clinical data systems in medical practices. Incentives could be linked to billing requirements, for example, or to evidence of quality improvement and implementation of best practices. It is important to note that electronic data systems should be designed primarily to assist in patient care so that they can be used effectively and the data can be coded accurately. However, the design of such systems, especially with respect to confidentiality and consistency in terminology and coding, should reflect the need to pool data across organizations (Stead, 1998).

New regulations to protect the privacy of health information could limit access to data in patient records that may be needed for the National Health Care Quality Data Set. On December 20, 2000, DHHS announced the final rule to protect the confidentiality of patients' medical records, formulated in response to one of the provisions of the Health Insurance Portability and Accountability Act (HIPAA) of 1996 (Health Insurance Portability and Accountability Act, 1996; U.S. Department of Health and Humans Services, 2000a). Under this final rule, patients have considerable control over how their health information is used. Health plans, health care clearinghouses, and health care providers who conduct certain transactions electronically must obtain patient consent to release their medical records. However, certain exceptions are allowed when the need for access to information for the public good outweighs the need to protect individual privacy. The Quality Report may be one of these cases, given that information may be disclosed without individual authorization for the "oversight of the health care system, including health assurance activities" (U.S. Department of Health and Human Services, 2000b).

INCREASING ACCESS TO THE
NATIONAL HEALTH CARE QUALITY DATA SET

The data sources required to support a comprehensive set of measures of health should be made available as the National Health Care Quality Data Set. However, all information in the data set cannot be included in the Quality Report. As explained in Chapter 5, both the print and the web versions of the report should be selective in what they contain. To capture the attention and interest of consumers, the media, policy makers, and other audiences, neither version should be overly long or detailed.

The Agency for Healthcare Research and Quality should make it easy for researchers and other policy specialists to use the data to explore trends, developments, and patterns in health care quality. The data set may be too large to place on the Web in its entirety. However, the agency should develop comprehensive public use data sets, along with all appropriate documentation, to the extent feasible. Where possible, researchers should be able to download data for analysis with statistical software. It would also be helpful if researchers could readily generate summary statistics, along with additional simple analyses such as cross-tabulations and other kinds of tables. Data that cannot be placed on the Web should be made as readily available as possible for use by researchers and other specialists.

SUMMARY

The focus of this chapter has been on data sources for the National Health Care Quality Report. The chapter has presented selection criteria to help guide the choice of data sources for the National Health Care Quality Data Set, along with a preliminary evaluation of how well several public and private data sources meet the criteria. As explained in the chapter, the Agency for Healthcare Research and Quality should pursue both short- and long-term strategies in choosing data sources. In the short term, the realization of the committee's vision for the Quality Report will be restricted by the limitations of existing data sources in terms of content, data format, and representativeness of the data with respect to the entire population. According to the committee's preliminary evaluation, MEPS combined with CAHPS has the potential to serve as an important data source for the Quality Report in the areas of patient centeredness and timeliness. However, this will have to be supplemented with other public and private data sources to adequately measure safety and effectiveness.

At the same time, AHRQ should pursue a long-term strategy. Although population surveys will remain the best way of examining patient centeredness and some aspects of timeliness, AHRQ should encourage the development and broad-scale implementation of electronic clinical data systems that will provide the best data to evaluate effectiveness and particular aspects of the timeliness of care (for example, the time elapsed between diagnosis and the start of treatment). New data sources will also have to be developed to examine health care safety. Ultimately, a new health information infrastructure based on existent and new data sources (including computerized clinical data systems, population surveys, and specialized data systems) will be essential to generate an adequate database for the production of the Quality Report. This new health information infrastructure should also include data on specific population subgroups and should closely articulate local-, state-, and national level data systems.

The committee is aware that considerable obstacles must be overcome in order to achieve this vision. HIPAA and regulations concerning the patient's right to confidentiality can potentially restrict access to medical records. The lack of uniform data standards impedes the aggregation of data from local to national levels as advocated by the committee. In addition, the very nature of the subject—quality of care—requires access to a wide range of information that cannot be found in any single data source or combination of existent data sources. The Quality Report should be an instrument for driving change in federal data policy such that needed data that are not currently available are collected. Although considerable, these barriers are not insurmountable, and only by making headway in this direction will it be possible to adequately assess and track the quality of health care delivery in the United States.

REFERENCES

Agency for Healthcare Research and Quality. 2000a. *From the Pipeline of Health Services Research—CAHPS: The Story of the Consumer Assessment of Health Plans* [on-line]. Available at: http://www.ahrq.gov/research/cahptrip.htm [Nov. 17, 2000].
Agency for Healthcare Research and Quality. 2000b. Consumer Assessment of Health Plans (CAHPS): *Fact Sheet* [on-line]. Available at: http://www.ahrq.gov/qual/cahpfact.htm [Feb. 18, 2001].
Agency for Healthcare Research and Quality. 2000c. *Overview: Healthcare Cost & Utilization Project (HCUP), 1988–97* [on-line]. Available at: http://www.ahrq.gov/data/hcup/hcup-pkt.htm [Nov. 17, 2000].
Agency for Healthcare Research and Quality. 2000d. *Household Component* [on-line]. Available at http://www.meps.ahrq.gov/Data_Pub/HC_TOC.htm [Jan. 3, 2001].
Agency for Healthcare Research and Quality. 2000e. *Overview of MEPS* [on-line]. Available at: http://www.meps.ahrq.gov/WhatIsMEPS/Overview.htm [Jan. 3, 2001].
Agency for Healthcare Research and Quality. 2000f. *What Is MEPS?* [on-line]. Available at: http://www.meps.ahrq.gov/whatis/htm [Jan. 3, 2001].
Agency for Healthcare Research and Quality. 2001. *CCFS Data Center (CCFS-DC)* [on-line]. Available at: http://www.meps.ahrq.gov/datacenter.htm [Jan. 24, 2001].
Arispe, Irma. 2000. Federal Data Sources for a National Quality Report. Presentation at the Institute of Medicine Workshop, "Envisioning a National Quality Report on Health Care," May 23.
Arispe, Irma, 2000a. Personal communication, November 27. National Center for Health Statistics.

Balas, E. Andrew, Farah Jaffrey, Gilad J. Kuperman, Suzanne A. Boren, Gordon D. Brown, Francesco Pinciroli, and Joyce A. Mitchell. 1997. Electronic communication with patients. Evaluation of distance medicine technology. *Journal of the American Medical Association* 278(2):152–159.

Blumberg, Steven, 2000. Personal communication, December 4. Centers for Disease Control and Prevention (CDC).

Centers for Disease Control and Prevention. 2000a. *Tracking Major Health Risks in America: The Behavioral Risk Factor Surveillance System* [on-line]. Available at: http://www.cdc.gov/nccdphp/brfss/at-a-gl.htm [Dec. 13, 2000].

Centers for Disease Control and Prevention. 2000b. *The National Immunization Survey*, [Online]. Available at: http://www.cdc.gov/nis/default.htm [Dec. 22, 2000].

Centers for Disease Control and Prevention. 2000c. *HIP: National Nosocomial Infections Surveillance (NNIS) System*, [Online]. Available at: http://www.cdc.gov/ncidid/hip/NNIS/@nnis.htm [Nov. 17, 2000].

Cohen, Steven B. 2000. Existing Data Sources to Support the DHHS National Health Quality Monitoring Initiative (draft). Unpublished.

Cynamon, Marcie L., 2000. Personal communication, November 30. CDC.

Darby, Charles, 2001. Personal communication, February 3. Agency for Healthcare Research and Quality (AHRQ).

Dartmouth Medical School, Center for the Evaluative Clinical Sciences. 1998. *The Dartmouth Atlas of Health Care, 1999*. Chicago: American Hospital Publishing.

Dickey, Wayne, 2000. Personal communication, December 1. CDC.

Economic and Statistics Administration and National Telecommunications and Information Administration. 2000. *Falling Through the Net: Toward Digital Inclusion: A Report on Americans' Access to Technology Tools*. Washington, D.C.: U.S. Department of Commerce. Available at: http://www.esa.doc.gov/fttn00.htm.

Eggers, Paul W., 2000. Personal communication, November 30. National Institute of Diabetes and Digestive and Kidney Diseases.

Elixhauser, Anne, 2000. Personal communication, November 20. AHRQ.

Elstein, Paul, 2000. Personal communication, December 1. Health Care Financing Administration (HCFA).

Eppig, Frank, 2000. Personal communication, December 1. HCFA.

Fowles, Jinnet B., Anne G. Lawthers, Jonathan P. Weiner, Deborah W. Garnick, Doris S. Petrie, and R. Heather Palmer. 1995. Agreement between physicians' office records and Medicare Part B claims data. *Health Care Financing Review* 16(4):189–199.

General Accounting Office. 1991. *Medical ADP Systems: Automated Medical Records Hold Promise to Improve Patient Care*. Washington, D.C.: U.S. Government Printing Office.

Gold, Marsha. 2000. Data Sources and Potential Indicators for a National Quality Report. Commissioned paper for the Institute of Medicine Committee on the National Quality Report on Health Care Delivery.

Hankey, Benjamin F., Lynn A. Ries, and Brenda K. Edwards. 1991. The Surveillance, Epidemiology, and End Results Program: A national resource. *Cancer Epidemiology, Biomarkers and Prevention* 8(12):1117–1121.

Hannan, Edward L., Albert L. Siu, Dinesh Kumar, Harold Kilburn, and Mark R. Chassin. 1995. The decline in coronary artery bypass graft surgery mortality in New York State. *Journal of the American Medical Association* 273(3):209–213.

Hannan, Edward L., Michael J. Racz, James G. Jollis, and Eric D. Peterson. 1997. Using Medicare claims data to assess provider quality for CABG surgery: Does it work well enough? *Health Services Research* 31(6):659–678.

Health Care Financing Administration. 1999. *Health Care Financing Review: Medicare and Medicaid Statistical Supplement, 1999.* Baltimore, Md.: U.S. Department of Health and Human Services.

Health Care Financing Administration. 2000a. *HCFA: Medicare, Medicaid, and the State Children's Health Insurance Program (SCHIP)* [on-line]. Available at: http://www.hcfa.gov [Dec. 4, 2000a].

Health Care Financing Administration. 2000b. *Medicare Basics Overview* [on-line]. Available at: http://www.medicare.gov/basics/overview.htm [Nov. 17, 2000b].

Health Insurance Portability and Accountability Act of 1996. 1996. *Statutes at Large.* Vol. 110, Sec. 1936.

Healthcare Research and Quality Act. 1999. *Statutes at Large.* Vol. 113, Sec. 1653.

Iezzoni, Lisa I. 1997. Assessing quality using administrative data. *Annals of Internal Medicine* 127(8):666–674.

Institute of Medicine 1997. *The Computer-Based Patient Record. An Essential Technology for Health Care* (revised edition). eds. Dick Richard S., Elaine B. Steen, and Don E. Detmer. Washington, D.C.: National Academy Press.

Institute of Medicine. 2000. *To Err Is Human: Building a Safer Health System.* eds. Linda T. Kohn, Janet M. Corrigan, and Molla S. Donaldson. Washington, D.C.: National Academy Press.

Institute of Medicine. 2001. *Crossing the Quality Chasm: A New Health System for the 21st Century.* Washington, D.C.: National Academy Press.

Institute of Medicine and National Research Council. 2000. *Enhancing Data Systems to Improve the Quality of Cancer Care.* eds. Maria Hewitt and Joseph V. Simone. Washington, D.C.: National Academy Press.

Jencks, Stephen F. 2000. Clinical performance measurement—A hard sell. *Journal of the American Medical Association* 283(15):2015–2016.

Jencks, Stephen F., Timothy Cuerdon, Dale R. Burwen, Barbara Fleming, Peter M. Houck, Annette E. Kussmaul, David S. Nilasena, Diana L. Ordin, and David R. Arday. 2000. Quality of medical care delivered to Medicare beneficiaries. *Journal of the American Medical Association* 284(13):1670–1676.

Johnson, Clifford L., 2000. Personal communication, December 19. Centers for Disease Control and Prevention.

Joint Commission on Accreditation of Healthcare Organizations. 2000a. *Welcome Page: Who We Are* [on-line]. Available at: http://www.jcaho. org/who_we_are.html [Nov. 17, 2000].

Joint Commission on Accreditation of Healthcare Organizations. 2000b. *Core Measures Implementation Plan* [on-line]. Available at: http://www.jcaho.org/perfmeas/ coremeas/implement.html [Nov. 17, 2000].

Joint Commission on the Accreditation of Healthcare Organizations. 2000c. *Sentinel Event Policy and Procedures* [on-line]. Available at: http://www.jcaho.org/sentinel/ se_pp.html [Dec. 4, 2000].

Jollis, James, Marek Ancukiewicz, Elizabeth DeLong, David B. Pryor, Lawrence H. Muhlbaier, and Daniel Mark. 1993. Discordance of databases designed for claims payment versus clinical information systems. *Annals of Internal Medicine* 119(8):844–850.

Kinsella, Audrey. 1998. Home telecare in the United States. *Journal of Telemedicine and Telecare* 4(4):195-200.

Lohr, Kathleen. 1990. Use of insurance claims data in measuring quality of care. *International Journal of Technology Assessment in Health Care* 6(2):263–271.

Lefkowitz, Doris. 2000. Memo to Thomas Reilly, October 10. AHRQ.

Lu-Yao, Grace L., Michael J. Barry, C. H. Chang, John H. Wasson, and John E. Wennberg. 1994. Transurethral resection of the prostate among Medicare beneficiaries in the United States: Time trends and outcomes. Prostate Patient Outcomes Research Team (PORT). *Urology* 44(5):698–699.

Malin, Jennifer L., Steven M. Asch, Eve A. Kerr, and Elizabeth A. McGlynn. 2000. Evaluating the quality of cancer care: Development of cancer quality indicators for a global quality assessment tool. *Cancer* 8(3):701–707.

McDonald, Clement J., J. Marc Overhage, Paul. Dexter, Blaine Y. Takesue, and Diane Dwyer. 1997. A framework for capturing clinical data from computerized sources. *Annals of Internal Medicine* 127(Part 2):675–682.

McGlynn, Elizabeth A. 2000. QA Tools and the National Quality Report. Presentation to the Institute of Medicine Committee on the National Quality Report on Health Care Delivery, August 21.

National Center for Health Statistics. 1995. *NCHS Instructions for Classifying Underlying Causes of Death, 1995.* Hyattsville, Md.: U.S. Department of Health and Human Services. Available at: http://www.cdc.gov/nchs/data/2amanual.pdf.

National Center for Health Statistics. 1999. *Programs and Activities*, DHHS Publication No. 99-1200. Hyattsville, Md.: U.S. Department of Health and Human Services.

National Center for Health Statistics. 2000a. *NAMCS/NHAMCS Frequently Asked Questions (FAQ's)* [on-line]. Available at: www.cdc.gov/nchs/about/major/ahcd/faq.htm [Dec. 5, 2000].

National Center for Health Statistics. 2000b. *NHANES-National Health and Examination Survey—Homepage* [on-line]. Available at: http://www.cdc.gov/nchs/nhanes.htm [Nov. 17, 2000c].

National Center for Health Statistics. 2000c. *National Health Interview Survey* [on-line]. Available at: http://www.cdc.gov/nchs/nhis.htm [Nov. 17, 2000a].

National Center for Health Statistics. 2000d. State and Loca Area Integrated Telephone Survey [on-line]. Available at: http://www.cdc.gov/nchs/slaits.htm [Nov. 17, 2000].

National Center for Health Statistics. 2000e. *National Vital Statistics System* [on-line]. Available at: http://www.cdc.gov/nchs/nvss.htm [Jan. 24, 2001b].

National Committee for Quality Assurance. *NCQA Overview* [on-line]. Available at: http://www.ncqa.org/Pages/about/overview3/htm [Sept. 25, 2000].

National Committee on Vital and Health Statistics. 2000. *Report on Uniform Data Standards for Patient Medical Record Information.* Available at: http://ncvhs.hhs.gov/hipaa000706.pdf

Palmer, R. Heather. 1997. Quality of care. *Journal of the American Medical Association* 277(23):1896–1897.

Peterson, Eric D., Elizabeth R. DeLong, James G. Jollis, Lawrence H. Muhlbaier, and Daniel B. Mark. 1998. The effects of New York's bypass surgery provider profiling on access to care and patient outcomes in the elderly. *Journal of the American College of Cardiology* 32:993.

Powell-Griner, Eve., 2000. Personal communication, November 31. CDC.

Quality Interagency Coordination Task Force. 2000. *Doing What Counts for Patient Safety: Federal Actions to Reduce Medical Errors and Their Im*pact. Rockville, Md.

Romano, Patrick S., Leslie L. Roos, Harold S. Luft, James G. Jollis, and Katherine Doliszny. 1994. A comparison of administrative versus clinical data: coronary artery bypass graft surgery as an example. Ischemic Heart Disease Patient Outcomes Research Team. *Journal of Clinical Epidemiology* 47(3):249–260.

Schappert, Susan M., 2000. Personal communication, December 19. Centers for Disease Control and Prevention.

Schilling, Brian, 2000. Personal communication, December 4. National Committee for Quality Assurance.

Schyve, Paul, 2000. Personal Communication. Joint Commission on Accreditation of Healthcare Organizations.

Sekscenski, Edward, 2000. Personal communication, December 1. Health Care Financing Administration.

Stead, William W. 1998. *Issues Related to Patient Medical Record Information: Testimony to National Committee on Vital and Health Statistics, Subcommittee on Standards and Security* [on-line]. Available at: http://www.mc.vanderbilt.edu/infocntr/ stead/medrec.html [Nov. 9, 2000].

Stead, William W., Randolph A. Miller, Mark A. Musen, and William R. Hersh. 2000. Integration and beyond: linking information from disparate sources and into workflow. *Journal of the American Medical Informatics Association* 7(2):135–145.

U.S. Department of Health and Human Services. 1999. *NCVHS Charter 1999* [on-line]. Available at: http://ncvhs.hhs.gov/99charter.htm [Dec. 6, 2000].

U.S. Department of Health and Human Services. 2000a. *Press Briefing on Federal Privacy Regulations* [on-line]. Available at: http://aspe.os.dhhs.gov/admnsimp/ final/brief2.htm [Feb. 6, 2001].

U.S. Department of Health and Human Services. 2000b. *HHS Fact Sheet: Protecting the Privacy of Patients' Health Information, Summary of the Final Regulation* [on-line]. Available at: http://aspe.os.dhhs.gov/admnsimp/pvcfact1.htm [Feb. 6, 2001].

Waidmann, Timothy A., and Shruti Rajan. 2000. Race and ethnic disparities in health care access and utilization: An examination of state variation. *Medical Care Research and Review* 57(1 Supplement):181–217.

Ware, John E., Mary K. Snyder, W. Russell Wright, and Allyson R. Davies. 1983. Defining and measuring patient satisfaction with medical care. *Evaluation and Program Planning* 6(3–4):247–263.

Weintraub, William S., Christi Deaton, Leslee Shaw, Elizabeth Mahoney, Douglas C. Morris, Candice Saunders, Debbie Canup, Stephanie Connolly, Steven Culler, Edmund R. Becker, Andrzej Kosinski, and Stephen J. Boccuzzi. 1999. Can cardiovascular clinical characteristics be identified and outcome models be developed from an in-patient claims database? *American Journal of Cardiology* 84(2):166–169.

Yang, Wei-Chung, 2000. Personal Communication, December 29. Research Data Assistance Center.

5

Designing the National Health Care Quality Report

The National Health Care Quality Report (also referred to as the Quality Report) offers an important way to increase awareness of quality issues, the amount of attention that audiences pay to quality, and the degree of involvement in efforts to improve it. To produce a report that achieves those goals, the Agency for Healthcare Research and Quality (AHRQ) should tailor reports to key audiences. This chapter provides an overview of how to produce such a report. It begins with a description of the audiences for the report and the goals that AHRQ should have in reaching each audience. The following sections provide an analysis of how audience needs should influence the presentation of data and the contents of the report. They also contain an examination of other important tasks, such as evaluating the strengths and weaknesses of the report following its release, promoting the report, and evaluating the longer-term outcomes associated with the goals of the Quality Report.

RECOMMENDATION

RECOMMENDATION 10: The National Health Care Quality Report should be produced in several versions tailored to key audiences—policy makers, consumers, purchasers, providers, and researchers. It should feature a limited number of key findings and the minimum number of measures needed to support these findings.

The Agency for Healthcare Research and Quality should produce a National Health Care Quality Report that will attract the attention and interest of policy makers, consumers, purchasers, providers, researchers, and other audiences. For some of these audiences, particularly policy makers, the findings should be "actionable." Currently, health care quality issues are poorly understood and receive little notice. The National Health Care Quality Report can become an important tool to promote a better understanding of health care quality, generate support for improvement, and highlight areas that need special attention.

To accomplish these goals, AHRQ should make the Quality Report relevant, engaging, easy to read, and easy to understand. Producing different reports for different audiences is an important and feasible way to do this. The print versions should be brief, be aimed at key audiences, and summarize key findings. Different versions of the report should be available on a web site tailored to specialized audiences as well as to the general public. While the Quality Report or family of reports should be focused and selective, it should draw on a comprehensive National Quality Report Data Set covering all aspects of quality as discussed in Chapter 4. This annual data set should also be available publicly on the Web in an accessible format to the extent feasible. The committee understands that some of the files will be made available only to researchers, and that other files containing extremely sensitive or identifying information will not be released at all in order to protect confidentiality.

Like the data set, the Quality Report should be produced annually as defined by law (Healthcare Research and Quality Act, 1999). The specific elements of the data set should be relatively stable in order to track changes in quality, although data may not have to be collected every year for every measure. In contrast, measures included in the Quality Report may vary from year to year based on the key findings selected, although some will be repeated from time to time to show changes in specific aspects of quality over time.

The report should not overwhelm either general or specialized audiences with information about health care quality. Instead, the content should be highly selective, relevant to current policy concerns, and fresh from year to year, even while preserving some continuity. Furthermore, the format employed should be designed so that differences across regions or groups and trends in health care quality are easily discernible.

AUDIENCES FOR THE NATIONAL HEALTH CARE QUALITY REPORT

The committee identified several groups of people or audiences that should be the focus of the Quality Report. Because audiences have different roles to play in supporting health care quality, the report must provide them with the kinds of information that meet their particular interests and needs. Audiences for the report include members of Congress and other policy makers in national and state government as well as consumers as the main audiences. Other important audiences include purchasers, providers, and researchers. The Quality Report should set specific goals in communicating with these audiences, including the following:

- *Policy makers.* The Quality Report should identify actionable areas of health care quality that deserve attention from policy makers.
- *Consumers.* The key goal with this audience is to raise awareness of important quality issues. Since relatively few consumers will see the actual report in print or on the Web, AHRQ should find ways to encourage the media to give it attention-getting, constructive, and lasting coverage, which will build public interest and understanding.
- *Purchasers.* The Quality Report should identify areas of health care quality that these groups can help to improve and aspects that they may have to focus on when evaluating the health plans they will offer to their employees.
- *Providers.* Health care providers, including clinicians, will have a special interest in the report findings since many will relate directly to their work. Quality Report findings should strongly encourage all those with a responsibility for providing high-quality health care to address areas in which improvement is seriously needed and to have a sense of personal satisfaction in those areas where progress has been made.
- *Researchers.* To the extent possible, researchers should have access to Quality Report data on the Web to develop new measures, refine existing ones, examine quality of care, and otherwise contribute to the dialogue on health care quality.

REPORT GUIDELINES

Defining the Content of the Quality Report

What should the Quality Report feature? AHRQ should at most select three to five key findings about health care quality for attention in the report. While it should present enough measures to clearly support these findings, it should also aim to present only 3 to 5 measures per finding for a total of 9 to 25 measures in the report. The Quality Report should highlight what the nation has achieved, where it has made progress, what needs improvement, and areas in which a high degree of variation exists.

Recent research on cognitive processing suggests that people can process only three to five "pieces" of information at one time (Halford, 1998; Hochhauser, 1999). An understandable temptation is to want to pack the report with more findings and measures in the hope of highlighting more information. However, this will lead to the ironic result of audiences learning less rather than more about the quality of care provided in the United States. When people are overwhelmed by information, they have a hard time differentiating and absorbing what is truly important. Often, even experts will cope with too much information by synthesizing findings. For instance, they may emphasize the importance of a single factor among several that were presented. This factor is usually something that is clear, precise, and understood (Hibbard, 1998; Hsee, 1996; Mellers et al., 1992; Slovic, 1992).

Findings in the Quality Report should be presented in a headline format. The content of the findings, of course, will depend on the evidence—what the measures and data show about the quality of health care delivery. Audience testing can also be used to fine-tune the wording of headlines, as discussed later in this chapter. Some examples of findings in headline format include the following: "Providers are getting patients more involved in their care"; "The nation is paying less attention to the importance of preventing condition X"; "Patients are less likely to wait for care in regions A and B"; and "The nation is giving the dying poorer-quality care now than before."

Findings could focus on a variety of aspects related to health care quality, including areas that

- demonstrate excellence by, for example, meeting clinical standards for treatment of particular health conditions;
- need improvement because, for example, they do *not* meet clinical standards for treatment of particular health conditions;
- show a high degree of variation, for example, from one year to the next;
- capture trends of improvement or deterioration; and
- indicate geographic disparities, for example, by state or region, or disparities across populations.

The guidelines for the National Health Care Quality Report should not be confused with the framework described in Chapter 2. While the report is selective, the framework is designed to ensure that quality measurement and data sources are comprehensive, that is, that enough data are gathered to support measures of the many important aspects of this complex topic. The framework provides a basis for the set of measures from which the Quality Report will draw. It is an analytical rather than a reporting framework.

Also, the Quality Report should not be confused with existing sources of comparative quality information for particular providers or organizations. There are many of these sources, including public- and private-sector organizations, accrediting bodies, national government agencies, state and local government agencies, individual health plans, other health organizations, and free or fee-based web sites (Bates and Gawande, 2000). The focus of most of these reports is on evaluating and comparing the performance of specific providers, institutions, or health plans. In contrast, the Quality Report will focus on the quality of care provided to the people of the United States by the system as a whole, rather than by a specific entity of the system. It will also provide information at a higher level than many of these reports by focusing on the national level complemented with information at the state level whenever possible.

Presenting Information in the Quality Report

Whatever the content of the Quality Report, it will contain some mix of data-based findings and other information on quality. The following sections present guidelines on how to most effectively present report contents to members of Congress and other key audiences, including consumers, purchasers, and providers. It should be noted that most of these guidelines should make the report more appealing to all audiences. There will be policy makers and other specialists who are so highly engaged in the issue of health care quality that they will read the report and find it useful, almost no matter what form it takes. Others, however, will benefit from efforts to make information on quality more meaningful and interesting. Box 5.1 summarizes these guidelines.

Making the Report Available in Print and on the Web

Making the report available in print and on the Web will allow AHRQ to deliver it in the format preferred by each audience. This does not mean that the content of the report in both media should be the same. Businesses, for example, issue annual reports in print and web versions (see Box 5.2). They make the print versions brief and engaging by presenting an overview of major trends and developments aimed at the general reader. The Web is used to present more detailed information to financial analysts, interested stockholders, and other specialists. However, efforts are made to make web sites appealing to specialists and generalists alike ("Annual Reports," 2000; "Corporate Annual Reports: Now More Readable, Credible, and Fashionable," 2000).

In producing the Quality Report, AHRQ should adopt the same practices used by businesses. The print version should be brief, engaging, and targeted at

---

BOX 5.1 Guidelines on Presenting Information in the Quality Report

- Make the report available in print and on the Web.
- Use benchmarks or standards for comparisons.
- Choose findings that have strong statistical evidence.
- Add salience to the issue of health care quality.
- Make health care quality actionable.
- Keep the Quality Report fresh.

policy makers, consumers, purchasers, providers, and the media. AHRQ should also consider not one, but several, print and Web versions for different audiences, that is, a "family of reports." For example, the one for policy makers should focus on highlighting problem areas in health care quality, while the one for consumers should focus on making the concept of quality understandable and relevant. For print reports, AHRQ should make use of accepted principles for presenting information in this medium (Schriver, 1997; Tufte, 1983; U.S. Securities and Exchange Commission, 1998). AHRQ should also evaluate the need for and feasibility of making the report available in other languages to increase access by the largest non-English-speaking populations in the United States.

The Web is a flexible enough medium to easily contain versions of the report for both generalists and specialists. For example, the Maryland Health Care Commission has a web site that contains several versions of a report on health care quality aimed at different audiences (see Box 5.3). As already mentioned,

---

**BOX 5.2 New-Style Annual Business Reports:
How to Serve Generalists and Specialists**

In the past few years, businesses have turned to new-style annual reports aimed at their two major audiences—shareholders and industry analysts. Some businesses produce eye-catching, engaging print reports to satisfy the general information needs of shareholders, placing financial data on the Web for analysts. Others, such as Merck & Co., Inc., have divided their reports into different parts for different audiences. According to Sharyn Bearse, director of corporate communications at Merck, "We found 85 percent of readers are influenced by what they see. If the cover is compelling, they'll open it up. If the call-outs, photos, lay-out and headlines capture their attention, they'll stop and read it" ("Corporate Annual Reports: Now More Readable, Credible, and Fashionable," 2000:1).

Some other innovations of new-style annual business reports include the following:

- *Themes.* Some annual reports have themes that change from year to year. Performance records, topical issues, and future plans are examples of themes.
- *Narratives.* Reports often present stories about employees or people helped by company products or about the process of developing a new product.
- *Data presentation.* Reports creatively present data by, for example, setting statistics against a background of colorful patterns or photos linked to the theme of the report.

SOURCES: "Annual Reports," 2000; "Corporate Annual Reports," 2000.

BOX 5.3 Maryland Health Care Commission's Health Maintenance Organization Quality and Performance Reports: Different Versions for Different Audiences

Which report is right for you? The web site for the Maryland Health Care Commission uses this question to guide users to the appropriate version of its HMO Quality and Performance Reports. The reports are available at http://www.mhcc.state.md.us/ in versions tailored for consumers, legislators and other policy makers, and specialists. The site briefly describes their contents, their purposes (e.g., comparison, evaluation, reference), and the kinds of people who might find them most useful.

Consumers can choose an "easy" version that provides basic overviews of managed care health plan benefits and performance ratings or an "interactive" version that allows them to select information only on the health maintenance organizations (HMOs) in which they are interested. The interactive report, which is also designed for use by employers and organizations, makes HMO comparisons easier. Legislators and other policy makers have a "policy-oriented" version that evaluates the strengths and weaknesses of Maryland's HMOs by comparing them to HMOs in the Mid-Atlantic region and elsewhere in the nation.

SOURCE: Maryland Health Care Commission, 2000.

---

the web site should also contain the measures and data set that the reports are based for use by researchers and other policy specialists. In addition, AHRQ should make use of accepted principles of good web design for the report web site (Nielson, 1999; Spool et al., 1999; Sun Microsystems, 1999). Including audio and video components for the web-based reports would make them more appealing to a general audience and more accessible to those with limited health literacy (that is, the ability to read, understand, and act on health care information) (American Medical Association, Ad Hoc Committee on Health Literacy for the Council on Scientific Affairs, 1999).

Using Benchmarks or Standards for Comparisons

Reports can summarize or synthesize findings in ways that limit the number actually presented and make the few that are chosen more meaningful to audiences. One of the most effective means is through use of benchmarks or standards. This involves presenting data on performance, processes, outcomes, or other items and comparing them in a straightforward manner to benchmarks established, for example, by what has occurred in previous years or what has been accomplished in similar areas. Data can also be compared to standards that are, for example, set by regulations, clinical guidelines, or expert groups. These comparisons can be general enough to encompass many discrete findings. At the same time, they can be more meaningful because they are more relevant to a greater number of people than a collection of discrete findings, which takes more effort to review and identify an interest in.

Using benchmarks or standards for comparison is an example of "evaluability," a new concept based on decision research (Hibbard et al., 2000; Hsee, 1996, 1998). The "evaluability principle" asserts that information is more likely to be used when it is presented in a way that makes it easier to map on an affective (good–bad or value-based) scale. That is, information is more likely to be used when it is easier to distinguish between better and worse options. When information is "evaluable," the differences among the comparisons are immediately evident to the reader, or at least the patterns in the data are immediately observable. Providing a context for understanding the information (for example, labeling care as "good," "fair," or "poor," rather than just providing comparative numbers) is another way to make the information more evaluable by and meaningful to consumers.

Although providing consumer-oriented information for plan selection is not an objective of the Quality Report, it is useful to note that experiments with consumers show that comparative performance information is more likely to be used and weighted in health plan choices when it is presented in an evaluable format than when the same information is presented with little attention to evaluability (Hibbard et al., 2000).

In showing a comparison of how the 50 states are doing on seven aspects of diabetes care, an evaluable presentation might summarize the information by giving a state a star for each measure that indicates adequate to good care (or some other threshold standard determined clinically or statistically). States with performance ranging from adequate to good in all seven measures of diabetes care would have seven stars and would pop out immediately to the reader and be easy to identify. This would also be true for states that have only one or no stars. Detailed data for all seven measures for each of the 50 states could also be shown, but the stars would provide a clear visual summary of the data.

On the other hand, an example of a less evaluable (but commonly used) presentation approach might be to show a number, representing a performance level, for each of the seven measures for each of the 50 states. It would be much more difficult to identify which states were high performers and which were poor performers in terms of diabetes care from such a data display.

An important attribute of evaluability is that it appears to operate outside the awareness of the individual. That is, the presentation format influences how people perceive and use information, but they are not conscious of this influence. This has implications for how data formats are tested. Report formats should be made as evaluable as possible, and testing with consumers should focus on how well they understand the information and the labels. However, consumer preferences for how the data should be presented may not actually facilitate the use of such data. Testing can also focus on how well users can discern patterns and easily pick out better or worse options. This is a more reliable indication of the evaluability of the format than consumer preferences, which may or may not facilitate the use of the data.

Choosing Findings That Have Strong Statistical Evidence

Some findings will have strong statistical evidence. For example, compared to others, they may be more robust (that is, consistent when tested with a wider range of assumptions or methodologies); significant at a higher confidence level; or supported by findings in the research literature. When selecting among the many findings that could be included in the Quality Report, those with stronger statistical evidence should be preferred.

Choosing Findings That Are Relevant to Prevailing Policy Concerns

AHRQ should also take into account various considerations that might make some quality topics more relevant to the report than others. These could include news events on certain quality concerns; public interest in particular health conditions; the policy agendas of administrations, congressional leaders, governors, and others; and findings from other government reports (Rushefsky and Patel, 1998).

Adding Salience to the Issue of Health Care Quality

A data-driven report on health care quality could easily be one of those important, but dry, documents that gets little attention. One way to personalize the issue of health care quality would be to spotlight findings that affect many people. Another approach could be to feature information on individuals, institutions, or other familiar focal points that personify a larger aspect of quality (also called narratives). In general, consumers prefer information on practical topics that could or do affect them or people like themselves (Blendon et al., 1998; Lubalin and Harris-Kojetin, 1999; Mennemeyer et al., 1997; Robinson and Brodie, 1997). They respond poorly to abstract, conceptual information (Eddy, 1998; Galvin, 1998; Marshall et al., 2000; Philipchalk, 1972; Yuille and Paivio, 1969). Policy makers and the media are also receptive to this kind of information (Beasley, 1998; Brodie et al., 2001; Graber, 1997; McDonough, 2001; Sharf, 2001).

Narratives can be presented in a variety of ways. These include

• using sidebars to highlight stories of people who illustrate statistical trends, for example, presenting the case of a child whose immunization record mirrors national norms;

- starting off a statistical presentation of trends in health care quality with an example of a health care provider whose involvement in health care quality is typical; and
- featuring case studies of institutions that have improved the quality of their health care delivery.

Including narratives to illustrate information also presented in statistical form can add salience to specific aspects of health care quality and make them more meaningful. Narratives appear to work best when combined with statistics by simultaneously engaging the reader emotionally through stories and analytically through data (Kopfman et al., 1998).

In addition, the report should present selected data at the state level, as well as by relevant population subgroups. In this way, it would make use of smaller units of analysis, which people might be able to identify with more easily. In addition, this would provide members of Congress and state policy makers with the kind of detailed information they need to target quality improvement initiatives.

As already mentioned, AHRQ should not necessarily use the framework's dimensions of components of quality and consumer perspectives on health care needs as categories for reporting. For example, AHRQ may wish to focus on quality health care for families, structuring the report around a handful of the main quality concerns of families. Although these concerns may fall into specific categories of the framework such as "effectiveness" or "staying healthy," audience research may reveal more meaningful ways to describe them in the report. Regardless of which labels are used for reporting, they should be tested, especially with the audiences that AHRQ believes might find them most relevant.

Making Health Care Quality Actionable

Policy makers, purchasers, and providers need information that will help them identify areas in which they can take effective action. To supply this information, the Quality Report should call attention to problem areas. In addition to developing long-term policy responses, executive and legislative policy makers must be able to identify the kind of incremental solutions that can be achieved within election periods. The Quality Report can help significantly by highlighting issues that lend themselves to feasible policy responses, such as immunization programs, improved access to care for specific groups, and increased appropriations for improved patient safety. In addition, purchasers and providers have responded to areas in which feasible solutions for improvement exist with innovative changes to improve quality (Bentley and Nash, 1998; Epstein, 1996; Erickson et al., 2000; Hannan et al., 1995).

BOX 5.4 Keeping an Annual Report Fresh:
AARP's State Profiles on Health Care

AARP (formerly the American Association for Retired Persons) has been producing annual reports on the status of health care since 1990, and its state profiles have changed with the times. The reports have always presented basic information on each state such as demographics, health status data (e.g., morbidity rates), and the use of medical services such as emergency rooms and prenatal care. However, they have also included new data to keep up with new developments. As managed care has grown, the reports have added statistics on coverage, performance, and state oversight activities. As the uninsured have gained more attention, the reports have presented more specific information on those with and without coverage. The reports have also tracked the impact of initiatives such as the State Children's Health Insurance Program (S-CHIP) and the Health Insurance Portability and Accountability Act (HIPAA). In addition, they have responded to rising concern over specific medical conditions, such as the prevalence of obesity, by providing new data.

As the producer of the report, AARP's Public Policy Institute uses different ways to identify new topics. In part, it relies on feedback from state networks, which convey what AARP members, policy makers, and others are interested in. It also responds to new developments in health care and issues in the news. From time to time, it surveys those on its mailing list for feedback. In deciding on content, the institute first looks at whether reliable data are available. The importance and timeliness of the topic are other prominent considerations.

SOURCES: Brangan, 2000; Lamphere et al., 1999; Landsverk, 1999; U.S. Department of Health and Human Services, 1996.

Placing Quality in Positive and Negative Frames

High-quality health care has many positive benefits, and the Quality Report should explain what they are. As discussed in Chapter 3, the measure set for the report should be balanced so that it can provide a complete picture of the quality of care in both its positive and its negative aspects. However, poor-quality health care has many negative consequences, and the report should also explain what they are. Placing selected information about quality in a negative frame is one way to draw attention because research shows that people are more influenced by negative frames (Hibbard et al., 2000; Kahneman and Tversky, 1984; Tversky and Kahneman, 1981). A negative frame has another advantage: it puts information on quality in a form that the media will find useful since it often highlights negative events or outcomes (Graber, 1997).

Keeping the Quality Report Fresh

AHRQ should guard against an annual report containing little that is new. Although some areas of health care quality may be so important and so changeable that the Quality Report (or "family" of reports) should feature updates on them each year, AHRQ should emphasize findings in different areas, touching on aspects of quality that seem especially relevant in a particular year or bringing to light aspects of quality that deserve greater attention. For example, the report could be kept fresh by spotlighting health conditions that are frequently in the news, featuring information that is especially relevant to consumer concerns, or focusing on new developments in health care policy. See Box 5.2 (on annual business reports) and Box 5.4 (on keeping annual policy reports fresh) for ways in which these publications can remain distinctive from year to year.

AUDIENCE TESTING THE NATIONAL
HEALTH CARE QUALITY REPORT

Audience Testing Before Report Releases

It is essential that AHRQ conduct audience research in writing and producing the report: each release needs the kind of specific feedback that can come only from testing it with the kinds of people who are likely to use it (Backer et al., 1992; McGee et al., 1999; Rubin, 1994). Audience testing can be performed in a number of ways, including in-depth or cognitive interviews, focus groups, random sample surveys, and experiments. Each has advantages and disadvantages in terms of the kinds of data produced, the strengths and weaknesses of those data, their expense, the ease of conducting them, and other issues of feasibility (McGee et al., 1999). In conducting testing, AHRQ should keep in mind the unconscious factors that can influence audience reaction to content and format. Testing at different stages of production provides different kinds of feedback. It also saves time and money and provides the kind of evidence needed to create a more effective audience-centered product (U.S. Department of Health and Human Services, 2000). Testing is especially critical for web site development since dissatisfied users are unlikely to visit the site again (Nielson, 2000; Schriver, 1997).

Before conducting pre-tests of report material, AHRQ should undertake formative audience research that will help guide basic aspects of developing the Quality Report. These basic aspects could include

- what the term "health care quality" means to audiences;
- how audiences might use information on quality;
- which components of quality audiences are most and least interested in; and
- how different audiences prefer to receive information on quality.

Formative research can be done in several different ways. In part, it builds on secondary data gathered by other agencies and organizations. In part, it also involves gathering primary data through interviews, focus groups, experiments, and other means designed to provide direct feedback on the Quality Report itself (U.S. Department of Health and Human Services, 2000; Weinreich, 1999).

Pre-testing is conducted while the print and web versions of the report are being designed. For the print version, pre-testing might involve exploring audience preferences on the cover, the order of topics, content, design, graphics, and overall length of the report. Researchers may test prototypes or examples from material that could serve as templates. For the web version, the material to be pre-tested might include the home and first page and navigation tools, in addition to areas also explored for the print version.

Testing is performed on mock-up material developed with the feedback gathered in pre-testing. It can be used to examine whether issues identified in pre-testing have been adequately addressed. It can also be used to identify new issues that have arisen from interpreting pre-testing results.

Evaluative Testing of Report Releases

After each Quality Report (or family of reports) has been released, further audience testing is necessary to improve subsequent versions and gain insights that could be applied to other AHRQ material (Kotler and Andreason, 1996; Kotler and Roberto, 1989; Rossi and Freeman, 1993). In particular, evaluative testing should track the audiences that read the report, what they did or did not like about it, and how they learned about the report. It should also assess the report's impact.

Important questions to ask include the following:

• *Audience readership.* Which audiences read the report? Which segments of which audiences especially used it? Which did not? Why?

• *Strengths and weaknesses of the report.* Which sections did audiences read? Which sections appealed to which audiences? Was the report interesting to read? Was it relevant to audience needs? What would audiences like to see changed?

• *Distribution of the report.* How did audiences learn about the report? How did they receive the report? When did they receive it?

• *Impact of the report.* Did audiences use the report in work they do on health care quality? How? Was it timely? Are there specific policy changes that it helped to bring about? Is public opinion on health care quality different as a result of the report? Is public understanding broader? Are communities or regions developing measurement and reporting systems to track Quality Report indicators at their levels? Did the report affect the efforts of low-performing areas? Did the report lead to local improvement efforts?

Specific computer programs have been developed to evaluate web sites. These automatically gather data on usage, including how often a site is visited, whether it is operating efficiently, and whether users like it. More specific information that can be gathered includes the number of hits and page views overall and by page; user session length overall and by page; user activity by day of week and hour of day; the page used prior to exiting the site; top paths to the site; data files that are downloaded; and server response times, among others (Kotler and Roberto, 1989).

Automated surveys can be supplemented with surveys available for users to complete on the web site. Candidate questions include users' interests (for example, research, policy) and satisfaction (for example, how they liked the site; how they would improve it; and if they were able to find the topics they were interested in). Web-based surveys can also include a text box for unstructured responses that can provide greater insights into how the report and web site could be improved (Nielson, 2000).

PROMOTING THE QUALITY REPORT

No matter how great the effort to design a report with audiences in mind, it will not have an impact unless those audiences learn about it in the media in ways that make them want to read it or learn more about it. To do this, it will be important to generate publicity at and between release times to let people know about the report and its significance (Backer et al., 1992; Kotler and Andreason, 1996; Kotler and Roberto, 1989). For an example of media attention to a similar national report on health care quality, see Box 5.5.

Communication Channels

To reach national, state, and local consumers, policy makers, and other audiences, the Quality Report must attract attention from many levels of print, broadcast, and electronic media or communication channels. Given the diversity of audiences, multiple communication channels and activities will be required. To get attention from wire services that provide news to many national and local newspapers, AHRQ should study the desirable coverage they have given to other reports. AHRQ should provide them with the information they need to give the Quality Report similar or better treatment. In addition, AHRQ should consult the "daybooks," which are compilations used by many wire services to describe the kinds of events and topics that interest them. To identify other print and broadcast outlets, AHRQ should also research how the media have covered other reports and consult media directories for background and contact information. Attention from Internet news sources is important as well. AHRQ should distribute press kits and releases to print and broadcast news outlets, as well as

---

BOX 5.5 Newspaper Coverage of the National Health Service Performance Indicators

What kind of media coverage might the Quality Report receive? One way to find out is to examine the kind of coverage received by a similar report. The National Health Service's "Quality Report on Healthcare" in England is comprehensive, containing 49 indicators, including 7 composite measures that summarize 18 discrete measures. It focuses mainly on the quality of care in hospitals.

Coverage of the latest version of the report (July 2000) by eight major daily newspapers revealed the following problems :

- limited coverage overall, with media complaints about the report's "phone book-sized bundle of figures";
- emphasis on negative outcomes, in this case poor performance in equity measures, and extreme outcomes, such as "good" and "bad" health authorities;
- poor explanation of statistical concepts, such as statistical significance and confidence limits;
- greater attention to more general measures, such as those on population health or hospitals; and
- limited coverage of trends in health care quality.

SOURCES: Appleby and Bell, 2000; Department of Health, 2000.

---

to on-line news services, electronic newsletters, and automatic mailing list servers (Weinreich, 1999).

With limited time between report releases, AHRQ will find it necessary to prioritize communication channels. Given the need to provide information to policy makers as soon as possible, AHRQ should prioritize those print, broadcast, and electronic sources that are most likely to reach them and their constituents. AHRQ should then turn its efforts to consumers and other key audience segments.

AHRQ must also work to attract media attention to the Quality Report and to quality issues throughout the year. It should not overlook the importance of pegging quality information to the news of the day—prominent quality-related events or crises should make the media more receptive to report-related press releases. Other newsworthy events could include public speeches, celebrity appearances, congressional hearings, and issue conferences on subjects that the report highlights (Corbett and Mori, 1999). AHRQ could also issue report updates that can be summarized in print form and placed on the Web. Data updates should also be placed on the Web. It should be noted that as new reports and data updates become available, it is important to maintain earlier archival versions of both on the web site, with links inserted to updates (Salzmann, 1998; Weinreich, 1999).

Partnerships

Partnerships are another way to distribute the report to targeted audiences. AHRQ should partner with other state and local government bodies and non-governmental organizations to distribute the report and focus attention on it through conferences, conventions, scientific seminars, newsletters, trade publications, workshops, hyperlinks, special events, and other forums and media. Partnerships would have the additional benefits of better targeting interested audiences at minimal cost. They may also attract resources that could include guest speakers, opinion articles, journal articles, and video programming (Weinreich, 1999).

An important way to keep the Quality Report in the public eye would be to use the capacity of the Department of Health and Human Services (DHHS) to generate news. The Quality Report should become an integral part of all of the programming, fieldwork, Internet communication, and press activities conducted by DHHS and its agencies, including AHRQ.

Evaluating the Promotion Plan

While AHRQ is creating its plan to distribute the Quality Report, it should also define a plan to evaluate the effectiveness of the distribution and to identify areas that should be improved. In particular, AHRQ should gather data on whether the report or notifications about the release of the report reached targeted audiences. It should also gather data on whether the report and release notifications were delivered in a timely manner. In addition, it should learn whether audiences who read or learned about the report in print, on the Web, or through the media would have preferred to be reached in a different way. AHRQ should also examine whether audiences were satisfied with getting additional information or other follow-up assistance they needed (U.S. Department of Health and Human Services, 2000).

AHRQ could choose many ways to carry out its evaluation, including interviews, focus groups, and surveys. Each has strengths and weaknesses, some of which are described in the section on audience testing methods. Whichever way is chosen, it is important to conduct these evaluations soon after the report is distributed so that memories are fresh and there is time to incorporate these findings into the distribution plan for the next release.

SUMMARY

This chapter contains an outline of the ways in which AHRQ should develop, promote, and evaluate the Quality Report. As explained, the Quality Report should not be a comprehensive document. Instead, it should contain a limited number of findings about quality and a limited number of measures to support those findings. The chapter also contains guidelines that can be used to help select findings for presentation in the report.

As also explained in this chapter, AHRQ should develop, promote, and evaluate the Quality Report for different audiences, especially members of Congress and other policy makers, consumers, and the media. To satisfy the different needs of different audiences in terms of content, accessibility and other areas, AHRQ should produce the report in print and web formats.

This chapter also contains an overview of how to let audiences know about the report. AHRQ should aggressively promote the Quality Report through the mass media and more specialized channels of communication, such as print and electronic newsletters. AHRQ should also seek to draw attention to the report at release time and between releases. It should employ private- and public-sector partnerships to encourage awareness and use of the report. Finally, as explained, AHRQ should evaluate the way each year's edition of the report was promoted, with the goal of improving its promotion in the following year.

AHRQ faces many challenges in developing, promoting, and evaluating the Quality Report in the ways that this chapter sets forth. In a report on complex, visible, and highly important issues such as national health care quality, there will be inevitable pressure to make it as comprehensive as possible in the hope of reaching as many people on as many subjects as possible. However, a strong body of evidence shows that a selective focus on the most important topics will be a far more effective means of communication. In addition, there will be pressure to save money by cutting back on development and evaluation activities. Here, too, a strong body of evidence shows that resources spent in these areas will make the National Health Care Quality Report a far more effective means of communication.

REFERENCES

Annual Reports. 2000. *Step-By-Step Graphics* 16(2):104–141.

American Medical Association, Ad Hoc Committee on Health Literacy for the Council on Scientific Affairs. 1999. Health literacy: Report of the Council on Scientific Affairs. *Journal of the American Medical Association* 281(6):551-557.

Appleby, John, and Andy Bell. 2000. Reporting NHS performance: How did the media perform? *British Medical Journal* 321:248.

Backer, Thomas E., Everett M. Rogers, and Pradeep Sopory. 1992. *Designing Health Communication Campaigns: What Works?* Newbury Park, Calif.: Sage Publications.

156   *ENVISIONING THE NATIONAL HEALTH CARE QUALITY REPORT*

Bates, David W., and Atul A. Gawande. 2000. The impact of the Internet on quality measurement. *Health Affairs* 19(6):104–114.

Beasley, Berrin. 1998. Journalists' attitudes toward narrative writing. *Newspaper Research Journal* 19(1):78–89.

Bentley, J. Marvin, and David B. Nash. 1998. How Pennsylvania hospitals have responded to publicly released reports on coronary artery bypass graft surgery. *Joint Commission Journal on Quality Improvement* 24(1):40–49.

Blendon, Robert J., Mollyann Brodie, John M. Benson, Drew E. Altman, L. Levitt, T. Hoff, and L. Hugick. 1998. Understanding the managed care backlash. *Health Affairs* 17(4):80–94.

Brangan, Normandy, 2000. Personal Communication, September 18. AARP.

Brodie, Mollyann, Ursula Foehr, Vicky Rideout, Neal Baer, Carolyn Miller, Rebecca Flournoy, and Drew Altman. 2001. Communicating health information thorough the entertainment media. *Health Affairs* 20(1):192–199.

Corbett, Julia B., and Motomi Mori. 1999. Medicine, media and celebrities: News coverage of breast cancer, 1960–1995. *Journalism and Mass Communication Quarterly* 76(2):229–249.

Corporate annual reports: Now more readable, credible, and fashionable. 2000. *PR News* 56(18).

Department of Health. 2000. *NHS Performance Indicators.* Leeds, England: National Health Service (NHS) Executive. Available at: http://www.doh.gov.uk/ nhsperformanceindicators.

Eddy, David M. 1998. Performance measurement: Problems and solutions. *Health Affairs* 17(4):7–25.

Epstein, Arnold M. 1996. The role of quality measurement in a competitive marketplace. Pp. 207–234 in *Strategic Choices for a Changing Health Care System.* eds. Stuart Altman and Uwe E. Reinhardt. Chicago: Health Administration Press.

Erickson, Lars C., David F. Torchiana, Eric C. Schneider, Jane W. Newburger, and Edward L. Hannan. 2000. The relationship between managed care insurance and use of lower-mortality hospitals for CABG surgery. *Journal of the American Medical Association* 283(15):1976–1982.

Galvin, Robert. 1998. Are performance measures relevant? *Health Affairs* 17(4):29–31.

Graber, Doris A. 1997. *Mass Media and American Politics.* Washington, D.C.: Congressional Quarterly Press.

Halford, G. S. 1998. Development of processing capacity entails representing more complex relations: Implications for cognitive development. *Working Memory and Thinking.* eds. R. H. Loie, and K. H. Gilhooly. East Sussex, U.K.: Psychology Press.

Hannan, Edward L., Albert L. Siu, Dinesh Kumar, Harold Kilburn, and Mark R. Chassin. 1995. The decline in coronary artery bypass graft surgery mortality in New York State. *Journal of the American Medical Association* 273(3):209–213.

Healthcare Research and Quality Act. 1999. *Statutes at Large.* Vol. 113, Sec. 1653.

Hibbard, Judith H. 1998. Use of outcome data by purchasers and consumers: new strategies and new dilemmas. *International Journal for Quality in Health Care* 10(6):503–508.

Hibbard, Judith, Peter Slovic, Ellen Peters, and Melissa Finucane. 2000. *Older Consumers' Skill in Using Comparative Data to Inform Health Plan Choice: A Preliminary*

Assessment, AARP, Public Policy Institute. Available at: http://research.aarp.org/ppi/index.html.

Hochhauser, Mark. 1999. Health maintenance organization report cards: communication strategies versus consumer abilities. *Managed Care Quarterly* 7(3):75–82.

Hsee, Christopher K. 1996. The evaluability hypothesis: An explanation for preference reversals between joint and separate evaluations of alternatives. *Organizational Behavior and Human Decision Processes* 67(3):247–257.

Hsee, Christopher K. 1998. Less is better: When low-value options are valued more highly then high-value options. *Journal of Behavioral Decision Making* 11:107–121.

Kahneman, Daniel, and Amos Tversky. 1984. Choices, values, and frames. *American Psychologist* 39:341–350.

Kopfman, J., S. Smith, K. Ah Yun, and A. Hodges. 1998. Affective and cognitive reactions to narrative versus statistical evidence organ donation messages. *Journal of Applied Communication Research* 26(3):279–300.

Kotler, Philip, and Alan R. Andreason. 1996. *Strategic Marketing for Nonprofit Organizations*. Upper Saddle River, N.J.: Prentice Hall.

Kotler, Philip, and Eduardo L. Roberto. 1989. *Social Marketing*. New York: The Free Press.

Lamphere, Jo Ann, Normandy Brangan, Sharon Bee, and Kelly Griffin. 1999. *Reforming the Health Care System: State Profiles 1999*, Washington, D.C.: AARP Public Policy Institute.

Landsverk, John. 1999. Patient race and ethnicity in primary care management of child behavior problems. *Medical Care* 37(11):1089–1091.

Lubalin, James S., and Lauren D. Harris-Kojetin. 1999. What do consumers want and need to know in making health care choices? *Medical Care Research and Review* 56(Supplement 1):67–102.

Marshall, Martin N., Paul G. Shekelle, Sheila Leatherman, and Robert H. Brook. 2000. The public release of performance data: What do we expect to gain? A review of the evidence. *Journal of the American Medical Association* 283(14):1866–1874.

Maryland Health Care Commission. 2000. *Comparing the Quality of Maryland HMOs*. Baltimore. Available at: http://www.mhcc.state.md.us.

McDonough, John E. 2001. Using and misusing anecdote in policy making. *Health Affairs* 20(1):207–212.

McGee, Jeanne, David E. Kanouse, Shoshanna Sofaer, J. Lee Hargraves, Elizabeth Hoy, and Susan Kleimann. 1999. Making survey results easy to report to consumers. *Medical Care* 37(3 Supplement):MS32–MS40.

Mellers, Barbara A., Virginia M. Richards, and Micahel H. Birnbaum. 1992. Distributional theories of impression formation. *Organizational Behavior and Human Decision Processes* 51:313–343.

Mennemeyer, Stephen T., Michael A. Morrisey, and Leslie Z. Howard. 1997. Death and reputation: How consumers acted upon HCFA mortality information. *Inquiry* 34:117–128.

Nielson, Jakob. 1999. *useit.com: Jakob Nielson's Website (Usable Information Technology)* [on-line]. Available at: http://www.useit.com [Dec. 7, 2000].

Nielson, Jakob. *The Alertbox: Current Issues in Web Usability* [on-line]. Available at: http://www.useit.com/alertbox [Jul. 17, 2000].

Philipchalk, R. P. 1972. Thematicity, abstractness, and the long-term recall of connected discourse. *Psychonomic Science* 27:361–362.

Robinson, Sandra, and Mollyann Brodie. 1997. Understanding the quality challenge for health consumers: The Kaiser/AHCPR Survey. *Joint Commission Journal on Quality Improvement* 23:239–244.

Rossi, Peter H., and Howard E. Freeman. 1993. *Evaluation: A Systematic Approach.* Newbury Park, Calif.: Sage Publications.

Rubin, Jeffrey. 1994. *Handbook of Usability Testing: How to Plan, Design, and Conduct Effective Tests.* New York: John Wiley & Sons.

Rushefsky, Mark E., and Kant Patel. 1998. *Politics, Power and Policy Making: The Case of Health Reform in the 1990s* . Armonk, N.Y.: M.E. Sharpe.

Salzmann, Jason. 1998. *Making the News: A Guide for Nonprofits and Activists.* Boulder, Colo.: Westview Press.

Schriver, Karen A. 1997. *Dynamics in Document Design: Creating Text for Readers.* New York: John Wiley & Sons.

Sharf, Barbara F. 2001. Out of the closet and into the legislature: Breast cancer stories. *Health Affairs* 20(1):213–218.

Slovic, Paul. 1992. Perception of risk: reflections on the psychometric paradigm. Pp. 117–152 in *Social Theories of Risk.* eds. Sheldon Krimsky, and Dominic Golding. Westport, Conn.: Praeger.

Spool, Jared M., Tara Scanlon, Carolyn Snyder, Will Schroeder, and Terri DeAngelo. 1999. *Web Site Usability: A Designer's Guide.* San Francisco: Morgan Kaufmann Publishers.

Sun Microsystems. 1999. *Sun Microsystems* [on-line]. Available at: http://www.sun.com [Dec. 7, 2000].

Tufte, Edward R. 1983. *The Visual Display of Quantitative Information.* Cheshire, Conn.: Graphics Press.

Tversky, Amos, and Daniel Kahneman. 1981. The framing of decisions and the psychology of choice. *Science* 211(4481):453–458.

U.S. Department of Health and Human Services. 1996. *Fact Sheet: Health Insurance Portability and Accountability Act of 1996* [on-line]. Available at: http://www.os.dhhs.gov:80/news/press/1996pres/960821.html [Jan. 15, 1998].

U.S. Department of Health and Human Services. 2000. *Healthy People 2010.* Washington, D.C.: U.S. Government Printing Office.

U.S. Securities and Exchange Commission. 1998. *A Plain English Handbook: How to create clear SEC disclosure documents.* Washington, D.C. Available at: http://www.sec.gov/news/handbook.htm.

Weinreich, Nedra Kline. 1999. *Hands-On Social Marketing.* Thousand Oaks, Calif.: Sage Publications.

Yuille, John C., and Allan Paivio. 1969. Abstractness and the recall of connected discourse. *Journal of Experimental Psychology* 82:467–471.

APPENDIX A

Workshop: Envisioning a National Quality Report on Health Care

PURPOSE AND STRUCTURE OF THE WORKSHOP

The general purpose of the workshop was to provide the Institute of Medicine Committee on the National Quality Report on Health Care Delivery with practical, state-of-the-art information on the definition and reporting of national indicators of health care quality.

The workshop involved more than 40 participants and was open to the public. The topics were organized in three parts: (1) Lessons to be Learned from Other Experiences; (2) Measuring the Dimensions of Health Care Quality; and, (3) Technical, Data, and Policy Issues.

Presenters were asked to focus on the practical or applied, rather than the theoretical, aspects of their subject. They were also asked to give their opinion regarding the proposed framework for the National Health Care Quality Report as it referred to the subject they are addressing. Those presenting on specific quality measures were asked to present evidence on why the measures should be included in the Quality Report and to comment on available data sources or data needs for implementing the quality measures proposed.

ISSUES ADDRESSED AT THE WORKSHOP

• The feasibility of measuring patient centeredness, safety, effectiveness, and efficiency as dimensions of quality of care.

• The availability and appropriateness of public and private data sources for national indicators of quality of care.

•The feasibility of translating experiences from other sectors and countries to measure quality of health care in the United States.

•The need for specific measures of quality for particular populations and tracking disparities in health care quality.

WORKSHOP AGENDA

May 22–23, 2000
Holiday Inn Georgetown—Mirage I Conference Room
2101 Wisconsin Avenue, N.W., Washington, D.C.

Monday, May 22, 2000

9:00 a.m.–9:05 a.m.	**Welcome** William L. Roper, M.D., M.P.H. *Chair, IOM Committee on the National Quality Report on Health Care Delivery*
9:05 a.m.–9:15 a.m.	**Introduction to the Workshop** Mark Smith, M.D., M.B.A. *Member, IOM Committee*

SESSION 1: Quality Indicators in Other Sectors and Other Countries: Issues of Measurement, Presentation, Process, and Accountability

9:15 a.m.–9:30 a.m.	**Measuring Consumer Satisfaction with Quality Across Industries—The American Customer Satisfaction Index** Claes Fornell, Ph.D. *University of Michigan School of Business Administration*
9:30 a.m.–9:45 a.m.	**Indicators of Educational Quality—The National Education Report Card (NAEP)** Peggy Carr, Ph.D. *National Center for Education Statistics*
9:45 a.m.–10:00 a.m.	**International Experiences in the Definition of National Indicators of Health Care Quality** R. Heather Palmer, M.B., B.Ch., S.M. *Harvard School of Public Health*

10:00 a.m.–10:30 a.m.   **Discussion: Lessons for the Designers of the**
                         National Quality Report on Health Care
                         Moderator: Michael Millenson
                         William M. Mercer, Inc.

10:30 a.m.–10:45 a.m.   Break

SESSION 2: Measuring Health Care Safety for the
National Health Care Quality Report

10:45 a.m.–11:00 a.m.   **Update on Federal Initiatives on Error Measures**
                         and Databases
                         Nancy Foster, Ph.D.
                         Gregg Meyer, M.D., M.Sc.
                         Agency for Healthcare Research and Quality

11:00 a.m.–11:15 a.m.   **Assessing and Reducing Errors in Health Care:**
                         The Purchaser Perspective
                         Suzanne Delbanco, Ph.D.
                         Leapfrog Group

11:15 a.m.–11:30 a.m.   **Using Information Technology to Ensure and**
                         Assess Safety in Health Care
                         David Bates, M.D., M.Sc.
                         Harvard Medical School

SESSION 3: Approaches to Measuring the Efficiency of
Health Care for the National Health Care Quality Report

11:30 a.m.–11:45 a.m.   **Efficiency, Productivity in Medical Care, and**
                         Medical Cost Increases
                         Jack Triplett, Ph.D.
                         The Brookings Institution

11:45 a.m.–12:15 p.m.   **Potential Measures of Efficiency of Health Care**
                         Mark McClellan, M.D., Ph.D.
                         Stanford University
                         Discussant: José Escarce, M.D., Ph.D.
                         IOM Committee

12:15 p.m.–12:45 p.m.   **Discussion: Measuring Safety and Efficiency for the National Quality Report**
Moderator: John Ware, Jr., Ph.D.
QualityMetric Inc.

12:45 p.m.–1:45 p.m.   Lunch

SESSION 4: Measuring Effectiveness and Appropriateness of Care for the National Health Care Quality Report

1:45 p.m.–2:00 p.m.   **Measuring the Appropriateness of Nursing Care**
Ora Strickland, Ph.D., R.N., F.A.A.N.
Emory University School of Nursing

2:00 p.m.–2:15 p.m.   **Considerations on the Use of Health Outcomes as Measures of Effectiveness**
John Ware, Jr., Ph.D.
QualityMetric Inc.

2:15 p.m.–2:45 p.m.   **Potential Measures of Effectiveness and Appropriateness of Health Care for the National Health Care Quality Report**
Elizabeth McGlynn, Ph.D.
Robert Brook, M.D., Sc.D.
RAND
Discussant: Sheldon Greenfield, *IOM Committee*

SESSION 5: Measuring Patient Centeredness for the National Health Care Quality Report

2:45 p.m.–3:00 p.m.   **Measuring the Patient's Role in Collaborative Chronic Disease Care and Its Link to Quality of Care and Outcomes**
Jessie Gruman, Ph.D.
Center for the Advancement of Health

3:00 p.m.–3:15 p.m.   **Measuring the Quality of Interpersonal Care and Patient Involvement in Care**
Sherrie Kaplan, Ph.D., M.P.H.
*Primary Care Outcomes Research Institute,
New England Medical Center*

3:15 p.m.–3:30 p.m.   **What Lies Ahead? Quality Measurement and the**
                             Future Role of the Consumer in Care
                             Michael Millenson
                             William M. Mercer, Inc.

3:30 p.m.–4:00 p.m.   **Developing Potential Measures of Patient**
                             Centeredness for the National Health Care
                             Quality Report
                             Christina Bethell, Ph.D., M.B.A., M.P.H.
                             Foundation for Accountability
                             Discussant: Judith Hibbard, Dr.P.H., *IOM Committee*

4:00 p.m.–4:15 p.m.   Break

SESSION 6: General Discussion on Measures for the
National Health Care Quality Report

4:15 p.m.–5:30 p.m.   **Discussion**
                             Moderator: Arnold Epstein, M.D., M.A.
                             IOM Committee

5:30 p.m.   Adjourn

Tuesday, May 23, 2000

SESSION 7: Issues to Be Considered in Selecting and Defining
Measures for the National Health Care Quality Report

9:00 a.m.–9:15 a.m.   **Defining Indicators and Indices to Track the**
                             U.S. Health Care System
                             Robert Rubin, M.D.
                             The Lewin Group

9:15 a.m.–9:30 a.m.   **Quality of Care Assessments: New Paradigms**
                             Barbara Starfield, M.D., M.P.H.
                             Johns Hopkins University

9:30 a.m.–9:45 a.m.   **Variability as a Measure of Quality: The Influence**
                             of Patient Preferences and Provider Practice
                             John Wennberg, M.D., M.P.H.
                             Dartmouth Medical School

9:45 a.m.–10:00 a.m.   **Monitoring Racial, Ethnic, and Socioeconomic Disparities in Health Care: Conceptual Issues and Practical Considerations**
David Williams, Ph.D.
University of Michigan

SESSION 8: *Available and Needed Data for the National Health Care Quality Report*

10:00 a.m.–10:15 a.m.   **Public Sources of Data and Possible Indicators for the National Health Care Quality Report**
Irma Arispe, Ph.D.
National Center for Health Statistics

10:15 a.m.–10:45 a.m.   **Potential Quality Indicators Using Private Data Sources and Future Data Needs for the National Health Care Quality Report**
Marsha Gold, Sc.D.
Mathematica Policy Research
Discussant: William Stead, *IOM Committee*

SESSION 9: *Technical and Data-Related Barriers to Producing a National Health Care Quality Report*

10:45 a.m.–11:30 a.m.   **Discussion**
Moderator: R. Heather Palmer, M.B., B.Ch., S.M.
Harvard School of Public Health

11:30 a.m.–11:45 a.m.   Break

SESSION 10: *Roundtable—What Do Policy Makers Want from the National Health Care Quality Report?*
Moderator: Robert Rubin, M.D., *The Lewin Group*

11:45 a.m.–12:30 p.m.   **Congress**
Cybele Bjorklund, M.P.H.
Senate Committee on Health, Education, Labor and Pensions

Jason Lee, Ph.D.
House Committee on Commerce

The States
Lee Partridge
American Public Human Services Association
John Colmers, M.P.H.
Maryland Health Care Commission

Other Policy Makers: Insurers
Donald Young, M.D.
Health Insurance Association of America

12:30 p.m.–1:00 p.m.	**Discussion: How to Produce a Report Useful to Policy Makers and Understandable to the Public**
1:00 p.m.–1:15 p.m.	Closing Comments Mark Smith, M.D., M.B.A., *IOM Committee*
1:15 p.m.	Adjourn

WORKSHOP SPEAKERS

IRMA E. ARISPE, Associate Director for Science, Division of Health Care Statistics, National Center for Health Care Statistics, Hyattsville, Maryland

DAVID W. BATES, Chief, Division of General Medicine, Brigham and Women's Hospital, Boston, Massachusetts

CHRISTINA BETHELL, Senior Vice President, Research and Policy, Foundation for Accountability (FACCT), Portland, Oregon

CYBELLE BJORKLUND, Deputy Staff Director, Senate Committee on Health, Education, Labor and Pensions, Washington, D.C.

ROBERT H. BROOK, Vice President and Director, RAND Health and Corporate Fellow, The RAND Corporation, Santa Monica, California

PEGGY G. CARR, Associate Commissioner, Assessment Division, National Center for Education Statistics, Washington, D.C.

SUZANNE F. DELBANCO, Executive Director, Leapfrog Group, Washington, D.C.

CLAES G. FORNELL, Donald C. Cook Professor of Business Administration and Director, National Quality Research Center, University of Michigan School of Business Administration, Ann Arbor, Michigan

NANCY FOSTER, Agency for Healthcare Research and Quality, Rockville, Maryland

MARSHA GOLD, Senior Fellow, Mathematica Policy Research, Inc., Washington, D.C.

JESSIE GRUMAN, Executive Director, Center for the Advancement of Health, Washington, D.C.

SHERRIE H. KAPLAN, Co-director, Primary Care Outcomes Research Institute, Tufts University School of Medicine, New England Medical Center, Boston, Massachusetts

JASON LEE, Health Policy Counsel, U.S. House of Representatives, Committee on Commerce, Washington, D.C.

MARK B. McCLELLAN, Assistant Professor, Department of Economics, Stanford University, Stanford, California

ELIZABETH A. McGLYNN, Senior Researcher, The RAND Corporation, Santa Monica, California

GREGG MEYER, Director, Center for Quality Measurement and Improvement, Agency for Healthcare Research and Quality, Rockville, Maryland

MICHAEL L. MILLENSON, Principal, William M. Mercer, Inc., Chicago, Illinois

R. HEATHER PALMER, Director, Center for Quality of Care Research and Education, Harvard School of Public Health, Boston, Massachusetts

LEE PARTRIDGE, American Public Human Services Association, Washington, D.C.

ROBERT J. RUBIN, President, The Lewin Group, Falls Church, Virginia

BARBARA STARFIELD, University Distinguished Professor, The Johns Hopkins University, Baltimore, Maryland

ORA STRICKLAND, Professor, Neil Hodgson Woodruff School of Nursing, and Director, Research on Special Populations of Veterans, Atlanta VA Medical Center, Atlanta, Georgia

JACK E. TRIPLETT, Visiting Fellow, Brookings Institution, Washington, D.C.

JOHN E. WARE, JR., President and Chief Scientific Officer, QualityMetric, Inc., Lincoln, Rhode Island

JOHN E. WENNBERG, Director, Center for Evaluative Clinical Sciences, Dartmouth Medical School, Hanover, New Hampshire

DAVID R. WILLIAMS, Senior Research Scientist, Survey Research Center, Institute for Social Research, University of Michigan, Ann Arbor, Michigan

DONALD YOUNG, Chief Operating Officer and Medical Director, Health Insurance Association of America, Washington, D.C.

Designing a Comprehensive National Report on Effectiveness of Care: Measurement, Data Collection, and Reporting Strategies

Elizabeth A. McGlynn, Ph.D. ,[1] Paul G. Shekelle, M.D., Ph.D.,[1,2] and Robert H. Brook, M.D., Sc.D.[1,3]

INTRODUCTION

This is an excerpt from a paper that was commissioned by the Institute of Medicine (IOM) Committee on the National Quality Report on Health Care Delivery to identify potential measures of effectiveness to include in a National Health Care Quality Report for Congress and the American public (McGlynn et al., 2000a).

One of the questions to consider in designing the report is how many measures to choose. We consider a continuum from a few (leading indicators) to many (comprehensive system) measures, which represent two conceptually distinct approaches to measuring quality nationally. Under the leading indicators approach, three to five specific measures of effectiveness would be selected across a few domains (for example, rates of mammography screening, prevalence of the use of beta-blockers, appropriateness of coronary angioplasty). This is the most common approach to quality measurement currently. Leading indicators may work well for drawing general conclusions about quality when they correlate highly with similar, but unmeasured, interventions and when repeated measurement and public reporting do not change the relationship of these indicators to unmeasured but related interventions. A leading indicator approach

[1] The RAND Corporation.
[2] Greater Los Angeles Veterans Affairs Healthcare System.
[3] UCLA Center for Health Sciences.

lacks face validity for summarizing performance because three to five specific measures will never satisfactorily represent care at a high level of aggregation (for example, care for chronic conditions). By contrast, a comprehensive system can represent the quality of care delivery on different dimensions by including a large number of measures applied to a population of interest and aggregated to produce index scores. A comprehensive system works well when there is evidence of variability within and between the diagnosis and management of different conditions and when the question being asked is framed at a high level (for example, how well the health system is helping the population to stay healthy; how much of a problem underuse is). Because the leading indicators approach is familiar, this appendix focuses on how a comprehensive approach to quality assessment for the National Health Care Quality Report might be implemented.

ASSESSING EFFECTIVENESS OF CARE

How good is the quality of care in America? That is the question many people would like to have answered if only the measures, the data, and the appropriate analytic framework were available. We begin by describing a new method for evaluating effectiveness that is under development at RAND because it offers a useful approach to assessing quality nationally.

Description of the QA Tools System

Under funding from public and private sponsors,[1] RAND has developed a comprehensive system for assessing the quality of care for children, adults, and the vulnerable elderly. We call this system QA Tools. We briefly discuss how the clinical areas were selected, how the indicators were chosen, what is included in the system, and how the system is being implemented.

Selecting Clinical Areas

We reviewed national data sources to identify the leading causes of morbidity and mortality and the most common reasons for physician visits in the United States for different age and gender groups in the population.[2] Table B.1 shows the list of 58 clinical areas included in the QA Tools system by population group: 20 include indicators for children, 36 for adults, and 23 for the vulnerable elderly. The clinical areas, broadly defined, represent about 55 percent

---

[1] Health Care Financing Administration, Agency for Healthcare Research and Quality, California HealthCare Foundation, Pfizer, and the Robert Wood Johnson Foundation.

[2] Age or gender groups: 0–1, 1–5, 6–11, 12–17, 18–50 (men separate from women), 50–64, 65–75, over 75.

of the reasons for ambulatory care visits among children; 50 percent of the reasons for ambulatory care visits and 46 percent of the reasons for hospitalization among adults; and about 50 percent of care for the vulnerable elderly.

Selecting Indicators

For each clinical area chosen, we reviewed the scientific literature for evidence that effective methods of prevention, screening, diagnosis, treatment, and follow-up existed (Asch et al., 2000; Kerr et al., 2000a,b; McGlynn et al., 2000a,b). We explicitly examined the continuum of care in each clinical area. For each clinical area, staff wrote a summary of the scientific evidence, and developed tables of the proposed indicators along with the level of evidence and specific studies in support of the indicator as well as the rationale for the indicator.

The indicators included in the QA Tools system are primarily process indicators. We deliberately chose such indicators because the system was designed to evaluate quality in the context of accountability, and process measures are frequently more suitable for such purposes. However, data are collected on a number of intermediate outcomes measures (for example, glycosylated hemoglobin, blood pressure, cholesterol) that could be used to construct additional clinical outcomes indicators. In many instances, the measures included in the QA Tools system examine whether interventions have been launched in response to poor performance on such measures (for example, whether persons who fail to control their blood sugar on dietary therapy are offered oral hypoglycemic therapy).

Expert panels were convened to evaluate the indicators and make final selections using the modified Delphi method developed at RAND and the University of California, Los Angeles (UCLA). The method has been shown to have a reproducibility consistent with that of well-accepted diagnostic tests such as the interpretation of coronary angiography and screening mammography (Shekelle et al., 1998a). It has been shown to have content, construct, and predictive validity in other applications (Brook, 1994; Kravitz et al., 1995; Selby et al., 1996; Shekelle et al., 1998b).

A total of eight expert panels were conducted on (1) children's care; (2) care for women 18 to 50 years old; (3) general medicine for adults; (4) oncologic conditions and human immunodeficiency virus (HIV); (5) cardiopulmonary conditions; (6, 7) selected conditions applicable to the vulnerable elderly; and (8) nursing home care. Panels were conducted as early as October 1995 (children's care) and as recently as April 1999 (vulnerable elderly). Table B.2 summarizes the distribution of indicators by type of care (preventive, acute, chronic); function of medicine (screening, diagnosis, treatment, follow-up, continuity); and modality (for example, history, physical examination, laboratory

TABLE B.1. Clinical Areas Included in QA Tools System by Population Group Covered

Clinical Area	Children	Adults	Vulnerable Elderly
Acne	X		
Adolescent preventive services	X		
Adult screening and prevention		X	X
Alcohol dependence		X	
Allergic rhinitis	X		
Asthma	X	X	
Atrial fibrillation		X	X
Attention deficit/hyperactivity disorder	X		
Benign prostatic hyperplasia		X	
Breast cancer		X	
Cataracts		X	
Cerebrovascular disease		X	X
Cervical cancer		X	
Cesarean delivery	X	X	
Chronic obstructive pulmonary disease		X	
Colorectal cancer		X	
Congestive heart failure		X	X
Coronary artery disease		X	
Dementia			X
Depression	X	X	X
Developmental screening	X		
Diabetes mellitus	X	X	X
Diarrheal disease	X		
End-of-life care			X
Falls and mobility disorders			X
Family planning and contraception	X	X	
Fever of unknown origin	X		
Headache		X	
Hearing impairment			X
Hip fracture		X	
Hormone replacement therapy		X	
Hospital care			X
Human immunodeficiency virus		X	
Hyperlipidemia		X	
Hypertension		X	X
Immunizations	X	X	X
Ischemic heart disease			X
Low-back pain		X	
Malnutrition			X
Orthopedic conditions		X	
Osteoarthritis		X	X
Osteoporosis			X
Otitis media	X		
Pain management		X	X

Peptic ulcer disease and dyspepsia		X	
Pharmacologic management			X
Pneumonia and influenza		X	X
Prenatal care and delivery	X	X	
Pressure ulcers			X
Prostate cancer		X	
Tuberculosis	X	X	
Upper respiratory tract infections	X		
Urinary incontinence			X
Urinary tract infections	X	X	
Uterine bleeding and hysterectomy		X	
Vaginitis and sexually transmitted diseases	X	X	
Vision impairment			X
Well-child care	X		
TOTAL			
Number of Clinical Areas	**20**	**36**	**23**

test, medication) (Malin et al., 2000; Schuster et al., 1997; Sloss et al., 2000). The categories are those selected by the research team and reflect terminology commonly used by health services researchers to describe different aspects of health service delivery. They also reflect the categories of care for which we sought to develop quality indicators (Table B.3 presents some sample indicators by type of care). However, a significant benefit of the QA Tools system is its adaptability to other frameworks.

Several projects to test the feasibility and utility of this approach to quality measurement are currently underway. Under funding from the Health Care Financing Administration (HCFA), data from medical records were collected in two health plans (one group model, one independent practice association [IPA]) for the 20 clinical areas related to women's health care. The preliminary analyses show variation in performance within and between health plans. Aggregate scores have been constructed in the categories described in Table B.2. Under funding from the Agency for Healthcare Research and Quality (AHRQ), data are being collected from two different managed care plans (one group model, one IPA) for the adult clinical areas. Under funding from the California HealthCare Foundation (CHCF), data will be collected from three medical groups in California for the children's and adult's clinical areas. Under funding from Pfizer, the set of quality indicators selected to assess the care of vulnerable elders is being pilot-tested in two managed care organizations. A separate set of indicators for evaluating nursing home quality was developed and will be tested under funding from CHCF. Finally, under funding from the Robert Wood Johnson Foundation (RWJ), we are testing a community-based implementation of this approach to quality measurement called the Community Quality Index (CQI) in

TABLE B.2 Summary of the QA Tools Indicators by Type of Care, Function of Care, and Modality

	Population			
Aspect	Children N (%)	Adults N (%)	Vulnerable Elderly N (%)	Total N (%)
Type of Care				
Preventive care	133 (32)	83 (14)	—	—
Acute care	175 (43)	188 (31)	—	—
Chronic care	102 (25)	340 (56)	—	—
Function of Care (Domain)				
Screening or Prevention	88 (21)	40 (7)	62 (25)	190 (15)
Diagnosis	126 (31)	216 (35)	51 (21)	393 (31)
Treatment	143 (35)	280 (46)	92 (37)	515 (41)
Follow-Up	53 (13)	75 (12)	22 (9)	150 (12)
Continuity	—	—	20 (8)	20 (2)
Modality				
Physical Exam	55 (13)	90 (15)	30 (12)	175 (14)
History	90 (22)	78 (13)	29 (12)	197 (15)
Laboratory or Radiology Test	96 (23)	163 (27)	13 (5)	272 (21)
Medication	58 (14)	144 (24)	77 (31)	279 (22)
Other Intervention	78 (19)	117 (19)	51 (21)	246 (19)
Other Contact	33 (8)	19 (3)	49 (20)	101 (8)
TOTAL	410 (100 %)	611 (100 %)	247 (100 %)	1268 (100 %)

12 communities that are participating in the Community Tracking Study. RWJ is funding RAND to conduct another round of this project, which will begin in February 2001. It will enable us to examine change in quality over time and will add a national sample to allow us to make national estimates of quality. The experience with this project provides considerable insight into the use of this tool for a National Health Care Quality Report.

TABLE B.3 Sample Indicators from QA Tools System ($N = 1,286$)

Category	Sample Indicator
Preventive care	Patients who have one or more first-degree relatives with colorectal cancer should be offered at least one of the following colon cancer screening tests beginning at age 40:
	• FOBT (if not done in the past 2 years) • Sigmoidoscopy (if not done in the past 5 years) • Colonoscopy (if not done in the past 10 years) • Double-contrast barium enema (if not done in past 5 years)
	Systolic and diastolic blood pressure should be measured on patients otherwise presenting for care at least once each year.
Acute care	Persons with hip fractures should be given prophylactic antithrombotics on admission to the hospital.
	If a patient has symptoms of urethritis, he should be tested for both chlamydia and gonorrhea or receive proper treatment for both.
Chronic care	If a child is started on pemoline, the health care provider should document the absence of hepatic disease prior to the start of therapy by history and baseline liver function tests.
	Patients with an FEV_1 or $PEFR \leq 70\%$ of baseline (or predicted) after treatment for an asthma exacerbation in the physician's office should be placed on an oral corticosteroid taper.
	Patients in any risk group with stage 2–3 hypertension should be offered pharmacotherapy.

NOTES: FEV_1 = forced expiratory volume at 1 second; FOBT = fecal occult blood test; PEFR = peak expiratory flow rate.

Implementation of the QA Tools System for a
National Health Care Quality Report

In this section, we discuss the methods by which the QA Tools system could be implemented to produce a national report on quality. In particular, we consider development of a sampling strategy, estimated sample sizes, data collection strategies, analysis and reporting, "actionability" of the information for policy makers, and the applicability of the system to special populations.

Developing a Sampling Strategy

The sampling strategy depends largely on the questions that the National Health Care Quality Report seeks to answer. If the purpose of the report is to provide a general snapshot of quality of care in America, a simple random sample of persons could be drawn. If the national report seeks to answer questions about variations in quality by region, race or ethnicity, urban versus rural, type of insurance, and so on, either a very large simple random sample would have to be drawn or a stratified sampling strategy would have to be developed. If one is interested in developing state-specific estimates, equal-sized samples could be developed for each state using either a random or a stratified approach and a national estimate produced from a weighted average.

Sample Sizes

Based on data from one of our pilot studies, we have estimated sample sizes for implementing the QA Tools system for a National Health Care Quality Report. Because the current state of information systems requires that we access paper copies of medical records, a clustered sampling design would enhance data collection efficiency. For example, a national snapshot sample could be concentrated in 12 metropolitan areas, as has been done with the RWJ-funded effort described above. The system is scored as the number of eligible care events received divided by the number of eligible events. If the summary score for a particular area (for example, quality of care for acute conditions, quality of care for hypertension) had an average adherence rate of 50 percent, a national sample of 500 persons would produce estimates with a 95 percent confidence interval (95% CI) ranging from 48.2 to 51.8 percent. Doubling the sample size increases the precision by one-tenth of a percentage point, which does not justify the additional costs.

To move beyond the simple national snapshot, a sample size of 500 might be selected for each subgroup of interest in the population. For example, if detecting a 1.8 percentage point difference in quality between men and women was adequate, a total sample of 1,000 people would be required (500 in each group). Similarly, if the national report included estimates about the quality of care experienced by people with particular chronic conditions, we might want to select 500 people with hypertension and/or 500 people with diabetes, in addition to the national snapshot sample. For some subgroup analyses, lower levels of precision might be adequate to identify differences in care that raise significant policy concerns.

To make state-level estimates of quality, adequate sample sizes would have to be drawn in every state. Because cluster sampling might not be used at the state level, a sample size of 400 has a 95% CI of ±1.2 percentage points. Using 100 cases per state would allow differences of 2.4 percentage points to be detected. Multiples of these sample sizes would have to be collected for each subgroup of interest at the state level.

Data Collection Strategies

We consider here how a supplement to the Medical Expenditure Panel Survey (MEPS) could be used to generate national quality-of-care scores using the QA Tools method. MEPS is a national probability survey of health care use, expenditures, sources of payment, and insurance coverage for the general U.S. population; a separate component of MEPS surveys nursing homes and residents of nursing homes as well. Detailed information about MEPS can be found on the AHRQ web site (Agency for Healthcare Research and Quality, 2000).

AHRQ and the National Center for Health Statistics (NCHS) could add collection and/or abstraction of medical records to the existing design. The current design of the RWJ study is similar to that of MEPS—data that provide information on utilization and financing of care are collected at the household and individual levels. Participants volunteer information about their health care providers and sign consents to release copies of medical records for research purposes. Because MEPS is a national probability sample, the addition of medical record data would allow national estimates of quality to be linked to information about utilization, expenditures, and insurance coverage. The National Health Care Quality Report could also take advantage of the indicators related to the vulnerable elderly as applied to both the household component subsample (adults with functional impairments) and the nursing home sample.

Analysis and Reporting

The basic approach to scoring starts with determining whether or not each person in the sample is eligible for each indicator in the set. This is simplified considerably by the way in which data are collected. Among those who are eligible for an indicator, we then determine whether the patient received the recommended care (or did not receive care that is contraindicated).

To create category scores, we take two approaches. The first is an indicator-based approach that sums all passes and divides by all eligibilities. It can be

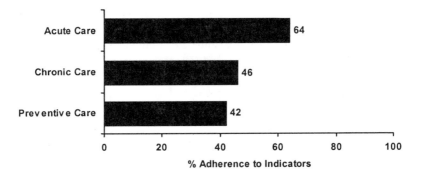

FIGURE B.1 An illustration of how to present QA Tools summary results.

characterized as the proportion of recommended care events that were received. The second is a patient-based approach that creates a summary score at the level of an individual patient. This can be characterized as the average proportion of recommended care received by an individual. The first approach allows individuals to be counted multiple times in the summary score if they have multiple eligible encounters with the system, which means that persons with more health problems and/or more serious problems will be weighted more in the score. The second approach makes individuals equal in their contribution to the score. In our pilot data, we have done the scoring both ways and find few differences in scores by the method used. Where we have found differences, they have been in both directions (i.e., the patient-based score can be higher or lower than the indicator-based score). Because different information is communicated using the different scoring approaches, both should be calculated. Figures B.1 and B.2 illustrate how the results from this approach might be presented.

"Actionability" by Policy Makers

The potential for using the results of this work to inform policy is significant, particularly if data are collected in a way that facilitates linking aspects of the organization and financing of care, as well as demographic characteristics, to variations in quality. If the QA Tools system were implemented at the individual health system level (for example, a managed care plan), certain conditions could be oversampled (for example, diabetes) to provide a focal point for quality improvement activities.

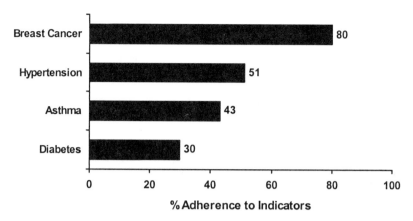

FIGURE B.2 An illustration of how to present condition-specific scores within chronic care categories.

Application to Special Populations

The QA Tools system includes a specific set of indicators targeted at the vulnerable elderly, a group responsible for significant health care utilization and expenditures. The system can also be applied to persons with chronic conditions and can facilitate comparisons of the care for chronic conditions among those with different insurance arrangements, socioeconomic status, and living in different areas of the country. The tool was developed to evaluate quality for a large portion of care and, as such, has focused on common conditions more often than rare conditions. However, the methodology and the software have been designed to facilitate the addition of new clinical areas, as well as to update existing indicators. Future work could add modules for persons with additional health problems (for example, pediatric cardiac illnesses).

CONCLUSION

The QA Tools system represents a feasible alternative to the leading indicators approach to quality measurement. This comprehensive approach is well suited to the requirements of a national report on quality and could be implemented by augmenting an existing national database.

REFERENCES

Agency for Healthcare Research and Quality (AHRQ). *Home Page* [on-line]. Available at: http://www.ahrq.gov [Dec. 11, 2000].

Asch S.M., E.A. Kerr, E.G. Hamilton, J.L. Reifel, and E.A. McGlynn, eds. 2000. *Quality of Care for Oncologic Conditions and HIV: A Review of the Literature and Quality Indicators.* MR-1281-AHRQ. Santa Monica, Calif.: RAND.

Brook R.H. 1994. The RAND/UCLA appropriateness method. *Clinical Practice Guideline Development: Methodology Perspectives*, eds. K.A. McCormick, S.R. Moore, and R.A. Siegel. AHCPR Pub. No. 95-0009, Rockville, Md.: Public Health Service.

Kerr E.A., S.M. Asch, E.G. Hamilton, and E.A. McGlynn, eds. 2000a. *Quality of Care for Cardiopulmonary Conditions: A Review of the Literature and Quality Indicators.* MR-1282-AHRQ. Santa Monica, Calif.: RAND.

Kerr E.A., S.M. Asch, E.G. Hamilton, and E.A. McGlynn, eds. 2000b. *Quality of Care for General Medical Conditions: A Review of the Literature and Quality Indicators.* MR-1280-AHRQ. Santa Monica, Calif: RAND.

Kravitz R.L., M. Laouri, J.P. Kahan, P. Guzy, et al. 1995. Validity of criteria used for detecting underuse of coronary revascularization. *Journal of the American Medical Association* 274(8):632–638.

Malin, J.L., S.M. Asch, E.A. Kerr, and E.A. McGlynn. 2000. Evaluating the quality of cancer care: Development of cancer quality indicators for a global quality assessment tool. *Cancer* 88:701–707.

McGlynn E.A., C. Damberg, E.A. Kerr, and M. Schuster, eds. 2000a. *Quality of Care for Children and Adolescents: A Review of Selected Clinical Conditions and Quality Indicators.* MR-1283-HCFA. Santa Monica, Calif: RAND.

McGlynn E.A., E.A. Kerr, C. Damberg, and S.M. Asch, eds. 2000b. *Quality of Care for Women: A Review of Selected Clinical Conditions and Quality Indicators.* MR-1284-HCFA. Santa Monica, Calif.: RAND.

McGlynn E.A., P.G. Shekelle, and R.H. Brook. 2000. Designing a National Report on Effectiveness and Appropriateness of Care: Measurement, Data Collection, and Reporting Strategies. Commissioned Paper for the Institute of Medicine Committee on the National Quality Report on Health Care Delivery.

Schuster M.A., S.M. Asch, E.A. McGlynn, et al. 1997. Development of a quality of care measurement system for children and adolescents: Methodological considerations and comparisons with a system for adult women. *Archives of Pediatrics and Adolescent Medicine* 151:1085–1092.

Selby J.V., B.H. Fireman, R.J. Lundstrom, et al. 1996. Variation among hospitals in coronary-angiography practices and outcomes after myocardial infarction in a large health maintenance organization. *New England Journal of Medicine* 335:1888–1896.

Shekelle P.G., M.R. Chassin, and R.E. Park. 1998a. Assessing the predictive validity of the RAND/UCLA appropriateness method criteria for performing carotid endarterectomy. *International Journal of Technology Assessment in Health Care* 14(4):707–727.

Shekelle P.G., J.P. Kahan, S.J. Bernstein, et al. 1998b.The reproducibility of a method to identify the overuse and underuse of medical procedures. *New England Journal of Medicine* 338:1888–1895.

Sloss E.M., D.H. Solomon, P.G. Shekelle, et al. 2000. Selecting target conditions for quality of care improvement in vulnerable older adults. *Journal of the American Geriatric Society* 48(4):363–369.

Submissions in Response to the IOM Committee's Call for Measures from the Private Sector[1]

Submitted by:	Name of Measure	Component of Health Care Quality	Consumer Perspective on Health Care Needs
American Diabetes Association (ADA)	Percentage of patients receiving one or more glycohemoglobin (HbA_{1c}) tests per year	Effectiveness	Living with illness
ADA	Percentage of patients with highest-risk HbA_{1c} level (HbA_{1c} greater than 9.5%)	Effectiveness	Living with illness
ADA	Percentage of patients assessed for nephropathy	Effectiveness	Living with illness
ADA	Percentage of patients receiving a lipid profile	Effectiveness	Living with illness
ADA	Percentage of patients with a low-density lipoprotein (LDL) less than 130 mg/dl	Effectiveness	Living with illness
ADA	Percentage of patients with blood pressure less than 140/90 mmHg	Effectiveness	Living with illness

---

[1] The committee issued its call for measures to the private sector from June to July, 2000. The Agency for Healthcare Research and Quality issued a separate call for measures to federal agencies after the committee had concluded its deliberations.

Submitted by:	Name of Measure	Component of Health Care Quality	Consumer Perspective on Health Care Needs
ADA	Percentage of patients receiving a dilated eye exam in the past year (or past two years if certain criteria are met)	Effectiveness	Living with illness
ADA	Percentage of patients with an annual foot exam	Effectiveness	Living with illness
ADA	Smoking cessation counseling	Effectiveness	Living with illness
American Medical Association (AMA)	Percentage of patients with diabetes receiving one or more HbA_{1c} test(s) per year	Effectiveness	Living with illness
AMA	Percentage of patients with diabetes receiving at least one lipid profile per year	Effectiveness	Living with illness
AMA	Percentage of patients with diabetes who had any test for microalbuminuria per year	Effectiveness	Living with illness
AMA	Percentage of patients with diabetes receiving a dilated eye exam per year	Effectiveness	Living with illness
AMA	Percentage of patients with diabetes with at least one foot exam per year	Effectiveness	Living with illness
AMA	Percentage of patients with diabetes who received an influenza vaccine in the past year	Effectiveness	Living with illness
AMA	Percentage of patients with diabetes who had a blood pressure reading at each visit	Effectiveness	Living with illness

Submitted by:	Name of Measure	Component of Health Care Quality	Consumer Perspective on Health Care Needs
AMA	Percentage of patients with diabetes with two or more visits per year	Effectiveness	Living with illness
American Nurses Association (ANA)	Patient satisfaction	Patient centeredness	Other
ANA	Mix of registered nurses, licensed practical nurses, and unlicensed assistive personnel in institutional settings	Safety	Getting better
ANA	Maintenance of skin integrity—prevention of nosocomial pressure ulcers. Percentage of patients with documented nosocomial ulcer on day of prevalence study	Safety	Getting better
ANA	Rate of patient falls and patient falls with injury. The rate per 1,000 patient-days at which patients fall and incur physical injury during their institutional stay	Safety	Getting better
American Psychiatric Association (APA)	Percentage of patients with a current diagnosis of chronic, moderate, or severe depression (not in remission) receiving an antidepressant medication or electroconvulsive therapy (ECT)	Effectiveness	Getting better

Submitted by:	Name of Measure	Component of Health Care Quality	Consumer Perspective on Health Care Needs
APA	Percentage of patients with a current diagnosis of depression with psychotic features (not in remission) receiving either a combination of an antidepressant medication and an antipsychotic medication, or electroconvulsive therapy	Effectiveness	Getting better
APA	Percentage of patients with a current diagnosis of depression that is mild and not chronic (not in remission) receiving medication and/or psychotherapy	Effectiveness	Getting better
Foundation for Accountability (FACCT)	Adult asthma: patient education	Effectiveness	Living with illness
FACCT	Adult asthma: peak flow meter use	Effectiveness	Living with illness
FACCT	Adult asthma: appropriate inhaler use	Effectiveness	Living with illness
FACCT	Adult asthma: patient experience and satisfaction	Patient centeredness	Living with illness
FACCT	Adult asthma: patient self-management knowledge and behavior	Effectiveness	Living with illness
FACCT	Adult asthma: patient ability to maintain daily activities	Effectiveness	Living with illness
FACCT	Breast cancer: mammography	Effectiveness	Staying healthy
FACCT	Breast cancer: early-stage detection	Timeliness	Staying healthy

Submitted by:	Name of Measure	Component of Health Care Quality	Consumer Perspective on Health Care Needs
FACCT	Breast cancer: informed about radiation treatment options	Patient centeredness	Living with illness
FACCT	Breast cancer: breast-conserving surgery	Effectiveness	Living with illness
FACCT	Breast cancer: radiation therapy following breast conserving surgery	Effectiveness	Living with illness
FACCT	Breast cancer: patient satisfaction with care	Patient Centeredness	Living with illness
FACCT	Breast cancer: experience of disease	Effectiveness	Living with illness
FACCT	Breast cancer: five-year disease-free survival	Effectiveness	Living with illness
FACCT	Diabetes: foot exam	Effectiveness	Living with illness
FACCT	Diabetes: frequency of HbA_{1c} testing	Effectiveness	Living with illness
FACCT	Diabetes: retinal exam	Effectiveness	Living with illness
FACCT	Diabetes: advice to quit smoking	Effectiveness	Living with illness
FACCT	Diabetes: HbA_{1c} under good control	Effectiveness	Living with illness
FACCT	Diabetes: lipid levels	Effectiveness	Living with illness
FACCT	Diabetes: smoking cessation	Effectiveness	Living with illness
FACCT	Diabetes: patient ability to maintain daily activities	Effectiveness	Living with illness
FACCT	Major depressive disorder: patient ability to maintain daily activities	Effectiveness	Living with illness

Submitted by:	Name of Measure	Component of Health Care Quality	Consumer Perspective on Health Care Needs
FACCT	Health risks: advice to quit smoking	Effectiveness	Staying healthy
FACCT	Health risks: awareness of health habits	Effectiveness	Staying healthy
FACCT	Health risks: smoking cessation	Effectiveness	Staying healthy
FACCT	Adolescent preventive care: counseling and screening to prevent risky behaviors	Effectiveness	Staying healthy
FACCT	Adolescent preventive care: counseling and screening to prevent unwanted pregnancies and sexually transmitted diseases (STDs)	Effectiveness	Staying healthy
FACCT	Adolescent preventive care: counseling and screening related to diet, weight, and exercise	Effectiveness	Staying healthy
FACCT	Adolescent preventive care: counseling and screening related to depression, mental health, and relationships	Effectiveness	Staying healthy
FACCT	Adolescent preventive care: care provided in a confidential and private setting	Effectiveness	Staying healthy
FACCT	Adolescent preventive care: helpfulness of counseling pro-vided	Patient centeredness	Staying healthy
FACCT	Adolescent preventive care: communication and experience of care	Patient centeredness	Staying healthy
FACCT	Early childhood development: getting anticipatory guidance from providers	Patient centeredness	Staying healthy

Submitted by:	Name of Measure	Component of Health Care Quality	Consumer Perspective on Health Care Needs
FACCT	Early childhood development: follow-up for children with an indication of risk for developmental problems	Effectiveness	Staying healthy
FACCT	Early childhood development: communication and relationship with providers	Patient centeredness	Not specified
FACCT	Early childhood development: helpfulness and effect of anticipatory guidance and counseling on confidence as a parent	Patient centeredness	Not specified
FACCT	Children with chronic conditions: how well doctors communicate	Patient centeredness	Living with illness
FACCT	Children with chronic conditions: getting care quickly	Timeliness	Living with illness
FACCT	Children with chronic conditions: patient education and teamwork	Patient centeredness, effectiveness	Living with illness
FACCT	Children with chronic conditions: coordination of child's care	Timeliness	Living with illness
FACCT– Robert Wood Johnson (RWJ)	Health status and quality of life (6 measures)	Effectiveness	Not specified
FACCT–RWJ	Healthy life style (3 measures)	Effectiveness	Staying healthy
FACCT–RWJ	Self-care efficacy (1 measure)	Patient centeredness	Staying healthy
FACCT–RWJ	Risk reduction counseling (3 measures)	Patient centeredness	Staying healthy

Submitted by:	Name of Measure	Component of Health Care Quality	Consumer Perspective on Health Care Needs
FACCT–RWJ	Getting needed care (2 measures)	Timeliness	Getting better
FACCT–RWJ	Medical home (2 measures)	Timeliness	Not specified
FACCT–RWJ	Access to specialized services (1 measure)	Timeliness	Getting better, living with illness
FACCT–RWJ	Consumer empowerment (2 measures)	Patient centeredness	Not specified
Joint Commission on Accreditation of Healthcare Organizations (JCAHO)	AMI, HF, PN—smoking cessation advice counseling	Effectiveness	Getting better
JCAHO	AMI—aspirin at arrival	Effectiveness	Getting better
JCAHO	AMI—reperfusion therapy: time from arrival to initiation	Effectiveness	Getting better
JCAHO	AMI—aspirin at discharge	Effectiveness	Getting better
JCAHO	AMI—beta-blocker at arrival	Effectiveness	Getting better
JCAHO	AMI, HF—LVEF <40% prescribed ACEI at discharge	Effectiveness	Getting better
JCAHO	AMI—beta-blocker at discharge	Effectiveness	Getting better
JCAHO	AMI—intrahospital mortality	Effectiveness	Getting better
JCAHO	HF—patients with atrial fibrillation prescribed warfarin at discharge	Effectiveness	Getting better
JCAHO	HF—diet, weight, and medication management instructions at discharge	Patient centeredness	Living with illness

Submitted by:	Name of Measure	Component of Health Care Quality	Consumer Perspective on Health Care Needs
JCAHO	HF—assessment of left ventricular function	Effectiveness	Getting better
JCAHO	PN—pneumonia screen or pneumococcal vaccination	Effectiveness	Staying healthy
JCAHO	PN—oxygenation assessment	Effectiveness	Getting better
JCAHO	PN—blood cultures	Effectiveness	Getting better
JCAHO	PN—antibiotic timing	Timeliness	Getting better
JCAHO	PN—empiric antibiotic regimen non-ICU	Effectiveness	Getting better
JCAHO	PN—empiric antibiotic regimen ICU	Effectiveness	Getting better
JCAHO	PR—vaginal birth after C-section (VBAC) rate	Effectiveness	Getting better
JCAHO	PR—third- or fourth-degree laceration	Effectiveness	Getting better
JCAHO	PR—neonatal mortality	Effectiveness	Other
JCAHO	SG—surgical site infection within 30 days (for selected surgical procedures)	Safety	Getting better
JCAHO	SG—timing of prophylactic administration of antibiotic	Timeliness	Getting better
Pamela Mitchell (American Academy of Nursing)	Patient fall injury rate	Safety	Getting better
Pamela Mitchell	Nosocomial infection (category of adverse events) (includes pneumonia and urinary tract infection in surgical patients; decubiti in all patients)	Safety	Getting better
National Committee for Quality Assurance (NCQA)—HEDIS	Effectiveness of care (16 measures)	Effectiveness	All

Submitted by:	Name of Measure	Component of Health Care Quality	Consumer Perspective on Health Care Needs
NCQA—HEDIS	Access or availability of care (5 measures)	Timeliness	All
NCQA—HEDIS	Satisfaction with experience of care (2 sets of measures—HEDIS/CAHPS 2.0H)	Patient centeredness	Several
NCQA—HEDIS	Health plan stability (2 measures)	Safety	Several
NCQA—HEDIS	Use of services (17 measures)	Not specified	Several
NCQA—HEDIS	Informed health care choices (1 measure)	Patient centeredness	Staying healthy
NCQA– HEDIS	Health plan descriptive information (8 measures)	NA	NA
Barbara Starfield	Primary Care Assessment Tool (child edition, adult edition, provider edition)	Effectiveness, patient centeredness	Staying healthy, getting better, coping with the end of life
U.S. Pharmacopoeia	Patient safety and medication error reporting system (standardized Medication Error Index)	Safety	Getting Better

NOTES: ACEI = angiotensin-converting enzyme inhibitor; AMI = Acute Myocardial Infarction Core Performance Measurement Set; CAHPS = Consumer Assessment of Health Plans Survey; HEDIS = Health Plan Employer Data and Information Set; HF = Heart Failure Core Performance Measurement Set; ICU = intensive care unit; LVEF = left ventricular ejection fraction; PN = Community-Acquired Pneumonia Core Performance Measurement Set; PR = Pregnancy and Related Conditions Core Performance Measurement Set; SG = Surgical Procedures and Complications Core Performance Measurement Set; VBAC = vaginal birth after cesarean section.

APPENDIX D
Selected Approaches to Thinking About Quality and the National Health Care Quality Report

The committee reviewed many of the approaches available to assess quality of health care and health care systems including those outlined in this appendix. Elements of these are part of the framework proposed by the committee in this report. The National Health Care Quality Framework rests on the Foundation for Accountability (FACCT) consumer reporting framework (Foundation for Accountability, 1997) and the health care system aims for quality improvement defined by the Institute of Medicine (Institute of Medicine, 2001). The framework builds on other efforts as well. The Institute of Medicine National Roundtable on Health Care Quality proposed a classification system for the different types of quality problems that exist in health care as problems of overuse, underuse, and misuse (Chassin and Galvin, 1998). To a large extent, these overlap with the quality components of effectiveness and safety in the National Health Care Quality Framework.

In their framework, Evans and Stoddart (1990) emphasize that the health care system is only one of several determinants of a person's health. Aspects such as how and where a person grew up, and his or her family, community, environment, and physical makeup can all influence health. Examining the context of health care goes beyond the scope of the National Health Care Quality Report (also referred to as the Quality Report), but the committee recognizes that health care does not operate in a vacuum and interested researchers can examine the data presented in the Quality Report in relation to frameworks of the determinants of health such as this.

The committee acknowledges the usefulness of Donabedian's (1966, 1980) classification of structure, process, and outcomes of care and considers his characterization of quality as an additional way of thinking about the types of measures that should be included in the Quality Report. The role of these three types of measures is discussed in Chapter 3.

The overall purpose of the system proposed by the President's Advisory Commission on Consumer Protection and Quality in the Health Care Industry was adopted by the committee for the National Health Care Quality Framework. The aims proposed by the commission are largely subsumed by the ones in the framework proposed by the committee (Advisory Commission on Consumer Protection and Quality in the Health Care Industry, 1998).

As discussed, many of *Healthy People 2010*'s focus areas are included in the National Health Care Quality Framework as suggested conditions for which to examine quality of care (U.S. Department of Health and Human Services, 2000).

Although the Health Plan Employer Data and Information Set (HEDIS) 2001 was developed to measure health plan performance rather than to track the quality of health care at the national level, specific HEDIS measures were considered as examples for the National Health Care Quality Data Set (National Committee for Quality Assurance, 2000). Some of the categories of measures, such as effectiveness, included in HEDIS 2001 overlap with the components of health care quality contemplated in the National Health Care Quality Framework.

Finally, as discussed in Chapter 1, the committee considered various international efforts in designing the framework. Several of the measure categories in the United Kingdom's National Health Service (NHS) Performance Assessment Framework are similar to those in the National Health Care Quality Framework. For example, "patient experience of the NHS" overlaps with the quality component of "patient centeredness," as does "effective delivery of appropriate health care" with "effectiveness" (Department of Health, 1999a, b, 2000).

A short description of each of the approaches examined by the committee follows. This description includes the definition of quality used (if applicable), a summary of the model or elements of the approach, including units of analyses, the intended audience, the main categories of measures, examples of measures, and brief comments on the nature of the framework or approach, including possible gaps, and the pros and cons when considering it for the National Health Care Quality Report.

CROSSING THE QUALITY CHASM: A NEW HEALTH SYSTEM FOR THE 21ST CENTURY

Description

- *Author:* Institute of Medicine (IOM), 2001.
- *Definition of Quality:* Adopted the IOM definition of quality as "the degree to which health services for individuals and populations increase the likelihood of desired health outcomes and are consistent with current professional knowledge." (Institute of Medicine, 1990:21)
- *Unit of Analysis:* Health care organizations and the system as a whole.
- *Audiences:* Policy makers, general public, patients, providers, administrators.

Categories

The aims for health care improvement are as follows:

- *Safety:* Avoiding injuries to patients from care that is intended to help them.
- *Effectiveness:* Providing services based on scientific knowledge to all who could benefit, and refraining from providing services to those not likely to benefit (avoiding overuse and underuse).
- *Patient centeredness:* Providing care that is respectful of and responsive to individual patient preferences, needs, and values and ensuring that patient values guide all clinical decisions.
- *Timeliness:* Reducing waits and sometimes harmful delays for both those who receive and those who give care.
- *Efficiency:* Avoiding waste, in particular waste of equipment, supplies, ideas, and energy.
- *Equity:* Providing care that does not vary in quality because of personal characteristics such as gender, ethnicity, geographic location, and socioeconomic status.

Comments

- *General:* This framework is grounded in the assumption that the health care system is in need of major restructuring. Specifying the aims that capture the desirable characteristics of a delivery system provides a common direction for the country's efforts to improve quality.

SOURCE: Institute of Medicine, 2001.

FACCT CONSUMER INFORMATION FRAMEWORK

Description

- FACCT's philosophy is that measures should reflect the needs and values of the consumer. The framework is a comprehensive approach to communicating health care quality information to consumers. It was originally defined for the Medicare program and tested with a broad section of consumers.
- *Author:* Foundation for Accountability, 1997.
- *Definition of Quality:* None specified.
- *Model:* The framework organizes comparative information about quality performance into five reporting categories based on how consumers think about their care. Emphasis is on consumer-relevant measures that are outcome- and patient-focused. FACCT has designed a multistep process to create composite scores for the measures. Measures come from a variety of sources including HEDIS, FACCT measurement sets, CAHPS (Consumer Assessment of Health Plans Survey), and public health databases. Performance is measured with respect to the population as a whole and for specific health conditions.
- *Audiences:* Consumers and purchasers.
- *Unit of Analysis:* Varies, includes health plans.

Categories and Measures

The Basics (getting the basics of access, communication, and service from provider and plan; data source is CAHPS):

- Doctor communication (e.g., provider who listens carefully and explains things clearly)
- Doctor access and service (e.g., can get an appointment quickly for routine care)
- Plan rules for getting care (e.g., have an easy time getting referrals to specialists)
- Plan information and service (e.g., receive clear information from plan)

Staying Healthy (help to avoid illness and stay healthy; data source is HEDIS):

- Screening for problems
- Immunizations
- Checkups
- Help for healthier living (e.g., proportion of patients who smoke who report being advised to quit smoking)

Getting Better (help to recover when sick or injured; data source is FACCT condition-specific patient surveys):

- Appropriate treatment and follow-up
- Experience and satisfaction with treatment
- Recovery and functioning

Living with Illness (help with ongoing, chronic conditions; data source is FACCT condition-specific patient surveys):

- Appropriate care
- Experience and satisfaction with care (e.g., score on provider communication or skill scale from FACCT asthma patient survey)
- Education and teamwork
- Day-to-day living (e.g., can maintain daily activities)

Changing Needs (caring for people and their families when needs change dramatically because of disability or terminal illness):

- Care for disabilities
- Caregiver support
- End-of-life care

Comments

- *General:* FACCT has designed a patient survey FACCT|ONE that addresses quality of care for people living with illness—specifically, asthma, diabetes, and coronary artery disease. It has also defined specific quality measurement sets for adult asthma, alcohol misuse, breast cancer, diabetes, major depressive disorder, health status, health risks, and consumer satisfaction. (Note: Lists of measures for each of these aspects are available, but measures are generally classified into "steps to good care," "experience and satisfaction," and/or "results," rather than the five categories listed above.)
- *Gaps:* FACCT has organized several groups to develop quality measures in gap areas such as children and adolescents, end of life, and HIV/AIDS. The availability of measures for each of the five categories of the framework varies.
- *Pros and Cons:* The purpose of the framework is to report information on quality to consumers, but it can also be used to define areas of measurement. Categories do not address a particular entity or provider, but rather the essential aspects of health care from a consumer viewpoint, so the framework can be used to measure the results of care regardless of the delivery system. The framework can be used to present information on quality measures from other sources and to present condition-specific quality data. The fact that it was de-

signed based on consumer research makes it particularly well suited for a report to the public.

SOURCES: Foundation for Accountability, 1997, 1999.

THREE-WAY CLASSIFICATION OF QUALITY PROBLEMS

Description

- *Author:* Mark R. Chassin, 1991.
- *Definition of Quality:* Chassin cites the IOM definition of quality of care—"the degree to which health services for individuals and populations increase the likelihood of desired health outcomes and are consistent with current professional knowledge" (Institute of Medicine, 1990:21).
- *Model:* This is a classification system for quality problems, rather than a model.
- *Unit of Analysis:* Not specified.
- *Audiences:* Researchers, policy makers.

Classification Categories

- *Underuse* is defined as "failure to provide an effective health care service when it would have produced favorable outcomes" (e.g., missed childhood immunizations, proportion of patients with depression not detected early) (Chassin, 1991:3472).
- *Overuse* is defined as "providing a health service when its risk of harm exceeds its potential benefit" (e.g., prescribing antibiotic for a cold, rate of inappropriate hysterectomies) (Chassin, 1991:3472).
- *Misuse* is defined as "avoidable complications of appropriate health care" (e.g., avoidable complications of surgery, patient injuries resulting from medication errors) (Chassin 1991:3472).

Comments

- *General:* Other important issues related to quality such as variations in care, physician training, and composition of the work force are seen as causal or explanatory factors related to specific problems of underuse, overuse, and misuse. For this reason, the system of quality problems is viewed as comprehensive.
- *Gaps, Pros and Cons:* This approach should be combined with a method for defining priorities among quality problems in terms of misuse, overuse, and underuse. If one can truly divide all quality problems into these three categories, the classification provides a clear and concise way to define quality

measures. It is not clear whether this classification and corresponding measures will provide enough feedback information to define policy and improve care based on the indicators. Also, it may place less importance on quality problems that do not fit directly into this classification system but should be considered as important measures for other reasons.

SOURCES: Chassin, 1991; Chassin and Galvin, 1998.

FIELD MODEL OF THE DETERMINANTS OF HEALTH

Description

- *Authors:* R.G. Evans and G. L. Stoddart, 1990.
- *Definition of Quality:* None specified since this is not the purpose of the model.
- *Model:* This model builds on Blum's (1981) and Lalonde's (1974) earlier health field framework that considered four determinants of health: environment, heredity, life-style, and health care services. The focus of the model is not on quality but on the determinants of health defined as social environment, physical environment, genetic endowment, health care, and individual biological and behavioral responses. Outcomes included in the model distinguish disease (as defined and treated by the health care system), health and functioning (as perceived by individuals), well-being, and prosperity. Health care is not considered the most important determinant of health and is most closely linked to illness. The conceptual model in Figure D.1 shows the elements in the model and the causal pathways among them.
- *Unit of Analysis:* The health care system and social determinants of health.
- *Audiences:* Policy makers, researchers.

Categories and Measures

The elements or categories in the model are shown in Figure D.1. This is not a model for quality assessment, so measures are not contemplated by the authors.

Comments

- *General:* The framework has broad appeal. In addition to being used in Canada (at the provincial and national levels), this model has reportedly been adopted by the U.S. Department of Health and Human Services for *Healthy People 2010*. It has also been used in the work of several Institute of Medicine committees (1997, 1999).

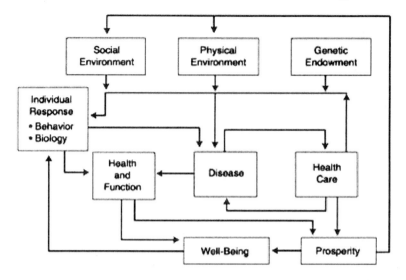

FIGURE D.1 Model of the determinants of health. SOURCE: Evans and Stoddart, 1990. Reprinted with permission from Elsevier Science.

- *Gaps, Pros and Cons:* The framework does not focus on quality so it would have to be combined with others. It is useful for examining the health care system within a broader context. If the goal of the health care system and of providing care is to improve health, this model can point to other factors that may influence health and should therefore be considered.

SOURCES: Evans and Stoddart, 1990; Institute of Medicine, 1997, 1999.

QUALITY ASSESSMENT TRIAD OF
STRUCTURE, PROCESS, AND OUTCOME

Description

- *Author:* Avedis Donabedian, first proposed in the 1960s.
- *Definition of Quality:* Quality is seen as a property of the medical care process and is defined as "the expected ability [of care] to achieve the highest possible net benefit according to valuations of individuals and society" (Donabedian, 1980:22). At the individual level, the process of medical care consists of technical and interpersonal aspects and is influenced by the amenities of the setting of care.
- *Model:* Donabedian's classic characterization of the approach to quality assessment includes elements of the structure of the health care delivery system, the process of care, and the outcomes of care. Structure refers to the resources

available, including characteristics of the providers and settings of care. Process refers to provider performance and includes normative behavior. Outcomes refer to any change in a patient's current and future health status that can be attributed to antecedent health care, including patient satisfaction. These three elements are causally linked so that structure affects the probability of good performance or the process of care, which in turn can affect outcomes such as health status and quality of life:

$$\text{Structure} \rightarrow \text{Process} \rightarrow \text{Outcome}$$

- *Unit of Analysis:* It may vary. It can focus on different levels of aggregation of the providers and recipients of care. In the case of the Quality Report, it could focus on the overall health care system as the provider and the general population as the recipient.
- *Audiences:* Health services researchers, providers interested in quality assurance.

Categories and Measures

The following list is a selection of the most relevant categories and measures for the Quality Report and is adapted from a schematic classification proposed by Donabedian in 1968 (Donabedian, 1980:Appendix B). Possible examples of measures not proposed by Donabedian but within his schema are in brackets rather than parentheses.

Characteristics of the Settings of Care (structure)

- Presence or absence of certain facilities or equipment related to specific care functions [e.g., proportion of hospitals with computerized adverse drug event systems]
- Accreditation [e.g., proportion of health plans accredited by the National Committee for Quality Assurance (NCQA); proportion with public reporting of quality data]
- Qualifications of health care professionals [e.g., proportion of board-certified specialist physicians; type and specialty of primary care provider]
- Geographic accessibility [e.g., average distance to hospital]

Characteristics of Provider Behavior in Management of Health and Illness (screening, diagnosis, treatment, referral, coordination, continuity) and Other Aspects (process)

- Frequency of recommended screening tests for a specific population
- Validation of diagnosis (e.g., comparison of admission and discharge diagnoses)

- Preventive management and supervision of certain diseases [e.g., proportion of diabetics who had an eye exam]
- Patterns of use of drugs, blood, and biologicals (e.g., total prescribed drug utilization per capita and per 1,000 physician visits)
- Surgical rates by type of procedures more open to abuse (e.g., hysterectomy)
- Patterns of multiple operations
- Number of providers involved in care of a single patient over a period of time or episode

Other Provider Behaviors Possibly Indicative of Strength or Weakness in the Organization of Care (structure)

- Staff turnover [e.g., turnover of primary care providers in health plans]

Client Behaviors Indicative of Defects in the Organization of Care or Relationship with Provider (process or outcome)

- Discharge against advice

Characteristics of Use of Service (process or outcome)

- Volume of care (e.g., utilization by certain population characteristics)
- Use by place of care (e.g., hospital, nursing home, home)

Characteristics of Health and Other Outcomes (outcome)

- General mortality, morbidity, and disability rates (check for trends, geographic variations)
- Mortality in special subgroups (e.g., infants, maternal, by race)
- Average number of days lost from work or school due to disability
- Case fatality rates and operative mortality rates by type of illness or operation
- Readmission rates of patients previously hospitalized due to mental illness
- Patient satisfaction

Comments

- *General:* Donabedian discusses several definitions of quality including an "absolutist" one that focuses on technical aspects, an "individualized" one that takes into account patient valuations of care, and a "social" one that takes into account the distribution of benefits. This last one would be useful in examining disparities. The author advocates the simultaneous use of process and outcome measures. Outcomes can be used as more inclusive, integrative measures of the total quality of care for a particular individual. Process measures allow for any needed corrective actions. Each can serve as a validity check on the other. Structural measures can supplement process and outcome measures and can be used to assess the capacity of the system to provide high-quality care. Aspects such as access to care, continuity, and coordination of care are attributes of care that can influence quality, yet are considered separate from it. They may or may not be used as quality measures. Client satisfaction is a consequence of care that can be used as a quality measure.

- *Gaps:* This framework focuses more on medical care than on health care, in general. It seems better suited for evaluating individual organizations or providers than the overall system; however, Donabedian stated it could be used for both.
- *Pros and Cons:* This is a very flexible framework that can be used with different conceptualizations of quality at different levels of aggregation. However, it does not contemplate the determinants of health beyond medical care, so the measures proposed tend to concentrate on the medical care process. It is based on a linear conception of the health care system that simplifies its use but may make interpretation of results more difficult. It is a well-known framework, used and built on by many others. For example, one of the proposals is to classify process measures into those that focus on technical aspects of care and those that focus on interpersonal aspects of quality (see, for example, McGlynn, 1996).

SOURCES: Donabedian, 1966, 1980.

PRESIDENT'S ADVISORY COMMISSION ON CONSUMER PROTECTION AND QUALITY IN THE HEALTH CARE INDUSTRY

Description

- *Author:* President's Advisory Commission on Consumer Protection and Quality in the Health Care Industry, 1998.
- *Definition of Quality:* Adopted the IOM definition of quality of care as "the degree to which health services for individuals and populations increase the likelihood of desired health outcomes and are consistent with current professional knowledge" (Institute of Medicine, 1990:21).
- *Model:* The commission did not have a model but declared that "the purpose of the health care system must be to continuously reduce the impact and burden of illness, injury and disability, and to improve the health and functioning of the people of the United States" (Advisory Commission on Consumer Protection and Quality in the Health Care Industry, 1998:2). The commission defined a set of national aims for improvement (see below).
- *Unit of Analysis:* National health care industry as a whole and individual sectors.
- *Audiences:* Several, but mainly policy makers.

Categories

There are six national aims for improvement of health care quality: (1) reducing underlying causes of illness, injury, and disability; (2) expanding research on new treatments and evidence of effectiveness; (3) ensuring the appropriate use of health care services; (4) reducing health care errors; (5) addressing oversupply and undersupply of health care resources; and (6) increasing patients' participation in their care.

Comments

- *General:* The authors point out that in defining objectives, policy makers must consider local needs as well as the needs of chronically ill, disabled, and vulnerable populations.
- *Gaps, Pros and Cons:* Objectives and measures corresponding to each aim must be defined in order to use this framework. Aims focus on clinical aspects of care but also recognize the need to consider service aspects such as access. They point out the need for developing measures of care for chronic conditions, disabilities, mental health, interpersonal aspects of care, functional outcomes, quality at the individual practitioner level, and summary measures of quality. The stated aims are useful in defining a framework for a national report because they have a national focus. The commission recommended the development of core sets of measures for each sector of the health care system, but one for the system as a whole is what is needed for the Quality Report.

SOURCE: Advisory Commission on Consumer Protection and Quality in the Health Care Industry, 1998.

HEALTHY PEOPLE 2010

Description

- *Author:* U. S. Department of Health and Human Services, 2000.
- *Definition of Quality:* Uses the IOM definition of quality as "the degree to which health services for individuals and populations increase the likelihood of desired health outcomes and are consistent with current professional knowledge" (Institute of Medicine, 1990:21).
- *Model:* The purpose of this framework, first developed in 1979, is to define a prevention agenda for the nation. *Healthy People 2010* has two overarching goals—"to increase quality and years of healthy life" and "to eliminate health disparities." These goals will be monitored through 467 objectives in 28 focus areas. *Healthy People 2010* also includes a reduced set of leading health indicators or focus areas reflecting major public health concerns. Improving ac-

cess to quality health services is one of them. Its objectives place an emphasis on areas where significant disparities in access to quality health services exist between the general population and vulnerable populations and where access to care is likely to affect years of healthy life. The framework of determinants of health draws from the Evans and Stoddart (1990) model. Policies and interventions can be used to improve health by targeting factors related to individuals and their environment, including access to quality health care.

- *Unit of Analysis:* The nation (can also apply to states and smaller geographic levels).
- *Audiences:* Policy makers in the health care arena and the general public.

Categories, Objectives, and Measures

Access to Quality Health Services. The goal of this focus area is to improve access to comprehensive, high-quality health care services. It includes four categories and specific objectives for each as listed below.

Clinical Preventive Services

- Persons with health insurance
- Health insurance coverage for preventive services (e.g., proportion of patients who have coverage for preventive services)
- Counseling about health behaviors (e.g., proportion of current smokers counseled about smoking at last visit)

Primary Care

- Source of ongoing primary care
- Usual primary care provider
- Difficulties or delays in obtaining needed health care (e.g., proportion in fair or poor health who report no visits in previous year)
- Core competencies in health provider training
- Racial and ethnic minority representation in the health professions
- Hospitalization for ambulatory care-sensitive conditions (e.g., reduce rate of pediatric asthma, pneumonia and influenza in elderly, and diabetes)

Emergency Services

- Delay or difficulty in getting emergency care
- Rapid pre-hospital emergency care (e.g., proportion who have access to rapidly responding emergency medical services [less than 9 minutes between call and arrival in urban areas])
- Single toll-free number for poison control center
- Trauma care systems

- Special needs of children

Long-Term Care and Rehabilitative Services

- Long-term care services
- Pressure ulcers among nursing home residents (e.g., reduce proportion of nursing home residents with pressure ulcers at stage 2 or greater)

Comments

- *General:* Criteria for the selection of *Healthy People 2010* leading indicators included the ability to motivate action by the public and others, the availability of data to measure progress, and relevance as a broad public health issue. The rationale for the focus of *Healthy People 2010* on access is that "adequate access to health care services can significantly influence patient use of the health care system and, ultimately, improve health outcomes. Consequently, measures of access to care provide an important mechanism for evaluating the quality of the Nation's health care system" (U.S. Department of Health and Human Services, 2000:1–4).
- *Gaps:* The authors recognize that there are gaps in this focus area (access to quality health services) regarding secondary and tertiary clinical care.
- *Pros and Cons:* Taking this framework into consideration in defining the Quality Report would facilitate the link with the *Healthy People 2010* objectives.

SOURCE: U.S. Department of Health and Human Services, 2000.

HEALTH PLAN EMPLOYER DATA AND INFORMATION SET

Description

- NCQA developed the Health Plan Employer Data and Information Set to assess health plan performance and continually revises it. HEDIS 2001 includes measures from CAHPS to assess member satisfaction with the quality of care provided by plans. Since 1996, NCQA has produced annual "Quality Compass" reports that include comparative HEDIS and accreditation data on health plans. Measures are reported yearly, except for a few that are reported only every two years.
- *Author:* National Committee for Quality Assurance, since 1996; latest version (HEDIS 2001) published in 2000.
- *Definition of Quality:* None specified.
- *Model:* HEDIS measures are selected through expert committees and draw on open calls for measures. The main criteria for the selection of measures are

relevance, scientific soundness, and feasibility. Measures fall into seven categories representing basic aspects of health plan performance thought to be important to purchasers and consumers. The first category, effectiveness of care, is the one most directly relevant to quality, although others may also contain useful measures depending on the selected conceptualization of quality of care.

- *Audiences:* Health plans and purchasers, including employers and consumers.
- *Unit of Analysis:* Health plans and the corresponding enrolled population.

Categories and Measures

Effectiveness of Care

- Childhood immunization status
- Adolescent immunization status
- Breast cancer screening
- Cervical cancer screening
- Chlamydia screening in women
- Controlling high blood pressure
- Beta-blocker treatment after a heart attack
- Cholesterol management after acute cardiovascular events
- Comprehensive diabetes care
- Use of appropriate medications for people with asthma
- Follow-up after hospitalization for mental illness
- Antidepressant medication management
- Advising smokers to quit
- Flu shots for older adults
- Pneumonia vaccination status in older adults
- Medicare Health Outcomes Survey

Access to or Availability of Care

- Adults' access to preventive or ambulatory health services
- Children's access to primary care practitioners
- Prenatal and postpartum care
- Annual dental visit
- Availability of language interpretation services

Satisfaction with the Experience of Care

- HEDIS/CAHPS 2.0H, Adult
- HEDIS/CAHPS 2.0H, Child

Health Plan Stability

- Practitioner turnover
- Years in business or total membership

Use of Services

- Frequency of ongoing prenatal care
- Well-child visits in the first 15 months of life
- Well-child visits in the third, fourth, fifth, and sixth years of life
- Adolescent well-care visits
- Frequency of selected procedures
- Inpatient utilization—general hospital or acute care
- Ambulatory care
- Inpatient utilization—non-acute care
- Discharge and average length of stay—maternity care
- Cesarean section rate
- Vaginal birth after cesarean rate
- Births and average length of stay, newborns
- Mental health utilization—inpatient discharges and average length of stay
- Mental health utilization—percentage of members receiving services
- Chemical dependency utilization—inpatient discharges and average length of stay
- Chemical dependency utilization—percentage of members receiving services
- Outpatient drug utilization

Informed Health Care Choices

- Management of menopause

Health Plan Descriptive Information

- Board certification or residency completion
- Practitioner compensation
- Arrangements with public health, educational, and social service organizations
- Total enrollment by percentage
- Enrollment by product line (member-years or member-months)
- Unduplicated count of Medicaid members
- Diversity of Medicaid membership
- Weeks of pregnancy at time of enrollment in managed care organization

Comments

- *Gaps:* HEDIS measures have evolved over time. The original clinical focus on preventive care has broadened, and the latest set includes some measures on the quality of chronic care. HEDIS contains measures for different age groups, including the elderly.

- *Pros and Cons:* HEDIS measures have gone through a rigorous selection process and are being used by many health plans. However, the focus is on the accountability of health plans, rather than on tracking health care quality at a national level. There is incomplete reporting of measures and health plans resulting in lack of representativeness at the national level. There is no explicit rationale for the categories of measures that were defined. However, measures within each category can be used in other frameworks and the HEDIS measure set is widely known and accepted. Vermont, for example, produces an annual health care quality report based on its own categories of quality but using HEDIS measures for the data (Vermont Program for Quality in Health Care, 2000).

SOURCE: National Committee for Quality Assurance, 2000.

NATIONAL HEALTH SERVICE (NHS) PERFORMANCE INDICATORS AND PERFORMANCE ASSESSMENT FRAMEWORK

Description

- *Author:* NHS Executive, United Kingdom, since 1998.
- *Definition of Quality:* Not explicit in source document.
- *Model:* The performance framework is based on a three-pronged strategy to improve quality: setting standards nationally, delivering standards locally, and monitoring standards externally. The six areas of the framework are interdependent. As stated, "From an initial view of the health of the communities (health improvement), they need to ensure that everyone with needs (fair access) receives effective care (effective delivery), offering good value (efficiency) and convenient, sensitive care (user/carer experience) so as to obtain good health outcomes (health outcomes of NHS care) and maximize the contribution to improved health (back to health improvement)" (Department of Health, 1999a:8). The framework is supported by 49 indicators (Department of Health, 2000). NHS states that the indicators are not direct measures of quality but can serve to draw attention to specific related issues.
- *Unit of Analysis:* Nation, NHS Trusts, NHS Health Authorities.
- *Audience:* Policy makers in health care arena and the general public.

Categories and Measures

Health Improvement

- Deaths from all causes (ages 15–64)
- Deaths from all causes (ages 65–74)

- Deaths from cancer
- Deaths from all circulatory diseases
- Suicide rates
- Deaths from accidents
- Serious injury from accidents

Fair Access

- Inpatient waiting list
- Adult dental registrations
- Early detection of cancer
- Cancer waiting times
- Number of general practitioners
- Practice availability
- Elective surgery rates
- Surgery rates—coronary heart disease

Effective Delivery of Appropriate Health Care

- Childhood immunizations
- Inappropriately used surgery
- Acute care management
- Chronic care management
- Mental health in primary care
- Cost-effective prescribing
- Returning home following treatment from a stroke
- Returning home following treatment for a fractured hip

Efficiency

- Day case rate
- Length of stay
- Unit cost of maternity unit
- Unit cost of caring for patients in receipt of specialist mental health services
- Percentage of generic prescribing

Patient/Carer Experience in the NHS

- Patients who wait less than 2 hours for emergency admissions
- Patients with operations canceled for nonmedical reasons on the day of or after admission
- Delayed discharge from hospital for people age 75 or over
- Percentage of first outpatient appointments that patient did not attend
- Percentage of outpatients seen within 13 weeks of general practitioner referral

- Percentage of those on waiting list waiting 18 months or more

Health Outcomes of NHS Care

- Conceptions below age 18
- Decayed, missing, and or filled teeth in 5-year-olds, average number
- Readmission to hospital following discharge
- Emergency admissions to hospital for people aged 75 or over
- Emergency psychiatric readmissions rates
- Stillbirths and infant mortality
- Breast cancer survival
- Cervical cancer survival
- Lung cancer survival
- Colon cancer survival
- Deaths in hospital following surgery (emergency admissions)
- Deaths in hospital following surgery (non-emergency admissions)
- Deaths in hospital following a heart attack (ages 35–74)
- Deaths in hospital following a fractured hip

Additional Comments

- *General:* At the international level, England (Department of Health, 2000) and Australia (National Health Performance Committee, 2000) are two of the countries that have defined national strategies for evaluating the quality of health care. The information is reported at the national level as well as at the level of NHS Trusts (regional) and Health Authorities (local).
- *Gaps:* There is an attempt to cover ambulatory and hospital care. The framework includes indicators of structure, process, and outcomes of care.
- *Pros and Cons:* The objective of this framework is similar to the one for the U.S. National Health Care Quality Report since the purpose is to assess the quality of care delivery at the national level. This framework includes fair access necessary for reducing health disparities and one of the two overarching goals of *Healthy People 2010* (U.S. Department of Health and Human Services, 2000). The data collection and reporting system used is facilitated by the fact that England has a national health system and a uniform, centralized health information system.

SOURCE: Department of Health, 1999a, 1999b, 2000.

SELECTION OF QUALITY-OF-CARE MEASURES BASED ON BURDEN OF DISEASE AND EXPECTED IMPACT

Description

- *Authors:* Albert Siu, Elizabeth A. McGlynn, Hal Morgenstern et al. (1992) based on earlier work by Brook et al. (1977) and by Williamson (1978) and Williamson et al. (1968).
- *Definition of Quality:* "Difference between efficacy and effectiveness that can be attributed to care providers" (Brook and Lohr, 1985:711).
- *Model:* Instead of a model, the framework includes a process for the definition of conditions of interest in quality measurement. First, identify the major causes of mortality and morbidity in the United States by age and gender, add others thought to be important by experts but not on list due to problems of underreporting, and other reasons. Second, conduct a literature review of the availability and efficacy of medical care interventions (primary, secondary, or tertiary prevention) or health-related behavior changes that can reduce disease burden. Third, estimate expected reductions in deaths, bed-days, or other adverse outcomes for each disease or outcome of interest following the intervention in a particular population. Other considerations are the cost-effectiveness of the intervention, whether providers of interest can influence improvements in care considered, and the availability and feasibility of collecting quality-of-care information.
- *Unit of Analysis:* The authors apply the framework to health plans, but the initial selection is based on national estimates of expected impact on morbidity and mortality so it can be used at this level. The focus is on health problems exhibited by a population of interest.
- *Audiences:* Policy makers, mainly in health care arena.

Categories and Measures

The major causes of mortality and morbidity for the United States included in this framework are infant mortality and related conditions, otitis media, asthma, accidents and injuries, suicide, acute respiratory conditions, breast cancer, back conditions, coronary artery disease, arthritis, chronic bronchitis and emphysema, colorectal cancer, lung cancer, stroke and cerebrovascular disease, diabetes, and pneumonia. Additional conditions that do not necessarily meet all criteria but were considered a priority by experts include vaccine-preventable childhood infectious diseases, mental health problems, sexually transmitted diseases, dementia and incontinence, osteoporosis and hip fractures, and sensory impairments.

Examples of Measures for Target Conditions

- Prevention of low birth weight: process measures to focus on timeliness, frequency, and content of prenatal care.
- Childhood infectious disease: vaccine rates for diptheria–pertussis–tetanus by age 2.
- Treatment of otitis media: process measures regarding. use of antibiotics for treatment, etc.
- Treatment of diabetes mellitus: process and intermediate outcome measures to focus on access, glucose monitoring, eye screening, etc.
- Overuse of surgical procedures and prevention of complications: proportion of cardiac catheterizations, cholecystectomies, hysterectomies performed for indications rated appropriate; complication rates adjusted for age, sex, and comorbidities.

Comments

- *General*: A recent article by Woolf (1999) presents evidence of the effectiveness of various interventions and expected benefit that could be combined with this approach.
- *Gaps*: This framework does not take into account public valuations or utilities. It does not include structural measures. The framework tends to be biased toward clinical conditions rather than positive health, but the user has the discretion to alter the original list of problems selected for action using expert judgment.
- *Pros and Cons*: This framework is specifically designed from a public policy perspective. It can be combined with other frameworks, such as Chassin (1991), to examine quality-of-care problems of overuse, misuse, and underuse. Different methods for assessing the burden of disease can be used, such as the newer disability-adjusted life-years proposed by the World Bank (1993). It is also possible to do sensitivity analysis of the effect of changes in the assumptions on the target conditions selected for quality measurement. The conditions selected and the estimates will have to be revised as new information and therapies become available. The initial selection criteria are explicit and replicable, but others used to modify the original list are not as clear.

SOURCE: Siu et al., 1992.

REFERENCES

Advisory Commission on Consumer Protection and Quality in the Health Care Industry. 1998. *Quality First: Better Health Care for All Americans*. Washington, D.C.: U.S. Government Printing Office.

Blum, H. 1981. *Planning for Health: Generics for the Eighties.* 2nd ed. New York: Human Sciences Press.

Brook, Robert H., Allyson Davies-Avery, Sheldon Greenfield, L. J. Harris, T. Lelah, N. E. Solomon, and John E. Ware, Jr. 1977. Assessing the quality of medical care using outcome measures: An overview of the method. *Medical Care* 15(Supplement):1–84.

Brook, Robert H., and Kathleen Lohr. 1985. Efficacy, effectiveness, variations, and quality—Boundary-crossing research. *Medical Care* 23(5):710–722.

Chassin, Mark R. 1991. Quality of care: Time to act. *Journal of the American Medical Association* 266(24) 3472–3473.

Chassin, Mark R., and Robert W. Galvin. 1998. The urgent need to improve health care quality: Institute of Medicine National Roundtable on Health Care Quality. *Journal of the American Medical Association* 280(11):1000–1005.

Department of Health. 1999a. *The NHS Performance Assessment Framework.* London: NHS Executive. Available at: http://www.doh.gov.uk/nhsexec/nhspaf.htm.

Department of Health. 1999b. *Quality and Performance in the NHS: High Level Performance Indicators.* London: NHS Executive. Available at: http://www.doh.gov.uk/nhshlpi.htm.

Department of Health. 2000. *NHS Performance Indicators.* Leeds, England: NHS Executive. Available at: http://www.doh.gov.uk/nhsperformanceindicators.

Donabedian, Avedis. 1966. Evaluating the quality of medical care. *Milbank Memorial Fund Quarterly* 44:166–203.

Donabedian, Avedis. 1980. *Explorations in Quality Assessment and Monitoring,* Vol. 1. Ann Arbor, Mich.: Health Administration Press.

Evans, R. G., and G. L. Stoddart. 1990. Producing health, consuming health care. *Social Science and Medicine* 31(12):1347–1363.

Foundation for Accountability. 1997. *Reporting Quality Information to Consumers.* Portland, Ore.: FACCT.

Foundation for Accountability. 1999. *Sharing the Quality Message with Consumers.* Portland, Ore.: FACCT.

Institute of Medicine. 1990. *Medicare: A Strategy for Quality Assurance,* Vol. 2. ed. Kathleen Lohr. Washington, D.C.: National Academy Press.

Institute of Medicine. 1997. *Improving Health in the Community: A Role for Performance Monitoring.* eds. Jane S. Durch, Linda A Bailey, and Michael A. Stoto. Washington, D.C.: National Academy Press. Pp. 126–65; 360–373.

Institute of Medicine. 1999. *Leading Health Indicators for Healthy People 2010.* eds. Carole A. Chrvala and Roger J. Bulger. Washington, D.C.: National Academy Press.

Institute of Medicine. 2001. *Crossing the Quality Chasm: A New Health System for the 21st Century.* Washington, D.C.: National Academy Press.

Lalonde, Marc. 1974. *A New Perspective on the Health of Canadians.* Ottawa: Health and Welfare, Canada.

McGlynn, Elizabeth A. 1996. Developing a quality measurement strategy. *QMAS conference—Measuring health care for value-based purchasing. Quality Measurement Advisory Service.* Available at: http://www.qmas.org.

National Committee for Quality Assurance. 2001. *HEDIS 2001,* Vol. 1. Washington, D.C.: NCQA.

National Health Performance Committee. 2000. *Fourth National Report on Health Sector Performance Indicators—A Report to the Australian Health Ministers' Conference*, Sydney, Australia: NSW Health Department.

Siu, Albert L., Elizabeth A. McGlynn, Hal Morgenstern, Mark H. Beers, David M. Carlisle, Emmett B. Keeler, Jerome Beloff, Kathleen Curtin, Jennifer Leaning, Bruce C. Perry, Harry P. Selker, Andrew Weisenthal, and Robert H. Brook. 1992. Choosing quality of care measures based on the expected impact of improved care on health. *Health Services Research* 27(5):619–650.

U.S. Department of Health and Human Services. 2000. *Healthy People 2010.* Washington, D.C.: U.S. Government Printing Office.

Vermont Program for Quality in Health Care. 2000. *The Vermont Health Care Quality Report* [on-line]. Available at: http://www.vpqhc.org.

Williamson, J. W. 1978. Formulating priorities for quality assurance activity. Description of a method and its application. *Journal of the American Medical Association* 239(7):631–637.

Williamson, J. W., M. Alexander, and G. E. Miller. 1968. Priorities in patient care research and continuing medical education. *Journal of the American Medical Association* 204(4):303–308.

Woolf, Steven H. 1999. The need for perspective in evidence-based medicine. *Journal of the American Medical Association* 282(24):2358–2365.

World Bank. 1993. *World Development Report 1993: Investing in Health.* Oxford, England: Oxford University Press.

APPENDIX E

Quality Measure Selection Criteria

This appendix includes summaries of the criteria used in or proposed by the U.S. Department of Health and Human Services working group on the National Health Care Quality Report; Donabedian's quality assessment triad of structure, process, and outcomes; the Foundation for Accountability's Child and Adolescent Health Measurement Initiative; National Committee for Quality Assurance; President's Advisory Commission on Consumer Protection and Quality in the Health Care Industry; *Healthy People 2010;* and *Measuring Health Performance in the Public Sector*, National Research Council. Many of the selection criteria correspond to conceptual frameworks outlined in Appendix A. As discussed in Chapter 3, the most common criteria are relevance, meaningfulness or applicability, health importance or improvement, evidence-based, reliability or reproducibility, validity, and feasibility.

U.S. DEPARTMENT OF HEALTH AND HUMAN SERVICES WORKING GROUP ON THE NATIONAL HEALTH CARE QUALITY REPORT

The U.S. Department of Health and Human Services (DHHS) has proposed the following criteria based on the Health Employer Data and Information Set (HEDIS) list of desirable attributes for measures and the indicator selection criteria from *America's Children: Key National Indicators of Well-Being* (Federal Interagency Forum on Child and Family Statistics, 2000). (See individual summaries of each in this appendix.)

212

Essential Criterion. Measures must meet this criterion to be rated on the desirable criteria that are listed below.

1. *Objectively based on substantial research.* The specific activity or intervention addressed by the measure must have a body of research showing effectiveness. The submitting organization should briefly describe the findings and give several key references.

Desirable Criteria. Measures are rated ("high," "medium," or "low") based on the following criteria.

2. *Relevance.* The measure should address features of health care systems that are relevant to the target audience of policy makers, health professionals, and consumers.

• *Meaningfulness.* The measure should be meaningful to at least one of the audiences. Decision makers should be able to understand the clinical and economic significance of differences in how well systems perform on the measure. The meaningfulness of a measure is enhanced if benchmarks and targets are available.

• *Health importance.* The measure should capture as much of the health care system's activities relating to quality as possible. Factors to be considered in evaluating the health importance of a measure include the type of measure (e.g., outcome versus process), the prevalence of the medical conditions to which the measure applies, and the seriousness of the health outcomes affected.

• *Strategic importance.* The measure should encourage activities that deserve high priority in terms of using resources most efficiently to maximize the health of their members. In general, measures that are of high clinical importance, of high financial importance, and cost-effective will also have high priority.

• *Controllability.* There should be actions that health care systems can take to improve their performance on a measure. If the measure is an outcome measure, there should exist one or more processes that can be controlled by the system that have important effects on the outcome. If the measure is a process measure, the process should be substantially under the control of the system, and there should be a strong link between the process and desired outcomes. If the measure is a structural measure, the structural feature should be open to modification by the system, and there should be a strong link between the structure and desired outcomes. The measure's time period should capture the events that have impact on clinical outcomes and reflect the time horizon over which the health care system had control.

• *Timeliness.* The data must be sufficiently current to be relevant to the audience. Submitting organization must give time from event to available data.

3. *Scientific soundness*

• *Clinical evidence.* There should be evidence documenting the links between the interventions, clinical processes, and/or outcomes addressed by the measure.

• *Reproducibility.* The measure should produce the same results when repeated in the same population and setting.

• *Validity.* The measure should have face validity (i.e., it should make sense logically and clinically). It should correlate well with other measures of the same aspects of care (construct validity) and capture meaningful aspects of this care (content validity).

• *Accuracy.* The measure should accurately measure what is actually happening.

4. *Richness of data.* Data are available to report the measure by race or ethnicity, socioeconomic status, state, and/or other geographic region.

5. *National representativeness of data.* The classification scheme attempts to order existing data sources under consideration in terms of their capacity to produce national estimates as well as their relevance. A measure's data sources should be classified as either A, B, C, or D, with justification.

SOURCE: U.S. Department of Health and Human Services, 2000a.

DONABEDIAN'S QUALITY ASSESSMENT TRIAD OF STRUCTURE, PROCESS, AND OUTCOMES

1. *Inclusivity or definitional range*
   • Technical versus interpersonal care
   • Medical versus psychosocial need
   • Diagnostic, therapeutic, preventive, anticipatory, and rehabilitative care
   • Individual, familial, or social responsibility
   • Cost containment versus quality enhancement
   • Parsimoniousness
2. *Scientific validity*
   • Causal validity
   • Scientific currency
3. *Measurement reliability and validity*
   • Explicitness, specification, objectiveness of the criteria
   • Specification of the referent and matching with the criteria
   • Verification
     - Of the diagnosis
     - Of clinical data
4. *Relevance, pertinence*

- Differentiation, adaptation
- Uniformity, generality, transferability
5. *Practicability, feasibility, implementability*
  - Costliness of development, revision, and application
  - Timeliness, with regard to care
6. *Legitimacy, acceptability*
  - "Political" factors (e.g., sponsorship, representativeness, degree of participation, consensuality)
  - Other factors (e.g., inclusivity, causal validity, measurement validity, and practicability)
  - Justification

SOURCE: Donabedian, 1982:371.

FOUNDATION FOR ACCOUNTABILITY'S
CHILD AND ADOLESCENT HEALTH MEASUREMENT INITIATIVE

Following are the criteria and corresponding evidence of criteria for selecting domains and survey items for domains.

1. *Relevance.* Known importance to families and children demonstrated through family interviews and focus groups, family surveys, and consensus panel recommendations.

2. *Parsimoniousness.* Domains each provide distinct information; they may be related (e.g., correlated) but are conceptually distinct.

3. *Discrimination.* Direction and magnitude of differences in performance scores for children with and without a chronic condition.

4. *Reliability.* Internal consistency of a composite of items combined to create a content area or domain performance score.

5. *Feasibility.* Taken as a whole, the number of survey items required to construct a performance score for each domain is within the acceptable range for the National Committee on Quality Assurance's HEDIS measures.

6. *Applicability.* Survey domains and items will yield information valuable to purchasers and providers in addition to consumers.

SOURCE: Foundation for Accountability, 1999.

NATIONAL COMMITTEE FOR QUALITY ASSURANCE (NCQA)
HEALTH PLAN EMPLOYER DATA AND INFORMATION SET

Desirable attributes of HEDIS measures include the following:

1. *Relevance.* The measure should address features of health care systems that are relevant to purchasers and/or consumers for making choices between systems, that are useful in negotiating with systems, or that will stimulate internal efforts at quality improvement by systems.

- *Meaningfulness.* The measure should be meaningful to at least one of the audiences for HEDIS: individual consumers, purchasers, or health care systems. Decision makers should be able to understand the clinical and economic significance of differences in how well systems perform on the measure. The meaningfulness of a measure is enhanced if benchmarks and targets are available.
- *Health importance.* The measure should capture as much of the health care system's activities relating to quality as possible. Factors to be considered in evaluating the health importance of a measure include the type of measure (e.g., outcome versus process), the prevalence of the medical conditions to which the measure applies, and the seriousness of the health outcomes affected.
- *Financial importance.* The measure should be related to activities that have high financial costs to health care systems or to purchasers or consumers of health care.
- *Cost-effectiveness.* The measure should encourage the use of cost-effective activities and/or discourage the use of activities that have low cost-effectiveness.
- *Strategic importance.* The measure should encourage activities that deserve high priority in terms of using resources most efficiently to maximize the health of their members. In general, measures that are of high clinical importance, high financial importance, and cost-effective will also have high priority.
- *Controllability.* There should be actions that health care systems can take to improve their performance on a measure. If the measure is an outcome measure, there should exist one or more processes that can be controlled by the system that have important effects on the outcome. If the measure is a process measure, the process should be substantially under the control of the system, and there should be a strong link between the process and desired outcomes. If the measure is a structural measure, the structural feature should be open to modification by the system, and there should be a strong link between the structure and desired outcomes. The measure's time period should capture the events that have impact on clinical outcomes and reflect the time horizon over which the health care system had control.
- *Variance among systems.* If the primary purpose of the measure is to differentiate among health care systems, then there should be potentially wide variations across systems with respect to the measure.
- *Potential for improvement.* If the primary purpose of the measure is to support negotiations between health care systems and purchasers, or to stimulate self-improvement by health care systems, there should be substantial room for systems to improve their performance with respect to the measure.

2. *Scientific soundness*

- *Clinical evidence.* There should be evidence documenting the links between the interventions, clinical processes, and/or outcomes addressed by the measure.
- *Reproducibility.* The measure should produce the same results when repeated in the same population and setting.
- *Validity.* The measure should have face validity (i.e., it should make sense logically, clinically, and if it focuses on a financially important aspect of care, financially). It should correlate well with other measures of the same aspects of care (construct validity) and capture meaningful aspects of this care (content validity).
- *Accuracy.* The measure should accurately measure what is actually happening.
- *Case-mix adjustment or risk adjustment.* Either the measure should not be appreciably affected by any variables that are beyond the health care system's control ("covariates"), or any extraneous factors should be known and measurable. If case-mix and/or risk adjustment are required, there should be well-described methods either for controlling through risk stratification or for using validated models to calculate an adjusted result that corrects for the effects of covariates.
- *Comparability of data sources.* The accuracy, reproducibility, risk-adjustability, and validity of the measure should not be affected if different systems have to use different data sources for the measures.

3. *Feasibility*

- *Precise specification.* The measure should have clear operational definitions, specifications for data sources, and methods for data collection and reporting.
- *Reasonable cost.* The measure should not impose an inappropriate burden on health care systems. Either the measures should be inexpensive to produce, or the cost of data collection and reporting should be justified by improvements in outcomes that result from the act of measurement.
- *Confidentiality.* The collection of data for the measures should not violate any accepted standards of member confidentiality.
- *Logistical feasibilty.* The data required for the measure should be available to the health care system during the time allowed for data collection. The measure should not be susceptible to cultural or other barriers that might make data collection infeasible (e.g., inpatient or physician surveys, there may be cultural or personal barriers that lead to biased responses; these would have to be addressed).
- *Auditability.* The measure should be auditable (i.e., it should not be susceptible to manipulation or "gaming" that would be undetectable in an audit).

Methods to verify retrospectively that reported results accurately portray delivered care should be suggested.

SOURCE: National Committee for Quality Assurance, 2000:10–11.

PRESIDENT'S ADVISORY COMMISSION ON CONSUMER PROTECTION AND QUALITY IN THE HEALTH CARE INDUSTRY

Examples of criteria for evaluating *individual measures* include scientific soundness (i.e., reliable, valid, appropriately adjusted), importance of the quality concern, relevance to various users, potential to foster improvements in health status or well-being, evidence basis, interpretability, "actionability" (i.e., degree to which steps can be taken to address the concern), feasibility, and ease and cost-effectiveness of measurement.

Examples of criteria for evaluating *measurement sets* including addressing the full spectrum of health care, incorporating measures of multiple dimensions of quality (e.g., technical quality, accessibility, acceptability), including various types of measures (e.g., structure, process, outcome), representativeness, and measurement burden (i.e., concise, not redundant; measurement can be conducted with a minimal burden on providers and health care organizations).

SOURCE: Advisory Commission on Consumer Protection and Quality in the Health Care Industry, 1998:81.

U.S. DEPARTMENT OF HEALTH AND HUMAN SERVICES: *HEALTHY PEOPLE 2010*

Criteria for *Healthy People 2010* objectives follow.

• The result to be achieved should be important and understandable to a broad audience and relate to the two overarching *Healthy People 2010* goals.

• Objectives should be prevention-oriented and should address health improvements that can be achieved through population-based and health service interventions.

• Objectives should drive action and suggest a set of interim steps that will achieve the proposed targets within the specified time frame.

• Objectives should be useful and relevant. States, localities, and the private sector should be able to use the objectives to target efforts in schools, communities, work sites, health practices, and other settings.

• Objectives should be measurable and include a range of measures— health outcomes, behavioral and health service interventions, and community capacity—directed toward improving health outcomes and quality of life. They should count assets and achievements and look to the positive.

- Continuity and comparability are important. Whenever possible, objectives should build on *Healthy People 2000* and those goals and performance measures already established.
- Objectives must be supported by sound scientific evidence.

SOURCE: U.S. Department of Health and Human Services, 2000:2–4.

NATIONAL HEALTH SERVICE (NHS)
PERFORMANCE INDICATORS (UNITED KINGDOM)

Criteria for assessing individual indicators follow.

- *Attributable.* Indicators should reflect health and social outcomes that are substantially attributable to the NHS through its roles as service provider, advocate for health, and interagency partner.
- *Important.* Indicators should cover an outcome that is relevant and important to policy makers, health professionals, and managers (and resonates with the concerns of the public).
- *Avoids perverse incentives.* An indicator should be presented in such a way that managers can act upon it without introducing perverse incentives. There should be no incentive to shift problems onto other organizations. Where this is the case, a counterbalancing indicator should be considered alongside.
- *Robust.* Measurement of the indicator should be reliable, and coverage of the outcome measured should be high, although sampling may be appropriate for some indicators. In particular, data should be robust at the level at which performance monitoring is undertaken.
- *Responsive.* An indicator should be responsive to change, and change should be measurable. It should not be an indicator in which change will be so small that monitoring trends becomes difficult. Consideration should be given to whether the rate at which change can be expected to occur makes the indicator relevant for performance-monitoring purposes.
- *Usable and timely.* Data should be readily available within a reasonable time.

SOURCE: Department of Health, 1999: Appendix B.

LEADING HEALTH INDICATORS FOR
HEALTHY PEOPLE 2010

The initial charge to the Institute of Medicine committee from the U.S. Department of Health and Human Services was to recommend at least two potential indicator sets that would "(1) elicit interest and awareness among the general population, (2) motivate diverse population groups to engage in activities that will exert a positive impact on specific indicators and in turn, improve the overall health of the nation, and (3) provide ongoing feedback concerning progress toward improving the status of specific indicators." The committee was later directed that no more than 10 indicators should be included and that "any proposed indicator set should be supported by a conceptual framework around which the specific indicators could be organized." The committee had accepted 14 criteria for indicator development, but later decided on a set of 6 simple criteria that would be understandable to the general public.

Criteria for Individual Measures

• *Worth measuring.* The indicators represent an important and salient aspect of the public's health.
• *Can be measured for diverse populations.* The indicators are valid and reliable for the general population and diverse population groups.
• *Understood by people who need to act.* People who need to act on their own behalf or that of others should be able to readily comprehend the indicators and what can be done to improve the status of those indicators.
• *Information will galvanize action.* The indicators are of such a nature that action can be taken at the national, state, local, and community levels by individuals as well as organized groups and public and private agencies.
• *Actions that can lead to improvement are known and feasible.* There are proven actions (e.g., personal behaviors, implementation of new policies, etc.) that can alter the course of the indicators when widely applied.
• *Measurement over time will reflect results of action.* If action is taken, tangible results will be seen indicating improvements in various aspects of the nation's health.

Note: An indicator was required to fulfill all six criteria before it was accepted as a potential indicator for inclusion in a set.

SOURCE: Institute of Medicine, 1999.

INDICATORS FOR *MEASURING HEALTH PERFORMANCE IN THE PUBLIC SECTOR*, NATIONAL RESEARCH COUNCIL

The charge to the Panel on Performance Measures and Data for Public Health Performance Partnership Grants (PPGs) of the National Research Council was "to examine the state of the art in performance measurement for public health and to recommend measures that could be used to monitor the Performance Partnership Grant agreements to be negotiated between each state and the federal government." The committee used the following four guidelines to evaluate the measures proposed.

1. *Measures should be aimed at a specific objective and be result oriented.* PPG measures must clearly specify a desired public health result, including identifying the population affected and the time frame involved. Process and capacity measures should clearly specify the health outcome, or long-term objective, to which they are thought to be related.

2. *Measures should be meaningful and understandable.* Performance measures must be seen as important to both the general public and policy makers at all levels of government and they should be stated in nontechnical terms.

3. *Data should be adequate to support the measure.* Adequate data on the populations of interest must be available for the use of measures and must have the following characteristics:

- data to track any objective must meet reasonable statistical standards for accuracy and completeness;
- data to track any objective must be available in a timely fashion, at appropriate periodicity, and at a reasonable cost; and
- Data applied to a specific measure must be collected using similar methods and with a common definition throughout the population of interest.

4. *Measures should be valid, reliable, and responsive.* Measures should, as much as possible, capture the essence of what they purport to measure (i.e., be unbiased and valid for their intended purpose), be reproducible (i.e., reliable), and be able to detect movement toward a desired objective (i.e., be responsive).

SOURCE: National Research Council, 1999:9.

REFERENCES

Advisory Commission on Consumer Protection and Quality in the Health Care Industry. 1998. *Quality First: Better Health Care for All Americans.* Washington, D.C.: U.S. Government Printing Office.

Department of Health. 1999. *Quality and Performance in the NHS: High Level Performance Indicators.* London: NHS Executive. Available at: http://www.doh.gov. uk/nhshlpi.htm.

Donabedian, Avedis. 1982. *The Criteria and Standards of Quality.* Ann Arbor, Mich.: Health Administration Press.

Federal Interagency Forum on Child and Family Statistics. 2000. *America's Children: Key National Indicators of Well-Being.* Washington, D.C.: U.S. Government Printing Office.

Foundation for Accountability. 1999. *Key Questions and Decision Making Criteria, Child and Adolescent Health Measurement Initiative.* Living with Illness Task Force Meeting, Portland, Ore.

Institute of Medicine. 1999. *Leading Health Indicators for Healthy People 2010.* eds. Carole A. Chrvala and Roger J. Bulger. Washington, D.C.: National Academy Press.

National Committee for Quality Assurance. 2000. *HEDIS 2001*, Vol. 1. Washington, D.C.: NCQA.

National Research Council. 1999. *Health Performance Measurement in the Public Sector: Principles and Policies for Implementing an Information Network.* eds. Edward B. Perrin, Jane S. Durch, and Susan M. Skillman. Washington, D.C.: National Academy Press.

U.S. Department of Health and Human Services. 2000a. Proposed Measure Evaluation and Selection Process Criteria for Evaluating Candidate Measures.

U.S. Department of Health and Human Services. 2000b. *Healthy People 2010*, Washington, D.C.: U.S. Government Printing Office.

Glossary

Component of health care quality: refers to one of the attributes of health care quality, namely, safety, effectiveness, patient centeredness, and timeliness.

Conceptual framework: explains, either graphically or in narrative form, the main areas to be studied—the key factors, constructs, or variables—and the presumed relationships among them. Frameworks can be rudimentary or elaborate, theory driven or commonsensical, and descriptive or causal (Miles and Huberman, 1994:18).

Consumer perspectives on health care needs: refers to various reasons people seek health care at different points in the life cycle, namely, to stay healthy, get better, live with illness or disability, or cope with the end of life. Also referred to as consumer needs for health care.

Coping with the end of life: refers to getting help to deal with a terminal illness (adapted from Foundation for Accountability, 1997).

Effectiveness: refers to providing services based on scientific knowledge to all who could benefit and refraining from providing services to those not likely to benefit (avoiding overuse and underuse) (Institute of Medicine, 2001).

Efficiency: avoiding waste, including waste of equipment, supplies, ideas, and energy (Institute of Medicine, 2001).

Equity: refers to providing care that does not vary in quality because of personal characteristics such as gender, ethnicity, geographic location, and socioeconomic status (Institute of Medicine, 2001).

Getting better: means getting help to recover from an illness or injury (Foundation for Accountability, 1997).

Living with illness or disability: means being able to get help in managing an ongoing, chronic condition or in dealing with a disability that affects function (adapted from Foundation for Accountability, 1997).

Measure: a standard of dimension; a fixed unit of quantity or extent; an extent or quantity in the fractions or multiples of which anything is estimated and stated; hence, a rule by which anything is adjusted or judged (*Webster's Revised Unabridged Dictionary*, 1913).

Patient centeredness: refers to health care that establishes a partnership among practitioners, patients, and their families (when appropriate) to ensure that decisions respect patients' wants, needs, and preferences and that patients have the education and support they need to make decisions and participate in their own care.

Quality of care: the degree to which health services for individuals and populations increase the likelihood of desired health outcomes and are consistent with current professional knowledge (Institute of Medicine, 1990:21).

Safety: refers to avoiding injuries to patients from care that is intended to help them (Institute of Medicine, 2001).

Staying healthy: means getting help to avoid illness and to remain well (Foundation for Accountability, 1997).

Timeliness: refers to obtaining needed care and minimizing unnecessary delays in getting that care.

REFERENCES

Foundation for Accountability. 1997. *Reporting Quality Information to Consumers*, Portland, Ore.: FACCT.

Institute of Medicine. 1990. *Medicare: A Strategy for Quality Assurance*, Vol. 2. ed. Kathleen Lohr. Washington, D.C.: National Academy Press.

Institute of Medicine. 2001. *Crossing the Quality Chasm: A New Health System for the 21st Century.* Washington, D.C.: National Academy Press.

Miles, Matthew B., and A. Michael Huberman. 1994. *Qualitative Data Analysis.* Thousand Oaks, Calif.: Sage.

Webster's Revised Unabridged Dictionary. 1913 ed. Springfield, Mass.: G.C. Merriam Co.

Acronyms and Abbreviations

ACSI	American Customer Satisfaction Index
AHCPR	Agency for Health Care Policy and Research
AHRQ	Agency for Healthcare Research and Quality
AMA	American Medical Association
AMI	acute myocardial infarction
BRFSS	Behavioral Risk Factor Surveillance Survey
CABG	coronary artery bypass graft
CAHPS	Consumer Assessment of Health Plans Survey
CDC	Centers for Disease Control and Prevention
CHCF	California HealthCare Foundation
CPI	Consumer Price Index
CSFII	Continuing Survey of Food Intakes by Individuals
DHHS	Department of Health and Human Services
DQuIP	Diabetes Quality Improvement Project
FACCT	Foundation for Accountability
FEHBP	Federal Employees Health Benefit Program
FOBT	fecal occult blood test
GP	general practitioner

HCFA	Health Care Financing Administration
HCQIP	Health Care Quality Improvement Program
HCUP	Healthcare Cost and Utilization Project
HEDIS	Health Plan Employer Data and Information Set
HIPAA	Health Insurance Portability and Accountability Act of 1996
HIV	human immunodeficiency virus
HMO	health maintenance organization
HOS	Health Outcomes Survey
IOM	Institute of Medicine
IPA	independent practice association
JAMA	*Journal of the American Medical Association*
JCAHO	Joint Commission on Accreditation of Healthcare Organizations
MCBS	Medicare Current Beneficiary Survey
MEPS	Medical Expenditure Panel Survey
MHCC	Maryland Health Care Commission
NAEP	National Assessment of Educational Progress
NAMCS	National Ambulatory Medical Care Survey
NAS	National Academy of Sciences
NCDB	National Cancer Data Base
NCHS	National Center for Health Statistics
NCQA	National Committee for Quality Assurance
NCVHS	National Committee on Vital and Health Statistics
NHAMCS	National Hospital Ambulatory Medical Care Survey
NHANES	National Health and Nutrition Examination Survey
NHIS	National Health Interview Survey
NHS	National Health Service
NIS	National Immunization Survey
NIS	Nationwide Inpatient Sample
NQF	National Quality Forum
NRC	National Research Council
NVSS	National Vital Statistics System
PHC4	Pennsylvania Health Care Cost Containment Council
PRO	peer review organization
QI	quality indicator
QuIC	Quality Interagency Coordination Task Force
S-CHIP	State Children's Health Insurance Program
SEER	Surveillance, Epidemiology, and End Results Program

SID	State Inpatient Database
SLAITS	State and Local Area Integrated Telephone Survey
STD	sexually transmitted disease
VPQHC	Vermont Program for Quality in Health Care
WHO	World Health Organization

Biographical Sketches of Committee Members

WILLIAM L. ROPER (Chair) is Dean of the School of Public Health, University of North Carolina at Chapel Hill (UNC). Before joining UNC in July 1997, Dr. Roper was senior vice president and chief medical officer at Prudential Healthcare. In that capacity, he was responsible for medical management services for all Prudential health plans including functions of quality improvement and health care information management. Before coming to Prudential, Dr. Roper was Director of the Centers for Disease Control and Prevention (CDC), served on the senior White House staff, and was administrator of the Health Care Financing Administration (HCFA). Dr. Roper is a past president of the Academy for Health Services Research and Health Policy (formerly the Association for Health Services Research) and chairman of Partnership for Prevention. He is also a member of the Institute of Medicine and serves on its Council. Dr. Roper received his M.D. from the University of Alabama School of Medicine and his M.P.H. from the University of Alabama at Birmingham School of Public Health.

ARNOLD M. EPSTEIN (Vice-Chair) is John H. Foster Professor and chair of the Department of Health Policy and Management at the Harvard School of Public Health. He is also chief of the Section on Health Services and Policy Research in the Department of Medicine at Brigham and Women's Hospital. In 1993–1994, Dr. Epstein worked in the White House on policy issues related to quality management. His research interests focus on quality of care and access to care for disadvantaged populations. His present research includes studies designed to clarify whether differences in surgical procedures by race and gender represent overuse or underuse, and the development of clinical and policy interventions to deal with any inequities that reflect problems in quality of care. He is also examining quality management for Medicaid managed care and public reporting of quality performance data including HEDIS (Health Plan Employer Data and Information Set) 3.0. He serves on the Executive Committee of the Joint Commission on Accreditation of Healthcare Organizations' (JCAHO's) Advisory Council on Performance Measurement, and the Performance Measurement Coordinating Council that jointly advises JCAHO and the National Committee for Quality Assurance (NCQA). He is also president-elect of the Academy for Health Services Research and Health Policy and a member of the Institute of Medicine. Dr. Epstein earned his M.D. from Duke University and an M.A. in political science from Harvard University.

BECKY J. CHERNEY is president and chief executive officer (CEO) of the Central Florida Health Care Coalition in Orlando, Florida. Representing 750,000 members from public and private employers, the coalition has been recognized nationally for its Quality Initiative. The initiative has clinical quality, overall community health status, and patient satisfaction components in place. Prior to assuming this position in 1994, Ms. Cherney served as a consultant to Florida's Agency for Health Care Administration. She was responsible for implementing the state's cutting-edge legislation for Community Health Purchasing Alliances. She spent 23 years in the private sector with three Fortune 500 companies. It was during her 11-year tenure with Tupperware International that she founded the coalition. Ms. Cherney is the founder of the Central Florida Women's Resource Center and has served as president of the Human Services Council and Florida Executive Women. She is currently serving her second appointed term on the Florida Board of Medicine. Ms. Cherney was named 1999's Businesswoman of the Year by the *Orlando Business Journal*. She is a graduate of the University of Wisconsin.

DAVID C. CLASSEN is an associate professor of medicine at the University of Utah and a vice president at First Consulting Group. Dr. Classen was formerly the associate hospital epidemiologist and a consultant in infectious diseases at LDS Hospital in Salt Lake City, Utah, and chair of Intermountain Health Care's Clinical Quality Committee for Drug Use and Evaluation. Dr. Classen is an expert in the development of computerized clinical decision support systems and epidemiological techniques to improve the use and safety of medications and the overall quality of care. His research interests are in the computer applications of epidemiological techniques to investigate clinical outcomes and the development of expert system technologies to provide decision support in the monitoring and prescribing medications. He received his medical degree from the University of Virginia School of Medicine and an M.S. degree in medical informatics from the University of Utah School of Medicine.

JOHN M. COLMERS is currently a program officer with the Milbank Memorial Fund. He was formerly executive director of the Maryland Health Care Commission (MHCC); an agency created through the merger of two existing health regulatory commissions. MHCC is charged with health care reform activities for the state, the development and adoption of a state health plan, and the compilation and analysis of health care data sets, among other responsibilities. Prior to the merger, Mr. Colmers was executive director of the Health Care Access and Cost Commission (HCACC), one of the organizations in the merger. HCACC implemented many initiatives, including report cards providing information on the quality and performance of health maintenance organizations and standards for the operation of electronic health networks. Before this position, Mr. Colmers was executive director of the Health Services Cost Review Commission, overseeing Maryland's all-payor hospital rate setting system. Mr. Colmers did undergraduate work at Johns Hopkins University, received his M.P.H. from the University of North Carolina, and has returned to Johns Hopkins University for doctoral study of health services research.

ALAIN C. ENTHOVEN is the Marriner S. Eccles Professor of Public and Private Management in the Graduate School of Business at Stanford University. He has been involved in health care-related public policy at both the federal and the state levels. Dr. Enthoven designed and proposed the Consumer Choice Health Plan, a plan for universal health insurance based on managed competition in the private sector, while serving as a consultant to U.S. Department of Health and Human Services (DHHS) Secretary Califano and the Carter administration in 1977. In 1997, he was appointed Chairman of the California Managed Health Care Improvement Task Force by Governor Pete Wilson to address health care issues raised by managed care to aid in policy decisions. He is a consultant to Kaiser Permanente and former chairman of the Health Benefits Advisory Council for CalPERS (California State employees' medical and hospital care plans). In 1998–99, he was the Rock Carling Fellow of the Nuffield Trust of London and visiting professor at the London School of Hygiene and Tropical Medicine. He has been a director of the Jackson Hole Group, the Institute for Healthcare Advancement, and PCS. He has received numerous awards including the President's Award for Distinguished Federal Civilian Service from John F. Kennedy, the Baxter Prize for Health Services Research, and the Board of Directors Award from the Healthcare Financial Management Association. He is a fellow of the American Academy of Arts and Sciences and a member of the Institute of Medicine (IOM). He is also a director of Caresoft.com; an Internet portal designed to empower consumers to receive a higher quality of health care. He holds degrees in economics from Stanford, Oxford, and the Massachusetts Institute of Technology.

JOSÉ J. ESCARCE is a senior natural scientist at RAND, where he is co-director of the Center for Research on Health Care Organization, Economics and Finance and director of the RAND–University of California, Los Angeles–Harvard Center for Health Care Financing Policy Research. Dr. Escarce has served on the Health Services Research Study Section at the Agency for Health Care Policy and Research (AHCPR) and is currently a member of the National Advisory Council for Health Care Policy, Research, and Evaluation of DHHS. He also serves on the National Advisory Committee of the Robert Wood Johnson Foundation Minority Medical Faculty Development Program and is past chair of the Health Economics Committee of the American Public Health Association. Dr. Escarce's research interests include physician behavior under economic incentives, access to care, and the impact of managed care on cost and quality. Dr. Escarce graduated from Princeton University, earned a master's degree in physics from Harvard University, and obtained his medical degree from the University of Pennsylvania, and his Ph.D. in health care systems from the Wharton School.

SHELDON GREENFIELD is the director of the Primary Care Outcomes Research Institute at the New England Medical Center. He is also professor of medicine at the Tufts University School of Medicine, medical advisor for the Tufts Managed Care Institute, and adjunct professor of public health at the Harvard School of Public Health. Dr. Greenfield has pioneered research in increasing patients' participation in care and using outcomes to determine the value of that participation. He was medical director of the Medical Outcomes Study which sought to compare systems of care, specialties, various aspects of interpersonal care, and resource use to outcomes, and in that position, he became one of the leading clinical outcomes researchers in the country. He was principal investigator of the Type II Diabetes Patient Outcome Research Team. Dr. Greenfield was chairman of the Health Care Technology Study Section for the AHCPR and is currently chairman of the Diabetes Quality Improvement Program, a joint venture of HCFA, NCQA, and the American Diabetes Association (ADA). He is a member of the Institute of Medicine and has served as chair of the IOM Workshop on the Measurement and Management of Quality in End Stage Renal Disease and as a member of the Committee on Setting Priorities for Practice Guidelines. Dr. Greenfield received his M.D. from the University of Cincinnati.

JUDITH H. HIBBARD is a professor of health policy in the Department of Planning, Public Policy and Management at the University of Oregon and clinical professor of public health and preventive medicine at the Oregon Health Sciences University. Her research focus is on consumer information and consumer choice issues in health care. One of her current studies focuses on the use of quality report cards to support informed decisions among Medicare beneficiaries. She is also an investigator on the Consumer Assessment of Health Plans Survey (CAHPS), serving on the Research Triangle Institute's team. In addition, she has examined the use of quality information among large purchasers of health care and the comprehension by consumers of quality-of-care indicators including condition-specific performance information. Her work on consumer information and decision making has been supported by contracts and grants from the Agency for Healthcare Research and Quality (AHRQ), HCFA, Robert Wood Johnson Foundation, and Public Policy Institute at AARP. Dr. Hibbard is currently a member of the HCFA and AHRQ workgroup on consumer information. She is also on the Framework Board for the National Quality Forum. She has an M.P.H. from the University of California at Los Angeles and doctor of public health degree from the University of California at Berkeley.

HAROLD S. LUFT is Caldwell B. Esselstyn Professor of Health Policy and Health Economics and director of the Institute for Health Policy Studies at the University of California, San Francisco. Dr. Luft is most commonly recognized for his research on managed care, but his investigations have covered a wide range of areas, including the volume–outcome relationship and quality of hospital care, risk assessment and risk adjustment, medical care utilization, health maintenance organizations, hospital market competition, and health care market reforms in various states and communities. He has also examined the role of large health care databases and new informatics tools in improving health care. He was a member of the AHCPR National Advisory Committee from 1994 to 1999 and served as the committee's chair from 1998 to 1999. Dr. Luft is a member of the board of directors of the Academy for Health Services Research and Health Policy. He is a member of the Institute of Medicine and has served on the IOM Technical Panel on the State of Quality in America and the IOM Committee to Design a Strategy for Quality Review and Assurance in Medicare. He received a Ph.D. in economics from Harvard University.

SCOTT C. RATZAN is senior technical advisor and population leadership fellow in the Global Bureau, Center for Population, Health and Nutrition at the U.S. Agency for International Development (USAID). He also is on the faculty at Yale University School of Public Health, Tufts University School of Medicine, and George Washington University Medical Center. Additionally, Dr. Ratzan serves as editor-in-chief of the *Journal of Health Communication*. Prior to joining USAID, he was executive director of health communication technology and educational innovation at the Academy for Educational Development. He was also founder and director of the Emerson–Tufts Program in Health Communication, a joint master's degree program between Emerson College and Tufts

University School of Medicine. Dr. Ratzan received his medical degree from the University of Southern California; a master's in public administration from the John F. Kennedy School of Government, Harvard University, and an M.A. in communication studies from Emerson College.

MARK D. SMITH is president and CEO of the California HealthCare Foundation. Dr. Smith is also a member of the clinical faculty of the University of California at San Francisco. Prior to joining the foundation, Dr. Smith was executive vice president of the Henry J. Kaiser Family Foundation where he was responsible for the Poverty and Health, HIV/AIDS Policy, and Changing Healthcare Marketplace Programs. Dr. Smith has written and spoken extensively on AIDS-related issues and the health care marketplace. He serves on the Committee on Performance Measurement (HEDIS) of the NCQA and has served on the editorial board of *Annals of Internal Medicine*. He holds an A.B. in Afro-American Studies from Harvard University, an M.B.A. in health care administration from the Wharton School at the University of Pennsylvania, and an M.D. from the University of North Carolina, and is certified in internal medicine.

WILLIAM W. STEAD is professor of medicine, professor of biomedical informatics, director of the Informatics Center, and associate vice chancellor for Health Affairs at Vanderbilt University. He is responsible for the Medical Center's working operation and decision support systems, the Medical Center Library, and an interdisciplinary faculty unit engaging in biomedical informatics research and training. Dr. Stead is editor-in-chief of the *Journal of the American Medical Informatics Association*, founding fellow of both the American College of Medical Informatics and the American Institute for Engineering in Biology and Medicine, and a member of the Institute of Medicine. He has served as president of the American Association for Medical Systems and Informatics and is currently president of the American College of Medical Informatics. Dr. Stead received his medical degree from Duke University and is certified in internal medicine and nephrology.

ALAN M. ZASLAVSKY is an associate professor of statistics in the Department of Health Care Policy at Harvard Medical School. His health services research interests focus on developing a methodology for quality measurement of health plans and understanding their implications. He has co-directed a team that studied the impact of individual characteristics on CAHPS reports and ratings as part of the development of a case-mix adjustment model for this population. He has specified software for analysis of CAHPS data that is used nationally and has analyzed the dimensions and sources of variation among reports on health plans. He is also involved in the development and evaluation of HEDIS clinical measures, including case-mix adjustment, as well as a study on the potential of cancer registry data for the evaluation of care provided by health plans. Dr.

Zaslavsky's statistical research interests include surveys, census methodology, small-area estimation, microsimulation models, missing data, categorical data, and Bayesian methodology. He is associate editor of the *Survey Methodology Journal*. Dr. Zaslavsky is a fellow of the American Statistical Association. He has served on several National Academy of Sciences panels on census methodology for the Committee on National Statistics and currently is on the Panel on Estimates of Poverty for Small Geographical Areas. He holds a Ph.D. in applied mathematics from the Massachusetts Institute of Technology.